The Used-Car Game:
A Sociology of the Bargain

The Used-Car Game:
A Sociology of the Bargain

Joy Browne

Lexington Books
D.C. Heath and Company
Lexington, Massachusetts
Toronto   London

HF
5439
.A8
B76

Library of Congress Cataloging in Publication Data

Browne, Joy.
 The used car game.

 Bibliography: p.
 1. Salesman and salesmanship — Automobiles.
2. Consumers. I. Title.
HF5439.A8B76   658.89'62922'2   72-12853
ISBN 0-669-85761-0

Copyright © 1973 by D.C. Heath and Company

Second printing May 1974.

Published simultaneously in Canada.

Printed in the United States of America.

International Standard Book Number: 0-669-85761-0

Library of Congress Catalog Card Number: 72-12853

To
R.M.N.
. . . the prototype . . .

Table of Contents

Introduction to the bargain. Examples in the literature. Groundwork for study as a field within sociology. Used car salesmen relevance. Uniqueness of product, duality of roles, triadic middleman. Social psychological use of bargain. The impact of control and competence on behavior.

Method and setting of study. Discussion of participant observation. Data collection. Related research. The importance of perspective. The advantages and disadvantages of an open-ended methodology.

The public view. The influence of the stereotype as a determinant of action. The importance of expectations. Documenting what we all "know." The public press as diary of the commonplace. Underscoring an impression in article, cartoon, book or legislation. The pervasiveness of an image.

A Very Significant Other. The Customer. Perspectives, occupied and indicated. Expectations of a customer's character and behavior. Obstacles to sales. Change and redefinition.

Appendixes

List of Figures

Preface

Man's scrutinization of man has some inherent difficulties. The debate on whether such study can succeed versus whether man should attempt any other study rages and will undoubtedly continue to rage. (See Karl Deutsch et al, *Science,* vol. 171. p. 450.) There will be no attempt here to adjudicate this argument, but rather to point out one of the more major problems such a study involves.

When a mathematician or a chemist seeks to describe his universe, he has a host of specialized, well-defined terms at his disposal. If he discovers something completely new, he is free to make up a term or an equation to describe his findings, if he follows the prescribed rules for doing so. Not so, the social scientist. He has nothing to rely on but his language of everyday. Whether he considers himself layman or specialist, he has only the words of the layman at his disposal since he is subject to the same culture as the subjects he describes and can discuss his findings only in these terms. He must use the language of everyday to describe the events of everyday. In theory, this should only prevent him from keeping his findings locked in esoterica, but in practice, the limitation is more confining than that. Because he is using words that "everybody knows" he often feels free to use them without definition, without rigor. If every word had one and only one meaning and there was some way to assess this point definitively, all would be well. Unfortunately, this is not the case. Words mean different things to different people.

The bargain is one such culprit. A bargain can mean something at half price, a deal struck between equals, a contract in a labor dispute, or something of extraordinary value. These meanings are certainly related, but they are not identical, and the use of a term in scholarly research must be uncluttered by doubt or variation, especially if we are to use it as an effective tool in understanding human action.

My purpose in this study is to lay the groundwork for using the baragin as a meaningful and well-understood concept in the study of man behaving. As I will point out, the concept has not lain unused, but rather undissected, undefined, unexplained. Since it is frequently used, I propose that now is the time to begin defining it in the hopes of making it a more useful tool with a view toward action, intervention, and understanding.

This study is a first step in setting forth how the concept has been used or misused in the past and the possibilities for the future. To this end, I have set about studying used car salesmen as they bargain on the used car lot. My study has been divided into an assessment of the situation in general, what could a bargain be, how might one think of it, how has it been used. On a pragmatic level, what is the place of the car in America? How is it likely to affect those dealing with it? How did I do my study and why?

Once this groundwork has been laid, I go on to show the sociological and psychological factors that influence the participants in this particular bargain, for this is a study of the sociology of a bargain, one located specifically in time and space. While it has relevance to the study of bargains in general, it is merely the first step. There is no such field of inquiry at this time, and this study is not an attempt to create one in a fell swoop. Rather, its intention is to point the way to fruitful study in the hopes of interesting others to carry on in the same or similar vein.

Human beings interacting with one another in unfamiliar or even familiar situations rely on appraisals formed over a long period of time. All of us entertain these expectations or stereotypes about individuals with whom we interact. The more important or problematic the interaction, the stronger our expectations expect it to be, as will be pointed out in the chapters that follow, expecially Chapter 3. Thus, the analysis of those expectations and thoughts about others who are significant in any encounter offers general insight into human behavior. The case of the bargain is certainly no exception. Four separate chapters are devoted to the impression, expectations, and emotions with which the human beings involved in this study face one another. They are exposed here partly by the nature of the interaction, partly by the nature of the research method, but without them, the study of a bargain would be incomplete and inaccurate. The chapters concern the public's view of the salesman and his view of his public. There is also a tacit acknowledgment of the customer's view of the salesman. The salesman's view of himself and his view of the other party of significance in the relationship, his boss (the house), is also included. (Note: The term 'house' is used by the salesman to mean either the dealership owner or the management, i.e. "they" as opposed to "we" — anyone in the company who is not a salesman.)

I have included these insights because they are the backdrop against which the bargain takes place. A customer comes to the salesman wanting to buy a car, expecting to get cheated. The salesman faces the customer knowing he is disliked, yet wanting to make a sale. The customer assumes the salesman is the final authority on the car; the salesman knows that he is not. The customer has his own self-image to maintain, usually in front of a wife or friend. The salesman also has an ego to protect, especially in front of his colleagues, who are also his competitors. The car is part of the customer's self-image and part of the salesman's income. Both salesman and customer expect to get cheated, yet neither wishes to appear the fool. The entire situation is then one of compromise and exchange, giving in and being stubborn, pleasing and being pleased, attacking and retreating; in a word, bargaining.

Responsibility for the successful outcome of the interaction lies with the man with least control over the situation, the salesman. His boundary conditions are the least specified. He is acting for another. He is the most distrusted and stands to lose the most, in salary, prestige, and dignity. The customer can go elsewhere;

the house can get another salesman. The salesman can go elsewhere, but he does not eat in the process. The final two chapters deal with how the salesman controls an uncontrollable situation and bargains with his house, himself, and his customer.

The final chapter deals with the possibilities for further study of the bargain and a reiteration of the groundwork established by this study. Appendixes on game theory and language follow, since both are germane but not integral parts of the study.

The emphasis is on definition with a view toward action in the form of successful intervention and prediction rather than simple description. Information is included because it is relevant to understanding action and is the kind of information that I feel we must ascertain if social scientists are to assist others in understanding and intervening in social situations.

Acknowledgments

The art of a graceful acknowledgment of indebtedness has always alluded me but this awkward attempt serves as proof of the triumph of gratitude over style. I wish to thank the following for their aid:

Blanche Geer: friend, mentor, editor and teacher who understood both my arrogance and my prose if not my punctuation.

Earl Rubington: for his inability to allow any printed snow jobs.

Elliott Krause: for his rejection of feudalism as a suitable model for IBM or a dissertation.

Mort Rubin: for unfailing kindness, good humor and carefully thought out criticism.

Stephen Miller: for a sense of perspective and humor in dealing with a rite of passage.

Laurie Amato: for understanding and disregarding my punctuation.

Patience Browne: for waiting that extra month to be born.

Carter Browne: for everything else.

1

Bargain, Brokerage, and Control

Haggling has always had an unpleasant connotation to most Americans. It conjures up images of far-off, exotic corners of the less-than-civilized world in sunlit bazaars filled with rugs, citrus fruits, flies, and pungent odors. Bargaining is the process carried on between an unsavory, robe-wrapped charlatan and an unsuspecting American tourist complete with camera and flowered sport shirt. Yet the bargaining of one who has with one who wants is a basic form of interaction. If we see the discrepancy between what one wants and what one has as motivating much human behavior, how people reduce this discrepancy must interest students of behavior. On the simplest level, the bargain can be seen as the compromise between one who wants and one who has. More formally: "an agreement between parties settling what each shall give and receive in a transaction between them . . . an agreement or compact viewed as advantageous or the reverse."[1]

The use of the bargain in resolving conflicting or competing postures is so common as to be taken for granted. For instance, on a private level, the struggle with conscience is often a set of rationalizations offered as fodder to an energetic superego, the "buying-off" of a "better self."

On a more global level, we resolve some of the most complex and crucial problems that face us as individuals, groups, nations, races or classes by means of a bargaining procedure. Strikes, treaties, disarmament talks, and sit-ins are some common examples. In between the two extremes of conscience and world politics at the interpersonal level, husbands and wives, fathers and children, teachers and students utilize the bargain. Still, we know little of the process itself. How do equals or near equals settle grievances without the intervention or arbitration of a third party? What is the trade-off between what can be gained and what can be lost by either party?

Considering its pervasiveness, the bargain has been specifically studied surprisingly seldom, although it has been used as a model without definition. This study describes the bargaining process as it occurs, as both inadvertently described in previous studies and specifically delineated in this one. The purpose here will be to offer an intentional discussion of what it means to bargain, how it occurs, and how it functions.[2,3]

As a concept, the bargain is much like the concept of commitment described by Howard S. Becker.[4] Everybody uses the term, but nobody defines it, an oversight which makes it not invalid, but inconvenient. In fact, much the same problems that are associated with this concept are associated with the bargain; as

1

Becker noted, commitment is "unscathed by so much as a single reference" in the literature although it was not infrequently utilized.

The bargain is not an unknown quantity in sociological studies; it is only undefined. For example, for Dalton, bargaining occurs during labor negotiations and, in a more general sense, when one of his managers declares that he "tried to make two plus two equal four, but sometimes I let it be 3.9 or 4.1"[5] or the informal, tacit bargain that is made with a prized secretary who is allowed to use the company postage meter for her Christmas cards in exchange for her services, goodwill, and loyalty.[6] Goffman's bargaining is for "face" or lost status that occurs between con man and mark that is part of "cooling the mark out."[7] To Freidson, bargaining occurs between doctor and patient on the kind of person each thinks the other is.[8] Miller's bargains are the give and take between medical student and faculty;[9] Becker and Geer discuss the compromises of faculty and students.[10] Roth's bargains are struck in a tuberculosis ward.[11]

McCall discusses bargaining as the process used to achieve different kinds of rewards during social functioning.[12] He separates out two stages of bargaining, including the negotiation of both social identities and interactive roles.

Backman discusses the emerging role of the bargain in the "changing role of social scientists with respect to governmental and private funding sources" by pointing out that the contract for information has to be reformulated on both sides.[13] Indik and Smith have even proposed collective bargaining as the alternative to violence in the solution of social problems in modern day America.[14]

The bargain is part and parcel of the researcher's life in the field. He is continuously negotiating for information with any group. Undeniably the bargain is significant, not only in the world at large but within the confines of social research as well.

The field of mathematical modeling of potential bargaining situations has received a certain amount of interest with the advent of relatively inexpensive computer time. Harsanyi,[15, 16] Joseph,[17] and others have discussed conflict in terms of problem solving with the bargain as model. Unfortunately, the mathematical model offers little to the sociologists past the most simplified schema. For interest, social power is discussed in terms of a change in behavior with power proportional to strength.

Other sociologists have concerned themselves with similar, if not identical, problems. Lipset discusses collective bargaining in *Union Democracy*.[18] This approach enjoyed a certain amount of popularity in the late fifties as a result of major strikes in the country.

Strauss et al. discuss negotiations in *Psychiatric Ideologies and Institutions,*[19] but with respect to fixed rules, regulations, and roles that are well understood by all participants.

The above listing is not exhaustive but rather indicative of the use of an undefined concept — an exhaustive list would require a thorough reading of every article written since the concept is "unscathed by reference" except in discussions of labor relations or when the word "bargain" occurs in the title itself. *Sociology Abstracts* lists few articles under "Bargain" in the last twenty years. All of them answer the criteria of using the word in the title or referring to labor negotiations. More than half of the entries were clustered in the late fifties when the country was plagued by major strikes. Three articles discussed mathematical modeling and referenced foreign relations. Only one was concerned with bargaining per se — in the Middle East.

The problem is one of definition and delineation, not description. This study is meant as a first step in this process — to specifically set out to describe the bargaining process which is neglected in the studies mentioned and to create a base of further systematic inquiry into this most significant and utilitarian concept. Hopefully within a short time, reference to an index will uncover a number of entries under the heading "Bargain."

Because bargains include at least two parties, how to study the process is a problem I deal with at some length in the next chapter. Suffice it to say at this point that in this preliminary foray into the rather uncharted land of bargaining, I chose to settle for depth rather than breadth and studied from a single vantage point. The ramifications of this decision will also be discussed in the final chapter. If the bargain is to become a useful tool in sociology, breadth will have to be acquired. The point of this study is to begin to study the process as it occurs and to thereby accumulate information on the delineation of the bargain as a conceptual tool.

Homans, in his plea to "bring men back in," supplies an additional rationale for the study as undertaken by urging the inclusion of real human beings in societal description:

If a serious effort is made to construct theories that will even begin to explain social phenomenon, it turns out that their general propositions are not about the equilibrium of societies but about the behavior of men.[20]

And, thus, if as he says, "the only inescapable office of theory is to explain,"[21] then a group that bargains with the least amount of subterfuge, frills, or facade should be the most parsimonious for the purposes of explanation, and it is on this basis that used car salesmen have been chosen to shed light on this "universal" of the bargain.

In addition to the intent of studying the bargaining process, it would greatly simplify understanding if the group studied used bargaining as a basic procedure — if the intent of the participants was also to bargain, thus eliminating the need to strip away other forms of behavior in order to arrive at the bargain. For this reason again I chose to study the used car salesmen — men who bargain daily in the course of making their living.

In this chapter I will discuss the general concept of the bargaining process, with emphasis on form, applications and ramifications including the idea of social control. I then turn to a discussion of the bargaining process as specifically employed by the used car salesman.

As is the case with any specific application, a number of unique features are present. Those that occur when the bargain is employed on the used car lot will be delineated before describing a general model of the bargain. Three elements of the general model are the product involved (the car), the duality of the roles involved (buyer becomes seller and seller becomes buyer at some point), and the fact that there are really three parties involved in any interaction (the customer, the salesman, and the dealer for whom the salesman works; a brokerage relationship.)

A psychologist, Irwin Deutsch, and his students have attempted to isolate and describe the bargaining situation in a laboratory setting, since they feel that the interaction has significance beyond the marketplace.

As experimental psychologists, they attempted to replicate bargaining situations in which participants could only achieve their respective goals successfully (passage on a blocked roadway) by cooperating and compromising with one another. The conclusions to the study offer generalized rules for defining a bargaining situation:

1. Both parties perceive that each party would be better off or no worse off because of the agreement than if no agreement were reached.
2. Both parties perceive that more than one agreement is feasible.
3. Both parties perceive each other to have conflicting preferences or opposed interests with respect to possible agreements.[22]

Deutsch does not paint a particularly rosy picture. He predicts that nothing very positive will occur since competition is involved which pits the participants against one another. In order for any agreement to be reached between the participants, he insists that the first of the three factors listed above must be stronger than either the second or third point combined in order that:

1. The stronger the cooperative interests as compared to the competitive, the more likely an agreement will be reached.
2. Bargainers are more likely to reach an agreement the more resources they have available for recognizing or inventing potential bargaining agreements and for communicating to one another once a potential agreement has been recognized or invented.[23]

Obviously, motivation is vital since the bargain highlights, among other things, the obstinancy of the beast:

Bargaining situations highlight the possibility that even where cooperation would be mutually advantageous, shared purposes may not develop, agreement may not be reached and interaction may be regulated antagonistically rather than normatively.[24]

Thus, it is possible to find human beings locked together by mutual dependence struggling against one another, even when logic or sheer opportunism should dictate otherwise.

Yet Deutsch's conclusions while interesting, insightful, and applicable were based on a nonlimited time factor seldom encountered outside the laboratory. Time is always a variable in human interaction, and its relevance, especially in a stressful situation, is undeniable. In this regard, at least, the used car salesman is a more useful paradigm since his interactions are extremely time dependent. The time of day, the time of the month, the time of the year, and the time in the model year are all significant. All the time in the world could obviously be a controlling factor if one participant were in a hurry; "waiting out" an opponent is an enviable position. In fact, the entire subject of control — who has the upper hand and is thereby in a position to determine the outcome — is crucial to the concept of the bargain. Within the bargaining context there is an incredible lack of control, both over the final outcome or even the intermediate steps. By its very nature, the course of events is not predictable since each participant depends on the actions of the other before he can determine his own next act. He cannot control, so he cannot predict. (This situation, incidentally, bears striking resemblance to Mead's concept of responsive interaction as an ongoing process.)

In addition, most participants in a bargain (especially on our car lot) are not particularly used to bargaining (or at least don't know that they are used to bargaining) which can result in feeling of incompetence that increases the feeling of helplessness and lack of control. This helplessness is quite often translated into a distrust of the other participant. Deutsch is quite explicit in his delineation of the importance of distrust in the bargain.[25]

It is likely that an individual will distrust another if he has no knowledge of the outcome and no control over his fellow participant. The less stable the situation, the less the direction of change or action can be predicted, the more likely it is that the participants will not trust one another.[26]

There are also sources of distrust that center around the individual's perception of himself rather than anything inherent in the situation. If the individual sees himself as less than competent and in danger of losing rather than gaining by the interaction, i.e., unable to substantively influence the outcome, he will undoubtedly enter the situation with suspicion.

On the other hand, if one enters a situation in which one *expects* to have no control to begin with, the experience is equally likely to be highly charged and most probably unpleasant. In summary, distrust can be based on either the inability to predict action or on the ability to predict an undesired action only too well. In addition to giving no clear motivation for parties to interact under these conditions, Deutsch's conclusions stemmed from experimentally controlled research on distrust. He designed his situations to study a resultant action which was defined as distrust. There is no need to create a situation to study the bargain and distrust in the case of the used car salesman. It already exists without a researcher's intervention.

As previously mentioned, understanding a situation characterized by lack of control would seem extremely relevant. No matter how strongly the dean may dislike, disagree with, or distrust the militant student occupying his office, at some point he is forced to deal with him simply because he is there and, as such, offers the dean no alternative. In the same sense, if a child is kidnapped, much as the parent distrusts the kidnapper, he must deal with him. If a demand exists for a product or service and there is only one game in town, when the product or service is greatly enough desired, no option but interaction remains.

Although some ingenious, if unsettling, studies[27, 28, 29, 30] have been reported on the effect of induced unpredictability, little work has been completed on interaction based on distrust, presumably because it is assumed to occur so seldom.

Yet, if interaction is interpreted in the strictly Meadian sense of emergent process, one action contingent on the previous ones both immediate and historical, then predictability is a theoretical impossibility. Any particular action is an outgrowth of a previous action and is evolutionary in nature. Human interaction is always unpredictable to a greater or lesser extent and is thereby grounds for mistrust if not distrust. Admittedly, some situations are more predictable than others. One particularly unpredictable situation is one in which both participants are completely dependent on the immediate past action of the other party with minimal historical information. Ideally, the most unpredictable situation is one in which strangers who know virtually nothing about one another are forced to reach an understanding over which neither has absolute control. This could suffice as a thumbnail sketch of salesman and customer about to come together on a used car lot. The basis, ramification, and rectification, while broadly sketched here, are the subject for many of the pages to follow. Yet other factors make car salesmen worthy of study and discussion.

Potentially, one of the reasons that bargaining may uncover, contribute to, highlight or cause hostility is that it is not an overly acceptable form of behavior in American society. It is seldom practiced formally and, as such, exists as an uncharted behavioral path. The unskilled would undoubtedly be uncomfortable at very least in such a situation. As Hall, a social anthropologist, states, practice at least makes comfortable:

Throughout the Middle East, for example, bargaining is an underlying pattern which is significantly different from the activity which goes under that name in our culture. Yet what is perceived on the surface (i.e., Arab methods of bargaining) looks familiar and is assumed to be the same. Nothing could be farther from the truth. Our first mistake is in the assessment of the value of bargaining in the Middle East and the role it plays in everyday life. Americans tend to look down on people who haggle. They restrict their serious trading to houses and automobiles . . . The American asks, "What percentage of the asking price shall I give as my first offer?" What he doesn't know is that there are several asking prices . . . the Arab has many different asking prices each with a different meaning. The American pattern is that the two parties have hidden prices above and below which they will not go, and an asking price which is perceived and thought of as having some sort of fixed relationship to the hidden prices.[31]

. . . The American pattern of bargaining is predicated on the assumption that each party has a high and a low point that is hidden (what he would like to get and what he will settle for). The function of the bargaining is to discover, if possible, what the opponent's points are without revealing one's own. The American in the Middle East, projecting his own unconscious pattern will ask,

"What percentage of the asking price do I give?" That is, "If he's asking ten pounds, will he settle for five?"[32]

The validity of these observations will be made clear in Chapters 7 and 8 on the actual bargaining technique between salesman and customer. Hall goes on to mention that there is a central pivotal point around which the bargaining centers. The nature of the bargaining is based on the deviation from that central point. If the customer is clearly out in left field, the bargain is unlikely to be consummated. If the vendor is way out of line, unless he's got himself a real sucker, he has probably talked himself out of a sale. (Occasionally, the salesman is so heavy-handed with his pigeon that he loses the sale.) As I will show, the actual selling price often depends on the salesman's view of the customer, so that bargain determines the price of the car in two distinct ways.

Hall has accurately described the bargain from the customer's point of view as evidenced by a customer encountered during the course of this research who described his method of dealing with used car salesmen: "Right away, I knock off twenty-five percent and I start to deal from there."

The salesman's method is more similar to the Arab's where there is a "let's-do-business one, the let's-not-do-business one, or the let's-fight asking price . . ."[33] The ramification of the bargain from the salesman's point of view is also more Arabic in nature: (an Arab explaining his technique)

. . . If you don't give a little in bargaining, the other fellow will back up. If he gives two steps, you have to give two steps. If you don't, he will back up four.[34]

Of course, this Arab was speaking about his dealings with other Arabs; this is seldom the case on the used car lot. Interestingly enough, however, salesmen report that an Arab or Lebanese is by far the worst kind of customer: ". . . cause he just won't stop. He'll get you down to bare bone and then want another $200 off." If Hall is correct in his analysis, one of the reasons the salesmen have such a hard time with their Arab customers is because they are both playing the same game by the same rules.

Because the bargain is not a well used technique in economic ventures, the possibility that the individual would feel a sense of competence is decreased. His feelings of incompetence foster his feelings of distrust. The customer's uncertainty increases the confidence of the salesman. We are now to the used car salesman and his use of the bargain, within the more generalized model of give and take in which lack of control and subsequent distrust are crucial.

The interactions of the salesman are a dramatic study in bargaining. From a situation of mistrust at least, and more likely distrust, he is able to not only function, but prevail. The customer not only buys from him, but conceivably will buy from him again and will send his friends and neighbors in to deal in the meantime.

In a world in which the strike, the sit-in, and the confrontation have become nearly commonplace, dealing with those disliked and mistrusted is becoming a most significant and useful technique. Sociological literature offers little in the way of either discussion or solution to the problem. Perhaps this is because human beings are assumed to deal with each other over protracted periods of time only if they trust each other. Garfinkle points out that if one party in an interaction distrusts another, the interaction terminates usually by one or both parties leaving the field or situation.[35]

Obviously, there are circumstances which could override this tendency. When interaction is obligatory, neither party can exercise the option of leaving the field; both must stay. This could be true because one party has something that the other wants or each has something that the other wants or needs. This need is at the basis of sales interaction. One party has, and the other needs. Or more realistically, one has a product and the other has a resource he is willing to trade for it.

The product here is a unique and even exotic object, the automobile. While less than one hundred years old, it has greatly influenced the American way of life. A car has unparalleled status in American life, widespread with societal as well as intrinsic value. In a country where there are as many registered cars as telephones (and even the most conservative estimate places the total number of automobiles at more than one for every two and a half men, women, and children), there can be little doubt as to the pervasive influence of the car.[36] Even in a year when the economy "turned down" and the automobile industry suffered its costliest strike in history, nearly 8.5 million new cars were sold in the United States.[37]

Buying a new car is not a strictly financial decision. An article entitled, "The New Cars," by Ben Kocivar, explains some of the appeal.

The Pony cars, which got their name and image from the fantastically successful Ford Mustang are in full gallop. Now the tricky bit in all this is that some are just cosmetic fakes. They only "look" tough and fast and are designed as relatively inexpensive rolling tricks for mild-mannered secretaries to achieve the "in" image.[38]

America's "love affair" with the automobile does not seem to have ended despite some lover's tiffs.[39] Image and status are intimately bound up with the function of the car, and these values influence behavior even if the dream is second-hand:

Used-car sales are also brisk, mainly for models costing less than $1,000. Auto-repair volume is up 10% from last year, partly because drivers are trying to nurse one more year from their old models.[40]

An item causing such an emotional stir must predictably elicit strong negative feelings when expectations are frustrated. Such is the case. The President's Committee on Consumer Interest states that Americans complain most about their automobiles:

Gripes included assertions that the vehicles complained about were no good to begin with, their warranties were a joke, their craftsmanship was miserable, the

repair charges exorbitant.[41]

The impact of the car in the United States cannot be denied. But all is not well in the consumer's mind about his image on wheels. And he has a bewildering display of "images" from which to choose. For it must be remembered that, unlike roses, cars are not all alike. A new car is definitely not like a used one. New cars are bought by a dealership at identical prices from the manufacturer regardless of quantity. The only possible difference in price on identical new cars is the distance from the factory and the dealer's overhead. Within any geographical area, these figures do not vary significantly. Because a customer can "shop around" and find an identical car elsewhere, price variations on a new car are negligible.

Similarly, options cost all dealers the same amount; the mark-up is also very similar. Since a difference of fifty dollars on a new car between dealers is exceptional, the sale of a new car by a dealer is often dependent on the personality of his salesman.

Buying a used car is a different story. Basically, the customer is buying a unique item — color, mileage, options, condition, make and model have already been determined on the car as it stands. The customer must decide how close the available vehicle comes to his wishes. More accurately, the salesman has only to convince the customer that this particular item is *exactly* what the customer is looking for, and then his job is done. The customer is not likely to find an identical car on another lot at a comparable price.

The car, with all of its cultural implications, is the third party to the action. People who don't care about another thing in the world seem to care about their car. According to those in the "know" "Mustang makes it happen," not to mention "making it great," by turning uptight spinsters into wavy-haired swingers. A Cadillac is not only the symbol of excellence, but elegance and opulence as well. Even though the Mercedes costs a cool $8,000, "isn't the safety of your family worth something?"[42]

The impact of the car was recently detailed in a column on consumer education in a local newspaper:

The car was a symbol of advancement, and we proudly drove it through town and sometimes parked it in front of the house rather than hide it in the garage. We were proud of it because it broadcast to everyone, "I can afford this luxury."

But that's just the point. The car ceased to be a luxury. It became a need, and not just one car was needed. In many households two cars are now as necessary as two bathrooms or two telephones.[43]

As the car changed status from luxury to necessity, there was an "unhealthy" change in the behavior and the public's subsequent general impression of the car salesman. This particular example is unique only in its completeness; the idea that used car salesmen were *once* the purveyors of questionable merchandise was a recurring theme during the time in the field:

Before the war, it was a matter of list price or nothing. Then after the war, there was a low supply and high demand, so you got a real inflated price which resulted in it being a high status item and then the name of the game was load 'em up with all the goodies. Then in the fifties, the competition was greater and by the mid fifties, salesmen were notorious for being deceptive. They'd even steal the registration . . . why a guy would drive in to look at a car and he'd stay around for awhile and you'd say, "look fella, you'd better buy cause I just sold your car to a wholesaler," and lots of times, he had. A guy would come into a dealer and he's afraid he's really going to be taken. It's not like that anymore, but you just try and convince some of these guys of that, but in a way, you can't blame 'em.

Another salesman wistfully recalled his own initial contact with a used car salesman when as a child his father drove home the family's very first automobile:

It was a real cold winter's day; everything was all froze up and he drove it up and it ran just fine, but then when he tried to start it up again, it wouldn't start. We looked inside it and under and there was this huge hole in the side of the engine, and the bastard that sold it to him had poured water into it till it froze and it lasted till he got home. It was defrosting all along the way and it was all melted by the time he got home and there wasn't a thing he could do about it. But now it's the old law of supply and demand again. We allow a guy to keep a car for thirty days and if he's not completely satisfied, he can bring it back and apply the price of it to another used car here if he decides he wants to trade.

Changing times have influenced conditions and, consequently, behavior. When "You can throw a rock and hit a Ford dealer on the South Shore," a dealer must adjust his actions accordingly. Although the supply of new cars is high (an estimated 9.6 million new American cars produced in 1970)[44] and the demand is slightly down in a recessional economy for new cars, the used car business is much less susceptible to the laws of supply and demand. Each used car is unique in the way that each new car is identical. As previously mentioned, the customer has no choice over color, condition, age or options on a used car, while he can exercise his choice over all of these in a new car. Most salesmen prefer selling used rather than new cars for this very reason, although almost all do both. There is also more money to be made in the sale of a used car.

In a not very surprising way, the history of the salesman and his product are inextricably woven. "An old horse trader" was seldom used as a term of endearment, and the car functionally replaced the horse. The history can be seen as reaching beyond the product, clear back to the function.

On the other hand, even if the history of buying cars had a history rivalling the purest endeavors of mankind throughout recorded history, the fact that a car is probably the second largest purchase (beyond that of a house) that most people ever make would lend an emotional air to the proceedings. Because a car is not expected to last as long as a house or to be nearly as good an investment, most customers face the prospect of buying a car with something less than the gay abandon envisioned in many car advertisements. The salesmen are well aware of this fact:

A car is the worst investment you can make. The moment you sign on the dotted line, the car is worth a third less than you paid for it, even if you just drive it around the block and bring it back.

This salesman was talking about buying a new car, but the feelings are pervasive enough to cover "pre-owned" cars as well.[45] Realizing that a car is a very poor investment adds to the customers' misgivings that he's buying "someone else's mistake" in a used car. (If something major wasn't wrong with the car in the first place, why would it have been traded?)

The trepidation with which a potential customer enters the used car lot can be seen as historical, fiscal, and emotional. The motivation for entering the lot in the first place can be seen as the "simple" need for a car. If the customer is just a "shopper," then his motivation is comparatively low and his competitiveness is rather high, and the possibility of a sale is reduced. One method the salesman can utilize to deal with this nonproductive state of affairs is to increase the customer's motivation by offering the customer what appears to be competitive advantage. This is often accomplished by means of a low-ball (an unrealistically low price on a car).[46]

A low-ball will hasten the process of returning a customer to a particular used car lot, and time is important to the salesman. His whole business orientation is time depedent; a man needs a car before he goes on vacation, the lot closes at nine, the month ends in two days, it's been a long day. All of these contingencies are both compelling and time dependent.

Time plays quite a different role and is relevant to both bargain and distrust (not to mention control) in that at some point in almost all instances, salesman and customer exchange roles. Nearly anyone who comes in to buy a used car is also trying to sell a used car (his own) and the distrust that the customer has of the salesman is likely founded on the knowledge of the customer's own behavior as salesman (and vice versa):

Boy, did I ever get the best of this guy when I sold my car. I told him that I had just had it in for a tune-up (I had taken it in and the mechanic said there wasn't anything he could do that wouldn't be a major repair and very expensive) and that the engine was only two years old (it had 90,000 miles on it) and that it did beautifully at 70 without a problem, except a little shimmy (that little shimmy would rattle your teeth; my mechanic told me it was suicidal to drive the thing over 70). He (the used car salesman) really trusted me, though, cause I told him about the shimmy and I showed him this little dent in the fender, so he thought I was a real honest guy . . . a slight shimmy between 70 and 72, jar your teeth . . . lethal . . . I really took him.

The fellow was chuckling himself silly, congratulating himself that he had fooled the unsuspecting salesman by "not exactly lying to him . . . I didn't tell him anything that wasn't the truth."

And, indeed, he hadn't, but he had been most careful to imply fairly neatly. This ex-customer considered himself clever and his actions more than justifiable on the basis of the assumed unscrupulous behavior of the used car salesman. The salesmen, as will be seen more clearly in Chapter 4, use identical criteria as the basis for their rationalizations and subsequent behavior. Sutherland[47] notes the same phenomenon on the part of the thief as do Goffman[48] and Maurer[49] in their discussion of "conning" — the mark is "asking for it" and therefore deserves what he gets.

In addition to two strangers dealing with one another over a product of which one is ignorant, whose value is in question, in an unfamiliar manner, the customer's disadvantage of not knowing price, technique, or value is somewhat offset by the salesman's lack of control as well. Although he knows more about the car than the customer and is presumably more adept at bargaining (assuming a non-Arabic customer), he has only a vague idea of what the car costs the dealership and, consequently, how much he can sell it for. The salesman acts in the capacity of broker between the customer and the house (who must sign off any sale the salesman makes before it becomes official).

The whole concept of acting on another's behalf as an intermediary is common in our culture.[50] This is a special case of that kind of situation where the middleman has something tangible to gain depending on his actions while also receiving something akin to a standard fee regardless of his actions. The salesman receives a percentage of the cash difference between the car he takes in trade and the car he sells, but only up to a rather limited amount ($25 to $35 depending on the dealership). Whether he gets that extra hundred for the car is quite often irrelevant in this context. In another context, he may not be empowered to sell the car at all if he doesn't meet a certain minimum that the house has in mind for the car (contingent on the intake price of the car, cost of repairs, appearance reconditioning, length of time on the lot, number of similar models available, etc.). All of these are relative unknowns to the salesman. The house simply doesn't tell him. If the salesman undercuts the house too often, or tries to, he will be fired. Yet, if he sells a certain number of cars per month, he will receive a cash bonus on each one. It thus behooves him to sell as many cars as possible since his commission on each one goes up as he sells more. The best way to sell a car is to lower the price. Because of all of these factors, the salesman is between the customer and the house. His own loyalties are financially split between them, not to mention his emotional ones (most salesmen are dependent emotionally and fiscally on being liked, even more than the rest of us).

Most literature deals with interactions between two groups. Yet, many interactions can be seen as occurring between three parties, even if the third party is unseen at the time. Stock brokers, real estate agents, welfare workers are only a few of those whose formal structure is based on three-party interaction. Seldom do informal interactions deal with less than three. A mother disciplining

a child must often consider not only her own preferences and wishes but also those of her husband. A teacher assigning a grade must consider not only the individual student, but the class, the department (a reputation as either a pushover or an unreasoning sadist is seldom a boost to one's career, especially before tenure is assured), and the university as a whole. In a very real sense, societal norms make intermediaries of us all. By observing this very specific form of brokerage, insight could conceivably be gained as to the process itself.

Simmel[51] was fascinated by the concept of three-person groups, but described them in a way not particularly relevant to the salesmen. Here, they are a "naturally" occurring grouping of three that exist not primarily for competition, but for less differentiated functioning. The alliances are a shifting thing as will be seen in later chapters and not easily predictable from a look at the list of players. Here, rather than having specific spheres of influence with essentially unlimited control within those spheres as Simmel details, the house, customer, and salesman have limited power. Authority is overlapping at best, undifferentiated at worst, making things a good deal more tangled. The idea is to sell a car, and all of these interactions are secondary and servant to that; the relationships occur only with respect to the goal.

In Simmel's discussions, the relationships occur first and any particular goal exists relative to those relationships.

Because of these shifting relationships within the brokerage schema, classical exchange theory receives a neat twist. As opposed to the usual theory, the currency of exchange is not primarily gratitude or indebtedness, although they very definitely do exist as secondary goals, but money, a complete flip-flop of Blau's concept of exchange.[52]

There should not be little doubt as to the importance of clarifying the uses of the bargain as a social paradigm. The frequency of its occurrence in both everyday functioning and sociological inquiry has been delineated.

It has been defined, with emphasis on the salient factors of control, predictability, trust, and competence or their absence as significant to understanding any ongoing process with the bargain as the underlying structure.

Used car salesmen have been presented as an appropriate group on which to model a study of the bargain because while on the one hand their product (the car) has some unique properties, their bargaining as a process is straightforward, intentional, and without subterfuge and, as such, is easy to study with minimal "surgery" necessary.

The influence of the product as unique to the relationship will be further highlighted in the pages that remain as will the cultural value of the used car salesman. The relevance, importance, applicability and complexity of the bargain as used by the salesman as well as used as a tool of human intercourse has only been hinted at; the remainder of the task lies in the pages to follow. The next chapter deals with how the study was conducted, conceptualized, and analyzed including a model for all the work to follow.

2   Procedure, Practice, and Perspective

It is amazing how seldom the crucial questions of sociological research are left both unasked and unanswered – how is a subject picked for study, why was it picked, and how is it to be studied?

The question of why often determines what group is to be studied in the case of a grant whose purpose is the collection of data in a certain field. In the particular case of the present study, no such constraints were involved; here, no grants were involved, no methodological commitment promised, no theory to be enhanced.

Used car salesmen were selected as a group worthy of study on the basis of the very personal experience of buying a used car. During discussions on various car lots, the salesmen seemed to be an extremely talkative, congenial group caught in an interesting dilemma. They were forced to deal with a public that made no bones about its feelings with regard to used car salesmen, and the feelings were far from complimentary.

On the basis of initial interest, I planned a short paper, but as the research progressed, a simple description of the occupation of used car salesmen seemed wholly inadequate to describe the findings.[1] The group appeared to be worthy of prolonged research for reasons specified in the preceding chapter. The question then became how best to study this group. The answer depended on what it was I was searching for. The choice of this group as opposed to the infinite set of groups to study dictated that I study men at work selling a product and, thereby, interacting with other human beings. My initial wish was to describe their situation on the used car lot in contrast to their behavior off the lot, but I changed my mind when I found access to their "off hours" limited and not of particular interest.

It became apparent that the give and take of the salesmen was their most salient characteristic and the one in which I was most interested. Action based on previous action and anticipating future behavior is descriptive of Mead's concept of emergent process, so a descriptive theory was inherent in the situation. It could be argued that my familiarity with Mead at least underscored the "inherent" nature of its existence, but so it can be argued that any researcher's knowledge (though no more or less than any other individual's previous experience) tends to structure a present situation (a Meadian thought in itself). Mead's concept did seem exceptionally apropos since emergent process, as a concept, has some fascinating gestalt properties:

... emergent properties are essentially relationships between elements in a

15

structure. The relationships are not contained in the elements though they could not exist without them and they define the structure.[2]

It is not surprising that Mead's concept of the whole being greater than the sum of the parts should be similar to the concepts of the Gestalt school since they were contemporaneous. But just as the principles of Gestalt psychology were poorly represented verbally, so, too, the quality of emergent process is much more than a word or even a concept; it is action, life. It moves and breathes so that when a situation such as this one is under scrutiny, where there is action and process and change, the result is not a study of the used car salesman or bargaining or control or competency or predictability, but human beings doing their best to get along, to survive, to get whatever it is that they feel makes their life liveable, tolerable or pleasant.

The question then becomes how best to study this process. The answer in this case was simple enough — watch it happen, be there while it was happening, watch behavior emerge. The only trouble with watching human interaction and trying to understand it is that the uninitiated (researcher) needs an informant and an informant can describe only his own view of the proceedings. The technique of participant observation solves part of the problem, but only part. By observing, action can be seen as it occurs and, later, questioning uncovers much of the latent meaning of action. But even the researcher can see through the eyes of only one participant at a time, and often a switch to the focus of another is impossible.[3]

In theory, in studying a bargain, it would undoubtedly be enlightening to be able to study all parties simultaneously, i.e., to be able to watch the action and interaction through each possible point of view. This, of course, is impossible not only because of the impossibility of being with more than one side at the same time physically but by the mutually exclusive nature of some relationships — you have to be "with" one side or the other to gain any information. Interaction between customer, house, and salesmen certainly fall into this mutually exclusive category. Because of the distrust factors involved, an observer, in order to be privy to anything deeper than the explicit verbal communication, must choose a side. Like any other choice, the choice of a side creates its own set of methodological, ideological, and moral dilemmas, what Becker calls the "hierarchy of credibility"[4] or the tendency to believe one group more than another. Because the researcher is both physically and emotionally "closer" to one group, a natural bias could be predicted which can only be overcome by a rigorous and painstaking delineation of his point of view.

I chose to study the salesman's view of the bargain because it deals with both the customer and the house and is thus pivotal and action centered.[5] Of crucial importance to an action-oriented study is entree or access to information.

Access to the salesman's point of view was never a problem. The men are delightfully easy to study. They talk and talk and talk. They are unselfconscious and most willing to explain what they're doing, saying, and thinking.[6] With a single exception, they were very willing to have me around while they talked with customers and would explain my presence by saying that they were "teaching me the ropes."

Seeing the world through their eyes was at once both natural and necessary.[7] In order to watch the situation as it developed, to observe process as it emerged, it was important to be there and to be a part of it. Because of the factors of distrust discussed in the preceding chapter, siding with more than one group at a time would have seriously jeopardized access to information. If neither side is sure where you stand, the likelihood of significant information acquisition is minimized.[8] For example, if I was seen to be on the house's side, the salesmen would have considered me a spy; if I spent a lot of time with the customer, out of hearing of the salesman, he would have suspected that I was giving the customer information on how to "get" the salesman. Obviously my actions were suspect from the point of view of both the customer and the house, but the salesmen explained my presence to the customer and I had to arrange entree originally through the house, so suspicion was minimized and I had access to the group I considered most crucial, the salesmen.

However, the major disadvantage of relinquishing the right or need to study all parties on equal terms (if such a thing is possible) is that the research must of necessity adopt a one-sided view of the proceedings. This limitation in this particular study is less shattering when the alternatives are considered.

Access to an informant before and after interaction is not only helpful but quite necessary unless one is willing to settle for and depend upon his own superficial, uninitiated version of what happened in an unfamiliar situation. The house is seldom on the scene during the actual bargaining and the only way you can ascertain a potential customer is if he has entered the lot of the showroom, so access prior to the interaction is impossible in his case.

On the other hand, it is virtually impossible *not* to glean a certain amount of information from both customer and house during the study. By just being there, conversation is invited, in the case of the customer when the salesman temporarily leaves the scene or, in the case of the house, when the entree is arranged. In addition, one of the untouted advantages of being a sociologist is that there are always a large but unofficial pool of unaffiliated "amateurs" in the "field" who are more than willing to offer their theories and "research" at nonprofessional gatherings if the conversation should lag. A casual reference to my research when asked what I was studying has never failed to elicit lengthy dissertations based on personal experience or secondhand documentations.

If it was ever in doubt, the supposition that salesmen are a cultural phenomenon is borne out by the fact that almost everyone has an opinion on them; they have either bought a used car from one, known someone who has bought a used car from one, or seen an ad, cartoon or article concerning used car sales and salesmen. The study could have theoretical and methodological substance at this point. I had achieved a way and a point of view through which to study bargaining.

At this point a theory and a compatible method had been achieved. A point of view became obvious, yet all this description ignores the near mystical transformation from the dryness of theory and methodology into the reality of useful technique. To say theory and methodology had been achieved sounds like the first plateau had been reached, whereas in actuality, the experience wás really quite different.

The filling out, the actualization, that theory is descriptive and technique a useful, usable tool ranks alongside the understanding of epsilon. Once you understand, the fact of not always having known borders on the incomprehensible. Yet, previous to the insight, Bernoulli and Riemann can make life fairly miserable.

The jump from rote to reason is the same "gut" understanding of the synchronization of clutch, brake and gas. Suddenly it's fun, and it's yours. At that point, the idea of participant observation is more exciting than the subject for study. The revelation is a truly joyous one that theory is real and that with a few minor alterations or altercations as the case may be, method works and really is an integral part of theory.

This feeling comes when there's a sense that you're seeing things the salesmen's way, when you begin to size up customers the same way they do, when their description is yours. Yet, you are still quite aware of it being your's and their's. When you begin to understand not the words but the concept they are discussing, you know you're finding their perspective and you're constantly aware that parts of it may be shared. But it's still basically their's; you know because you have to ask questions, some of it you just don't get, like a punch line that has to be explained. Your understanding and your conceptualization is continually shifting and rearranging and just plain changing to include new bits of information or to adjust to ideas that just don't fit.[9]

The words are fun and often a help. Understanding the vernacular, in addition to making you feel like you belong, gives "scientific" proof and insight into the thoughts that are expressed.[10, 11] The salesmen are pleased when you can understand the slang and seem to take a certain amount of pride in your knowledge; they like to share. But the words are only a part, doubly symbolic. It's when you and he arrive at the same price for a clunker and can size up the tire kickers from the hot prospects that a perspective becomes shared.

Yet, only parts of the perspective are shared. The words and thoughts and actions have to be filtered through my system. Perhaps the greatest single advantage of the method of actually being there while it's happening and writing it down as it happened before it is organized or analyzed is that anybody else can at least look at the data, the words, the sentences as they were before they became mine, before they were dissected, and see what they think. They can check out the vocabulary, the sentences, the descriptions without having to rely on my filtering system. It's there, unadulterated, untouched. The interpretation is carefully bounded and does not impinge upon the data, and therefore, cannot taint it.[12] Field data is recorded verbatim in the pages that follow, allowing the reader an opportunity to evaluate my conclusions.

And because the data is recorded as it was, upon rereading the notes, it all happens all over again, and its existence can be verified a second time. When it is first recorded, you're a part of it and trying mostly to remember, but afterward, upon rereading, you can watch and enjoy and think about it all over again. Mead's enthusiasm for the knife-edged present becomes quite justified,[13, 14] and sociology seems not only important, but enjoyable. Its importance is based not on its youth or the fact that it is radical or learned or rigorous or scientific or fundable, but because it is alive. It really is people doing their thing, just plain living, like everyone else only in their own way and by faithfully reporting it and painstakingly analyzing it, there is the possibility of a little more understanding, a bit more awareness, that perhaps can make us all a bit more human, a bit more able.

The participant observer is in a strange position by being both in and out of the world he is studying (perhaps as a microcosmic Frommian universe[15] in which man is both part and apart from his environment).[16]

Dealing with a group such as salesmen is explicitly delineated by Becker, who notes that in the study of deviancy, the sociologist tends to exhibit sympathy toward the deviant group under scrutiny. This choice can easily cloud, direct or distort the data.[17] The difficulty has been minimized here since this group is not particularly "deviant" although it most certainly has strong negative societal connotations associated with it. Another solution to Becker's fears is achieved by the fact that unretouched data is included, thereby minimizing a reader's dependence on a single interpretation.

Becker's point again emphasizes the limitations of the choice of theory and method; only one point of view can really be delineated. Here, statistical analysis is infeasible and data collection is nonstructured, but participant observation allows for the possibility of sidestepping facile superficialities for real insight into a dynamic process that a methodology less dependent on actual observation might miss.

Used car salesmen, for instance, are notorious for the cheerful, smiling, extremely friendly approach to the unsuspecting, naive customer. The assumption is that this is a phony facade of friendliness designed to make the customer trust the salesman. While this may be the case, there is another, more parsimonious explanation for their behavior. When used car salesmen are selling, interacting, things really move. It's exciting and lively and unpredictable and challenging and, as they admit, just plain fun. When no customers are around, their existence is unimaginably boring. There is nothing to do and nobody to see and all the time in the world to do it in. There is a lot full of cars to look at with which they are already painfully familiar and a small office in which to sit. Lots of coffee is fetched. Mealtimes become the high point of the day. Newspapers are thoroughly read, and a radio is an indispensible factor in their emotional survival. Clients are supposed to be called and postcards written and notes made. But, basically, they just sit.

The lethargy is overwhelming. If another salesman is on, there is somebody to talk to, but also someone to share the ups, so often it is an even longer time between action. So, part of the eagerness and friendliness with which the salesman greets the customer isn't feigned at all. In addition to having a sales prospect, he's very glad to have someone to talk to.

Participant observation imparts a liveliness to the data, but neither theory nor method is dictated. Neither a model nor a structure is obvious. To the contrary, while theory is definitely present, if sometimes obscure, hypotheses are operational if existent at all. They are used only so long as they are helpful; as such, they offer no format for a conceptualization of an entire study.

In participant observation, the model, the structure of the group is reflected by the configuration of the data. With apologies to Glaser and Strauss,[18] who cheerfully extol the virtues of grounded theory and emergent hypothesizing, this is not the easiest way to run an airline. Since a definite hypothesis was never involved, the endpoint of a study is seldom obvious. In this case, a research plan[19] was drawn up partially through the study on the basis of data acquired in the field, but the sense of "completeness"[20] was achieved quite independently of the plan. When different salesmen on different lots selling different kinds of cars began "repeating," saying things that other salesmen had said, I felt I was writing down the right things, conceptualizing appropriate behavior and watching the relevant things. This feeling of "being on the right track" is hard to delineate, yet quite compelling.[21]

The related question — "what can the data be compared to?" — is equally perilous without a pre-ordained model, and for the same reasons. If the technique employed in the field allows data to "assume its own shape," then references to other studies and "the literature" in general become crucial.

The group's quasi-deviancy brings up the point of the use of relevant literature within the study. This particular study has correlates in a semi-infinite group of areas, as do most studies, if reduced to the "basics." However, just as language is significant in determining thought and perspective of subjects, it becomes a trap for the unwary researcher. Language is a double-edged tool; it is not only evidence of structuring, but conversely, structures in itself. If I adhere to the literature on the professions, then I begin to structure my group in terms of how like or unlike other professions (assuming that the salesmen could be even remotely considered as such) they are, which could be totally irrelevant to the impact and excitement of the group. The point has been made (parenthetically) that the term "professional" can and is being applied to nearly every group and, as such, has lost much of its original meaning.[22]

The value judgment inherent in a label is also an added incentive to tread lightly in the sociological archives. There is a large temptation to tie the salesman in with the literature on deviant groups since they are a group rather out of the main stream, but if I succumb to the temptation, then I have structured my group in an exceedingly inappropriate way.[23]

Some elements involved in selling could be considered a "con," but, then, so could some elements in teaching, hunting, or combing one's hair. The question is, when considering an analogy, is more disservice done than information imparted or insight gained? Is it at all useful to consider salesmen criminal or deviant? Does this stance impart any knowledge or offer an information that is relevant?

Undoubtedly salesmen could be studied as *The Big Con*[24] revisited, but it would be just that. This group is a nearly unique combination of factors that can be studied and understood and abstracted to a great many human interactions, none of which deal with working, conning or driving. References to the literature are limited to central or basic considerations rather than facile, lifeless sorties into the literature.

One sociological subgroup of literature that will be occasionally referenced is that of exchange theory. Basically exchange theory uses the physical analogy of exchange to explain the more complex realm of social exchange. Here, the converse is true; instead of the more conventional relationship, in the used car game, sociological considerations are analogies for the actual physical exchange. Although any exchange can be seen as social, used car salesmen are dependent on both social and economic considerations. On the other hand, gratitude and reciprocity play a role, but it is secondary to the actual physical exchange. As Blau points out:

Two conditions must be met for behavior to lead to social exchange. It must be oriented toward ends that can only be achieved through interaction with other persons and it must seek to adapt means to further the achievement of these ends.[25]

Although buying and selling a used car can most certainly be seen in these terms, an additional constraint is that:

Social exchange is distinguished from strictly economic exchange by the unspecified obligations incurred in it and the trust both required for and promoted by it.[26]

The obligations incurred are in existence, but, ironically, trust is neither required nor promoted (necessarily) by the interaction.

Another variation on a sociological theme is offered by the three-part brokerage arrangement, a third kind of "naturally" occurring triad in addition to the two Simmel described,[27] since neither the nonpartisan third or the *tertius gaudens* seems particularly appropriate here. The triad present in this study functions quite differently than in terms of either an uninvolved third party or the third party who gains by throwing his weight to one of the two other parties.

As has been broadly hinted, the very dynamism of this group dictates an equally lively methodology and forbids a deadening, limp categorization to an inappropriate but well-traveled rut.

One of the classical sociological ruts (not so very well traveled) into which the present study offers insight is the concept of perspective. Becker and Geer delineate the definition and use of a group perspective in *Boys in White,* but discuss it within the confines of a medical school. Here, the concept of group perspective can be seen on an individual basis as it bumps up against others who do not share the perspective. How the generalized perspective as it applies to specific interaction can be seen, for the format of this research has assumed the shape of adversaries preparing to interact.

Participants involved in any interaction always have a set of experiences, expectations, and assumptions that they bring with them. If both are members of a larger group, one can safely assume that they have some experiences in common, some shared understanding which could be considered a common "culture." This set of preconceived notions will, to a certain extent, determine the course of the interaction on the basis of their communality. To the extent that both individuals have an identical base (a practical impossibility) the shape of the encounter can be predicted by either since both presumably have the same point of view, the same goals, apply the same criteria, obey the same rules, and thus (hypothetically) act in the same way. As one might guess this degree of similarity is seldom achieved, so most human interaction falls somewhere between unrealistic sameness and a similarly unrealistic difference. That extreme would be encountered when two individuals shared no common meeting ground, language, philosophy, behavioral norms, or the other commodities thought to be basic to "humanness."

This study will demonstrate how individuals with varying and occasionally conflicting views of the universe, their respective roles, goals, self-images, manage to successfully deal with one another – the bargain that occurs being the successful culmination of their attempts to deal with one another. Thus, the used car salesman may hopefully offer some insight into the process by which noncompatible individuals and their goals are made compatible. To facilitate this understanding, the study has been separated into chapters dealing with salesmen and their view of themselves, salesmen's view of customers, the salesman's view of the house, the customer's view of the salesman (which, in this case, is the idealized customer, the society's view of the salesman) and the culmination of these differing views in action.

The format of the study, because it is reflective of the underlying structure of the behavior, is of particular significance. The first chapter sets up a macrocosm, the universe of human action and the place of bargaining behavior in the world as it always was and always will be.

Next, the scope is narrowed to the slightly less global in looking at the cultural or societal view by focusing on a society's view of men who bargain. Ostensibly, this view is called the customer's view of the salesman, but is really a cultural reflection of a phenomenon.

The trilogy of the salesman's view of himself, his client, and his boss compose the three chapters that describe the view of the world from the salesman's perch. The importance of these differing views or perspectives lies in their existence as a determinant of action. Mead very neatly places the whole concept into a time frame by citing perspective or the organic resultant of experience, expectation, anticipation, self-image, shared understanding as the relationship of both past and future to the present.[28] Both past (experience) and future (anticipation) are distilled into immediacy in the present (action). This study offers an instantaneous look at this distillation at the moment conflicting views of past and future clash rather spectacularly, are molded and merged, between suspicious customer and successful salesman.

This clash, of course, is not a unique occurrence, but rather a paradigm for all human interaction where individuals are not identical in their views of themselves, each other, their situation, their goals, and their rules, yet deal with one another.

Finally, these differing views of the universe are brought together in the bargain, but not before the salesman attempts to alter the perspective of his adversary. In the final chapter, the link is again forged between the particular of the microcosm and the wider, universal applicability. The bargain again assumes larger proportions.

Two appendixes of particular interest have been included, one a glossary to add both flavor and insight to the actual functioning world of the salesman through the vehicle of his language. The second appendix is also intended to lend insight, but in a contrasting manner. It is a discussion of the utility of the game playing model to the study of human behavior, its strengths and weaknesses in this specific instance in terms of universal functioning. While not an integral part of the study, the discussion of perspective and definition of the situation leading to specific goals of behavior dictated by specific rules does point to the concept of the game. It is these perspectives, goals and actions that compose the study on the bargain. Thus, the final section is a treatise on why the "next logical step forward" was not taken.

3 Through a Windshield Darkly

The strength of expectation could not be denied by anyone who ever listened to Martin Luther King, Jr.'s speeches and could consequently predict the color of his audience from his accent. There are many examples of the strength of what we assume another's opinion to be to influence our action. The most common example of this assumption and its resultant behavior is the stereotype — the expectation that doesn't allow for deviation. It is no accident that the word originally meant:

... anything undistinguished by individual marks, as if produced from a stereotype [which is] a plate made by taking a mold or matrix of a printing surface and making from this a cast in type metal ... hence [with regard to action] to repeat without variation; to hackney.[1]

A more behavioral view logically enough follows suit:

... a relatively simplex condition, especially of a social group (e.g., "All Orientals look alike"). Stereotypes tend to be widely shared by members of a given society.[2]

The dumb football player, the dizzy blonde, the shiftless black, the avaricious Jew, the neurotic suburban housewife; the whole study of stereotypes would be lost without such societal assumptions, i.e., that the present (or future) situation is the same as a past one.

Stereotypes are the extreme of expectation, leaving no room for variation, yet in our daily lives we are all influenced by and act on the basis of notions gained from previous experience, either our own or someone else's that we are willing to accept as our own.[3] Hastorf and Cantril cleverly point out how these expectations influence the actions of those to whom they are directed as well as those who hold them in their description of a Dartmouth-Princeton football game.[4] They gleefully point out that what you "saw" was determined by who you were and which side you supported. As they summarized: "We do not simply "react to" a happening or to some impingment from the environment ... we behave according to what we bring to the occasion ..."[5]

Mead gives these perceived expectations a place of central importance in his diagram of man when he describes human-ness as consisting of an "I" and a "me":

The "I" is the response of the organism to the attitudes of the others; the "me" is the organized set of attitudes of others which one himself assumes. The attitudes of the others constitute the organized "me" and then one reacts toward that as an "I."[6]

This "I" and "me" are both part of the essential self:

We may have a better self and a worse self, but that again is not the "I" as over against the "me," because they are both selves. We approve of one and disapprove of the other, but when we bring up one or the other they are there for such approval as "me's." The "I" does not get into the limelight; we talk to ourselves, but do not see ourselves. The "I" reacts to the self which arises through the taking of the attitudes of others. Through taking those attitudes we have introduced the "me" and we react to it as an "I."[7, 8]

In terms of action and everyday functioning:

The "I" is his action over against that social situation within his own conduct, and it gets into his experience only after he has carried out the act. Then he is aware of it. He had to do such a thing and he did it. He fulfills his duty and he may look with pride at the throw which he made. The "me" arises to do that duty — that is the way in which it arises in his experience. He had in him all the attitudes of others, calling for a certain response; that was the "me" of that situation, and his response is the "I."[9]

In summary:

The "I," then, in this relation of the "I" and the "me," is something that is, so to speak, responding to a social situation which is within the experience of the individual. It is the answer which the individual makes to the attitude which others take toward him when he assumes an attitude toward them.[10]

Everyone is familiar with the feeling of doing what is expected, by taking a birthday present to a party, refraining from an off-color remark in polite company, of not going back on one's word. In some cases, the action is based on a tacit understanding and sometimes stated. In all cases mentioned and in countless others, the opinions, actions and very existence of the perceived "other" is fundamental to action.

Used car salesmen are not exempted from this chain. But, as discussed in earlier chapters, used car salesmen are not merely members of a society, doing a job; they have symbolic value in and of themselves.

The presidential campaign of 1968, if nothing else, convinced just about everyone that used car salesmen are a basic part of the American scene. "Would you buy a used car from this man?" undoubtedly did little to elect Richard Nixon to the highest office in the land, but it did epitomize a national cynicism toward the used car salesman. On the one hand, this makes them interesting subjects for study; on the other hand, it is nearly impossible to document some forms of cultural phenomena, i.e., what we all "know." Because we all know it to be true, "it" often remains unrecorded (a point historians and anthropologists also sadly lament). For this reason, what is not recorded is often as important as what is.

The dilemma is this: if we acknowledge that human beings often act on the basis of a perceived opinion that they attribute to "another" (he thinks I'm stupid) and that this perceived opinion is instrumental in understanding the first person's behavior, but also acknowledge the fact that what we all "know" (everyone knows that he thinks I'm stupid) is often left unrecorded, how do we obtain this potentially vital information?

In our world, the daily newspaper serves as the diary of the commonplace and as such, along with other non-"scientific" publications provides an insight into what "other" thinks of the used car salesman on a widespread basis. This form of documentation is not without precedent. Hughes, in his disucssion of others, cites politicians, playwrights and novelists as being sensitive to the gestures and attitudes of others and, therefore, reasonable sources of sociological data.[11]

Louis Wirth, in discussing consensus and mass communication, makes the point even stronger by suggesting, as far back as 1948, that: "Mass communication is rapidly becoming, if it is not already, the main framework of the web of social life."[12] Even more compellingly:

Consensus in mass democracies . . . is not so much agreement on all issues or even on the most essential substantive issues among all the members of society as it is the established habit of intercommunications . . .[13]

Thus, the very existence of information about used car salesmen in the popular press bespeaks consensus and shared understanding.

This chapter is intended to delineate the "me" of the used car salesman and when read with the three chapters that follow describing the "I" will complete a picture of the used car salesman self. This is the chapter of what others think of the salesman and since salesmen themselves presumably have access to the same newspapers as well as to the people who read the newspapers we can begin to talk about shared information.

So, although there is little "hard data" in the literature concerning either used car salesmen or the public's view of them, they are indeed a cultural phenomenon as evidenced by jokes, newspaper articles, fictional references, and the like; possibly they are the second most common source of jokes and unpleasantries, humbled only by the mother-in-law.

Working on this assumption, the majority of the information included in this chapter as representative of the "public" view of the salesman has been gathered from clippings, articles, occasional books that are generally available to the reading public.[14] Commentaries have also been gleaned from on-the-spot customers and informal "informants" who were aware of my research and had miscellaneous thoughts on the subject. Presumably the information that is recorded in the public press is representative of the public's view of the salesman as well as the salesman's view of the public's view of him.

The impact of this chapter is that the public at large has ideas about cars and car salesmen which it gleans from the public press. These ideas are over-whelmingly negative and, as such, are an obstacle to free and easy interaction between salesman and customer. As such, these stereotypes are an obstacle the salesman must overcome if he is to sell a car to a customer.

The following quote describing a fictional Detroit salesman is unusual only in the length and thoroughness of the description:

He cut his teeth selling used cars in Livernois, the used car capital of the world. He wore herringbone suits. His shoes were pointed and polished. On his right hand he wore a two-carat diamond ring. He lied glibly. He had no conscience, no pity for the suckers. He was the archetype successful young car hustler. The razzle-dazzle, near nefarious business suited him perfectly. In the Trenton streets and fields, down river, where he grew up, there were few holds barred. Livernois, with its stretchable rule, was but a sideward step, and he operated there with cocksureness and abandon . . . By the time he was thirty he was earning fifteen thousand dollars a year [in 1930]. He was independent and sought after. He switched back and forth among the big lots on used car row as the fancy suited him . . . [after his hair suddenly and mysteriously turned white at age thirty] . . . he was not at all dismayed. He was pleased. Suddenly he was distinguished. His car-salesman's mind leaped to the possibilities here unfolded. A distinguished used-car salesman! It was a natural . . . the grin looked, somehow, now honest and reassuring beneath the white hair. Now there'd be no more skeptics, no more wary shoppers looking at him out of the corners of their eyes to betray their distrust of a black-haired, fast-talking kid with a diamond ring . . . In those first few weeks with his new white hair, he cut a hell of a swath through the gullible shoppers. His income soared. Singing Sam, his current employer, fearing to lose him, offered him a chance to buy into the lot. But he looked at Singing Sam with a sudden distaste. Sam was a man with brown baggy trousers and a toothpick in his mouth.[15]

The character described above goes on to recount:

When I peddled cars, I lied about mileage and piston rings. They were normal lies, lies we called white lies. They were lies.[16]

It is important to remember this chapter in presenting what we all know is not concerned necessarily with the truth, objectivity or accuracy of the information but, rather, with its existence. That we all *do* know it means it serves as a potential basis for our actions.

A predominant view of the used car salesman chidingly asks whether or not "you would buy a used car and/or war from this man." The analogy of Nixon as a typically untrustworthy used car salesman is sufficiently strong to be the tacit basis of a political cartoon showing Nixon driving a beat-up combination jeep and tank saying, "Good heavens. It's a used car and I bought it."[17]

In fact, the commentary is so widespread that *Punch,* the British humour magazine, published a cartoon with a caricature of Ted Heath, the leader of the Conservative Party and then candidate for Prime Minister, in his boat, the Morning Cloud, smiling toothily with arms crossed, leaning out of the picture asking, "Would you buy a used boat from this man?."[18]

Even *Consumer Reports,* that bastion of the unstated and the conservative, ran a cartoon depicting Honest John's used car lot with Honest John himself, balding and with a tiny mustache, and a pipesmoking, rather disgruntled customer skeptically eyeing a car marked "clean" with John saying, "It's one of our better lemons, I must say."[19]

In terms of personality, car salesmen are thought of as dishonest, sleezy, and scummy. In an article having absolutely nothing to do with cars or salesmen, a movie star was quoted as saying: "The big studios are run by men with used-car dealers' mentality. We are going to bust them, he declared, grinning maliciously". . . ."the people running the studios are functioning illiterates . . ."[20]

Again, it should be stressed that the veracity of these statements is not as significant as their existence. Obviously, people believe them to be true to the extent that the phrase "used car dealers' mentality" is not thought to need explanation.

To a certain extent, it is only when these assumptions are challenged that their pervasiveness comes into focus. The *New York Times* reports that an auto sales manager was in the process of suing two high school girls for libel to the tune of a million dollars:

The plaintiff is Rudolph J. Moberg, an auto sales manager who is reportedly shown in a sequence about a minute long, discussing a business transaction on a car lot with a teenaged girl, while a rock record, whose lyrics treat narcotics pushing, furnishes background music.
"Sick America" is reported to be the title of the film. School officials involved will not discuss either the title or the incident.
. . . [Moberg] contends he was depicted as an unscrupulous car salesman and wrongly identified as having sold narcotics to teenagers.[21]

Unsafe from the hands of teeny-boppers, the beleaguered salesman suffers even at the hands of the women's page with reference to, of all things, weddings:

Weddings today are sold like used cars, mostly by the wrong person, with this or that gadget thrown in that you neither need nor want. "For just another hundred dollars," purrs the saleslady, "you can have lasagna or a taste of YOUR national dish added to the regular dinner." A wedding should be a ceremony, not a racket.[22]

Compliments, when they do appear, are backhanded: "I don't mean to say that all used-car dealers are dishonest," Mrs. [Bess Myerson] Grant said, "but . . . the evil reputation of the used car dealer isn't entirely undeserved."[23] She goes on to pooh-pooh the viewpoint of the dealers who admit that "a used car is a considerable gamble to both seller and buyer."[24]

Betty Furness adds her famous voice to those maligning the purveyor of the second hand dream in an extended column completely devoted to buying a car. She points out that he will "claim" ignorance when it suits him and cheat you if he can; specifically:

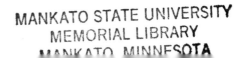

When I asked (Bob) Knoll what a woman should look for in a warranty, he said, "Nothing." He says that, good or bad, they don't differ enough to be a buying factor. A warranty is as good as the dealer's intentions or his ability to carry out its terms.

At price time, the dealer is going to ask you right off if you have a car to trade in. Try to keep it out of the original bargaining. Tell him you don't know whether you want to dispose of it or you might sell it to a friend. It can confuse the pricing aspect a lot. First, establish what you're going to pay for the new car. Then you can ask what the dealer will give you for your old car. You may make a better deal selling the old car privately. Beware of the dealer who tells you he'll give you $35,000 for your 1950 Chevrolet. He'll charge you $40,000 for a new one.[25]

Not only are used car salesmen purportedly unethical, unfair and a group against which one has to be constantly on guard, but they are so evil that nothing is too low to try on them, lying, cheating, chicanery, flattery, or if all else fails, a little sex.

In addition to lamenting the ethics and personality of used car salesmen, the mass media gleefully details the specific antics of the men.

A comic strip appropriately entitled "Gasoline Alley" by Bill Perry devoted an entire Sunday to a squinty eyed character with a bow tie on a used car lot. Slim and Clovia perpetrate a bit of a fraud on the hapless salesman in that they know more about the car than the salesman since it used to belong to Clovia's father, but they don't let on. They approach the salesman and specifically point out the car in question. The salesman tells them:

You're getting a snappy, smooth, honey of a deal here with an amazing lot of pluses . . . new paint and rubber and a price that's absolutely unfair to my boss.

If we weren't overstocked right now, you'd never steal it from us like you're goin' to. No ma'am.

To which Clovia replies:

Sir, couldn't we be a little more realistic? This paint isn't new and neither are the tires.

Miss, don't tell ME about this car. The man who traded it in is a PERSONAL friend of mine.

Clovia springs the trap by responding:

I'm even closer to him, mister, he's my father.[26]

The public's view of the salesman is further, albeit more subtly, shaped by the kind of want ad that recruits would-be salesmen. A large 7 x 7 inch ad is headlined with "$20,000-Automobile Sales":

We train you. You will be paid while attending a two week training course evenings. Yes, it's true. If you have the desire to earn more money, you owe it to yourself to answer this ad. Some of our men make more than $20,000. You can too at one of New England's largest Ford dealerships. Our constant growth has created excellent opportunities for creative, aggressive, individuals . . .[27]

The heavy emphasis on a healthy sum of money makes the appeal unidimensional to the prospective salesman. It also leaves little doubt as to the career motivation of a salesman in the mind of the casual reader. A customer who will very likely go in to buy a car with the idea that the salesman is going to make $20,000 this year will feel that beating him on the price is not only fair game, but a moral imperative.

An actual salesman-customer dialogue underlines the customer's view of the economic status of the used car salesman:

Customer: You're going to make a pile on this deal anyhow. How much do you make anyhow.

Salesman: Listen, we're the only ones without a union. [to me] Hey, that's what you can do, get us organized. The only place they got a union is in California. There they get 125 a week, guaranteed.

Customer: You get more than that.

Adding to their operating handicap, A Better Business Bureau quiz in the Boston Globe reports on some of the pitfalls the shopper may encounter:

A car dealer advertises that he sells his new cars "at cost." However, the dealer takes his invoice price from the manufacturer and then adds the cost of sales commissions, advertising, makeready, and overhead in order to arrive at his final "at cost" figure. (This practice is considered deceptive by the BBB.)

The salesman wrote "as is" on the sales slip for the used car he sold to Mr. Y., but he assured Mr. Y. that it was a good buy — in fine running condition. The purchaser soon found that the car was in very bad shape and needed expensive repairs. He tried to get the dealer either to make the repairs or to take the car back. The dealer refused. (The customer cannot force the dealer to make the adjustment.)[28]

The purpose of the article was to point out the most common ways the customer can be and often is hoodwinked by a less than scrupulous dealer.

Not to be outdone by BBB, AAA (American Automobile Association) reports that they receive so many complaints concerning used cars and dealers to warrant printing a guide to used car buying. The tone of the guide more than implies that a used car salesman is not the most reputable of all business men. The tips are prefaced by the statement:

Massachusetts motorists buy 3/4 of a million used cars in a year, and that many sales means some bad deals. If you're shopping for a used car, here are some tips from the Massachusetts consumers' council:

1. Buy from a reputable dealer. This is your most important protection.

2. Check the car; motor, transmission, suspension system, electrical system, cooling system, brakes and any evidence of accident damage. AAA suggests you take along a friend who is mechanically skilled if you're not.

3. Ask to road test the car. If the dealer wants to sell it, he'll let you drive it first. If he refuses, don't buy it.

4. Know the approximate market value. You can determine price ranges by comparison shopping and studying before you begin to negotiate.

5. Read your written sales contract before signing. All salesmen's promises should be put into writing signed by the dealer management and a copy given to you.

There is no standard warranty for a used car, but AAA offers these suggestions:

- Get your warranty in writing making certain that it spells out the protection you've been promised both for parts and length of service. (The words "30-day warranty" by themselves mean nothing.)

- If you're buying a recent used car, check for any unexpired warranty from the manufacturer. (If there is, make certain it also applies to your ownership and ask if any additional warranty fee is required.)

6. Have your car properly inspected. Your sales contract should specify that the car can pass state inspection at a disinterested station. Any improper inspection should be reported to the Registry.

7. Watch out for phony mileage and "bargains" (taxis, rental, leased, police or fleet cars that have been turned in). Look at other items that show wear: tires, pedals, floor mats, seats. Beware of cars that have been in public service.

8. Verify any so-called "one-owner" deal. This is one of the oldest claims in the book. Check it out; the dealer should be glad to tell you who the "original owner" was.

9. Compare your loan and insurance rates and terms. Use reputable sources known to you — your bank, insurance agency and AAA.[29]

Consumer boards have recently sprung to the rescue of the customer in dealing with "sharp practices and high pressure sales techniques" in the used car business. A New York group reported that since most automobiles sold in the city were used, consumer protection was necessary. They recommended following "minimal" provisions requiring used car dealers to:

Certify that a vehicle is safe to operate and capable of providing satisfactory service under normal use.

Inform the buyer that the certification is a guarantee, backed by the right to require the dealer either to repair or pay in full for repairs needed to make the automobile safe.

Refrain from writing into a sales contract a limit on liability — to a portion of the total sales price — for the repair of defects existing at the time of sale.

Refrain from taking deposits from more than one potential buyer on the same automobile at the same time.

The last requirement is aimed in part at variations of what is known in the trade as "bait and switch" — a tactic by which some dealers take a deposit on an automobile that appears to be going for a bargain price, subsequently announce that the vehicle has been sold to someone else and then try to upgrade the buyer with a different automobile selling at a higher price.[30]

The unscrupulous used car salesman could no longer force the helpless customer to buy a piece of junk against his will. If the article was not damning enough, the general counsel added that the purpose of the proposed legislation is to "... make it easier for buyers in the city "to get what they are legally owed" without having to go to court."[31] The salesman is finally indebted ("legally owes") to his customer.

Even articles purporting to be helpful, fair, and objective cast the salesman in a less than favorable light. Ralph Stein notes that a customer should "note prices but don't start any bargaining" until you know exactly what it is you want in a car.

... Until then, you're fair game. A smooth salesman will dizzy you with other models and other options so that you'll have no reference point from which to compare prices when you go to other dealers for the same make car.

You can get a considerable discount from the sticker price from almost any dealer (except on a Volkswagen) in a "clean deal" — that is, without a trade-in. If a dealer is anxious to sell you a car, he may be happy to end up with as little as $150 in clear profit. Sslesmen sometimes will even cut part of their commissions to make a sale.[32]

It might be noted here that although the popular press distinguishes between new and used car salesmen, this is seldom done at any agency. Since salesmen can sell both, it is unrealistic to consider the new car salesman a higher breed of cat. The action, both competitive and monetary, is in used cars.

The popular press also doesn't distinguish between a salesman and a dealer. The dealer is able to cut the price and can decide to take a bare profit on the car; the salesman is only whistling in the dark. He can try to get a customer a good deal, but has no final jurisdiction over the outcome of the sale in terms of price. Stein casts a further onus on the business:

One thing to watch out for is "low balling." Here's how the gambit works: suppose that most of the dealers ask around $4000 for the car you choose. One salesman, however, quotes a price of $3700. You turn down the other dealers and come back to the one where you got the low price. The salesman is all apologies. "The sales manager said no to that price," he says. "The price is $4000 now." The way to avoid such disappointment is to make sure the sales manager okays the quoted price before you leave the showroom — and in writing if possible.

Then comes the business of bringing out a little book which purports to list trade-in values. The expert will gladly show you this figure, which is usually what the car will bring if he wholesales it to the operators who buy used cars en masse. If there were such little books for, say, diamonds, the Cullinan would very likely be listed as worth $19.79. So pay no attention to the salesman's dramatics or his little book — just have him tell you exactly how much he'll allow you for your old car, and again, make sure the sales manager okays it.

These are some of the pitfalls of buying a car. The pleasures go without saying. There are of course *some* helpful, honest car dealers who go out of their way to make new car-buying a joy, but there are very, very few such paragons.[33]

Such reporting does little to comfort the customer. To the contrary it offers the customer the rationale for cheating the salesman before the salesman can cheat him. This side of the interaction will be dealt with elsewhere, but with respect to the above, it is worthwhile noting that the "low ball" when it is used is dependent on the greed of the customer who will try *another* place after being offered the ridiculous price. Salesmen seldom resort to this method because it makes it much harder to sell the car in the long run; the salesman now has to deal with an angry customer who feels he's being gypped. Thus they use the technique only on customers whom they feel are "wasting their time" by not being serious about buying and asking questions to which they already know the answers since they've seen the same car a number of times before.

The "little book" is not only a sham, but the guidepost of the average worth of any car on a national average, with *both* wholesale and retail value. The salesman's signature is as good as the manager's when he will give it (seldom before checking with the manager), and the customer is just asking for it when he is openly hostile to the salesman. If need be, any other salesman in the place can be passed off as the manager.

Consumer Corner has also done its part to cement an evil impression of the car salesman in the mind of the buying public. In an article concerning buying a car, the case of some poor, little old lady is cited:

The sale was complete but there was a little "mixup" with reading the serial number of the auto. When she called to straighten it out (you don't get registered until all the numbers match), the salesman said there "had been a little mistake" in the sale.

The lady has been undercharged!

For what? she asked.

She had been given a full tank of gas and a "final polish" and these items were extras she had not ordered and which had not been included on the bill.

She'd have to come up with the extra money, the salesman told her, or he would be in big trouble with his boss. Too bad for the salesman: he was up against a smart lady.

"I wouldn't want to cause you any trouble," she told him. "Cancel the sale!"

When the lady refused to back down, guess who did?

The salesman's final word on the matter was: "I'm going to go over the head of my boss and you won't have to pay."

The lady knows she won't have to pay, and she has that "over-the-head-of-my-boss" stuff figured too.

The moral: If you didn't order, don't pay . . . Next they'll want extra for the wheels![34]

While it is nearly impossible to classify any group as to political stance, without exception, the salesmen I have met have been politically conservative tending toward the far right. They take offense at "long haired, filthy, dirty, hippy types," are "law and order men" and fear greatly for what is happening to the country. They have been, also without exception, without college education, for as one put it, "What do you need a college education for in this business? You can get more smarts working here in a few months than you can get in years of college."

While self-analysis is not necessarily any more valid, legitimate, or useful than analysis by another, it can offer another dimension. The next chapter is composed solely of salesmen's views of themselves and each other. However, the views described in an article entitled "A lesson on how to avoid 'shims' selling mongers on pig farms" offers some self-revelations to the public and will, therefore, be used to conclude this chapter of the public view of salesmen while leading into the next, on their own view of themselves.

Excerpts from "Adventures in the Iron Trade" will also be used, with the balance of the "salesman's side" used elsewhere.

The "lesson on how to avoid 'shims' selling mongers on pig farms" is not an overly helpful lesson unless the reader intends in the not-too-distant future to open up a small, unaffiliated used car lot. What the article does accomplish in a pseudo-Runyonesque style is to allow the reader a keyhole view of the slightly naughty, slightly lurid, altogether unfamiliar world of the used car wholesaler. The bargaining techniques described in the article are the same ones that occur between customer and salesman, with the roles reversed (as they often are, even with the customer). A wholesaler has spotted a car in which he is interested, a white, '68 VW:

"Hi grouchy," he said. The manager acknowledged the greeting with a glance. Joe asked him, "You got anything good?"

"I've got a white '68 VW down in back," said the manager.

"I just looked at it. It's pretty rough. What to you need for it?"

"Eleven bucks ($1100)," was the manager's unenthusiastic reply.

Joe pushed back in his chair. "Ed Sullivan needs guys like you. You're a real comedian."

And that was the end of the interlude. The used car manager quoted a wholesale price that he knew was higher than Joe would be willing to pay. No transaction. Had he asked for perhaps $900 or even $950, Joe would have taken it on the spot, peeled off the payment in cash, slapped his dealer's plates on the car and driven it away. Then he would search for another dealer who would give him perhaps a $50 or $75 profit and then put the car on his lot for a list price anywhere from $1400 to $1500.

The wholesaler's view of the dealer is similar to the dealer's view of the wholesaler and both's view of the customer, not to mention the customer's view of both:

"There's not much glamour to it," Joe mused, "because you're dealing primarily with thieves. With some dealers you build up an honest relationship and you're straight with each other, but you have to watch out."

By watching out, Joe means that checks are routinely refused in wholesale deals. "When a strange wholesaler wants to do business with me by check, I tell him I'd rather have my car than his check."

Other hazards include having a whole car or part of it substituted between the time you buy and pick it up. "If you can, you drive them away on the spot," says Joe.[35]

In spite of this rampant distrust in every phase of the dealers' life, there is virtually no bitterness. The whole scene is treated as a game with winning or losing not being all that important.

According to the "salesman's side" this distrust is a "nuisance, i.e., the public's misconception of his nature":

...a misconception which a few unscrupulous blackguards, according to all dealers contacted, have brought on the whole profession.

For many people the used car salesman conjures images of fasttalk, hard eyes and the depressing prospect of steaming engines and sluggish pistons. He populates various sorts of detective novels and is often the target of television comedy writers.

Raymond Chandler had a typically skeptical line in *The High Window:* "We looked at each other with the clear innocent eyes of a couple of used car salesmen."

Even politicans and their puckish advisers have played upon this image. (One magazine noted for its smart-alecky attitude recently ran a picture of Mr. Nixon over the caption: "America, this time you bought his used car.")[36]

The fact that this kind of reputation does the men absolutely no good is evidenced by the fact that an association established within the profession does exist and

...when a local newspaper ran a series in 1959 detailing some sly practices by a few used car lots, the Association was revitalized to help out the beleaguered Good Name of honest used car dealers.

From the salesmen's point of view, what's the pull of the job if it carries such negative social connotations? The most commonly cited answer is simple if not overwhelming:

The pleasure for him? "The money," he says and begins to laugh at his own abruptness. (He makes in the neighborhood of $13,000 a year.) He much prefers the "horsetradin' " aspects of used car selling to work with new cars "where the customers beat you to death for $25."[37]

Another oft-given reason:

"I love to chisel (bargain) with the other guy."[38]

"It may sound funny but I don't care if I sell anything," he says, "In this kind of business it's not so much selling as matching up the customer with a car he can pay for." Most of the time he makes sure he has made a decent profit on the down payment because 75 per cent of the customers, he claims, don't come back with the rest that they owe.[39]

Another salesman echoes this reverse side of the used car credibility questions:

Echoing similar complaints by many in the used car business, he says, "The customer will absolutely tell you 50 lies to every one of yours."[40]

And for all this grief, the rewards are getting scantier and scantier:

Used car salesmen at new car franchises make between $10,000 and $14,000 a year, according to Jim Atkinson, who has been in the business over 10 years. The income of independent dealers can vary considerably, but the days of "making $70,000-80,000 a year like you could back in the 50s and early 1960s" are gone forever, Wayne Florence complains.[41]

The customer is not the only one with a preconceived notion of how the encounter will go. The salesman has an equally jaundiced view of the customer, his ethics, and motivations. As noted on the game board, these "self-images" and images of the other must be balanced and played off against one another before interaction can occur. The next chapter deals with the salesman's view of himself. The missing piece of the puzzle is obviously the customer's view of himself. The methodological impossibilities of this were discussed in Chapter 2. However, the ramifications of this balancing can still be seen in the chapters that follow.

4

Ya Can't Cheat An Honest Man

Just as the customer's expectations of the salesman will influence the customers' actions, not to mention the salesman's reaction, the salesman's anticipations will also influence the interaction. The last chapter dealt with the "societal" expectations that any customer can be expected to hold at the point of entering a used car lot. The next three chapters will deal with the salesman's expectations concerning his customer and his boss. To the extent that these perceptions form the basis of behavior, these viewpoints are crucial to the understanding of action.

These viewpoints or self-images are made up of at least two elements, what I think of myself and what I think others think of me. The two are in no way independent but, rather, organically interdependent. However, for the sake of clarity and understanding, they will be treated separately. This chapter will deal with the salesman's view of his customer − one of the "significant others" in his work. The next will deal with the way the salesman views himself.

Of course, all of the above is merely a simplified explanation of the Meadian concept of the self as composed of the "I" and the "me."[1] Remembering that any individual acts on the basis of a me, the self as object, seen through the eyes of "society" and the "I" as the actor, the subject who acts on the basis of this perceived "me," the differentiation of this "I" becomes quite difficult. To understand how the "I" part of the salesman reacts to what society expects of him is crucial to understanding the interaction between salesman and customer. But how does the researcher achieve this knowledge. If the salesman explains his actions to the researcher, then the salesman is seeing himself as object, through the veil of culture, but his very use of language and thus is describing his "me." To depend wholly on observation is perilous at best. Participant observation permits introspection on the part of the researcher if he feels comfortable in the role of participant, but the assumption that researcher and salesman share an "I" is an absurd temptation.

How, then, to assess the "I?" Unfortunately there is no easy methodological answer. The path I have chosen is a combination of all the possibilities described above; observation, introspection, and interview. The solution is only partially satisfactory, but was deemed worth the confusion and risk in the hope of trying to achieve at least a partial insight into the "I" of the salesman. The delineation of this "I" is most successful with respect to a specific subject.

In the same way that the public has a view of a used car salesman that influences interaction with the salesman (Chapter 3), the salesman has a view of the public which influences his interaction with the customer.

This viewpoint implies a predisposition to respond in specifiable ways and thus forms the basis of action. In the Meadian sense, this predisposition forges the link between past and future action.[2] The present is the dynamic, ephemeral, fleeting link between past and future and is the subject of this study. As such, it must be firmly couched in the participants' views of both past and future insofar as is possible, in order to be able to understand what effects this central action, this momentary present. This chapter constitutes another portion of defining the situation as Becker, Hughes and Geer define it in *Making the Grade:* "a set of ideas describing the character of the situation in which action must be taken."

Important here is the concept of perspective, the idea of shared understanding and meaning upon which action can be based and communicated. It will be dealt with only briefly here since it has already been discussed in Chapter 2.

Mead frequently alludes to perspectives (in terms of both definition[3] and defense[4]), although it is left to Becker and Geer[5] to demonstrate its methodological impact. This chapter will give examples of both occupied and indicated perspective as Mead delineates:

Meaning as such, i.e., the object of thought, arises in experience through the individual stimulating himself to take the attitude of the other in his reaction toward the object. Meaning is that which can be indicated to others while it is by the same process indicated to the indication individual. Insofar as the individual indicated it to himself in the role of the other, he is occupying his perspective, and as he is indicating it to the other from his own perspective, and as that which is so indicated is identical, it must be that which can be in different perspectives. . .[6]

The subject of this chapter is, then, the view of and resultant behavior toward customers on the part of the used car salesmen, the third in the trilogy of postures toward significant factors in the salesman's world that structures his action during the bargaining process. An interesting variation on the idea of an occupied perspective as defined above occurs here: not only the salesman's view of the salesman (Chapter 5), the salesman's view of the house (Chapter 6) and the salesman's view of the customer, but also the salesman's view of the customer's view of him (Chapter 3 and Chapter 4 taken jointly), a two-dimensional occupied perspective.

For example, 80 percent of the salesmen present at two different seminars devoted to advanced retail selling conducted by the Ford Marketing Institute I attended as a participant observer[7] concurred that customers think a used car salesman is:

. . . interested mainly in selling a car as opposed to interested mainly in helping the buyer make the decision that is in the buyer's best interest; are interested in making the highest profit for the dealer as opposed to giving the customer the lowest possible price; present a car in the most favorable light, neglecting some of its drawbacks, rather than explaining the weak points as well as the strong points of a car; try to get the customer to come to a decision favorable to the salesman rather than trying to help the customer to reach his own decision; exaggerate and stretch the truth rather than being reliable; do not worry about the customer being burdened financially, in contrast to not selling a car thought to be a financial burden to the buyer; are primarily interested in selling a car they need to sell in contrast to selling the car that's best for the customer.[8]

It should be remembered that these sentiments are the view that the salesman thinks the customer holds about him and are a shared perspective to the extent that such an overwhelming consensus was achieved.

Functionally, there is no difference between what the salesmen think about the customer and what they think the customer thinks about them, since either (or both) serve as the basis for action in terms of "attitudes"[9] or what Rose calls expectations:

The expectations ... specify or refer to a number of 1) meanings and 2) folkways or values, which together make up the culture or subculture of the group. A meaning is simply a definition of an object ... (it) usually indicates how an individual may act toward the object ... (whereas the folkway or value) indicates how an individual should or must act toward an object.[10]

The distinction between "may" and "should or must" is not particularly important here, but notice the similarity between this definition of expectations and the ideas involved in Mead's definition of perspective. Both are significant in that they offer a theoretical construct for understanding and explaining action.

Sutherland explained the pragmatic importance of a point of view in describing the "perspective" of a con man:

The con man has little difficulty in easing his conscience, for in the con, the sucker is always beaten while he is trying to beat someone else. The sucker is generally gloating over his prospective gain and has no sympathy for the person he expects to victimize so that the thief gets a feeling of sweet vengeance in beating him.[11]

Again, the importance of the data in this chapter is that it forms the abstract "past" and potential "future" upon which the emergent process of present will be based, the definition, importance and value of the customer to the salesman or in Meadian terms: ". . . value as the 'future character of the object in so far as it determines your action to it.' "[12]

The opinions expressed by the salesmen concerning the customer fall into five general categories, each with a resultant, justifiable (to them) course of action. Customers are misinformed, often to the point of ignorance, and thus are unfairly demanding; they are innocent and childlike, hence infinitely malleable; evil, disloyal with propensity toward greed and larceny and thus justly deserving of a "hard" time; the customer is "out to get you" thus making him fair game if "you are able to get him first"; and finally, but not insignificantly, the customer is a source of income and must, therefore, be protected. Diagramatically:

The Customer Is:	The Salesman Can:
A. Misinformed → Ignorance ∴ unfairly demanding	reject his demands as unfair
B. Innocent, Childlike ∴ malleable	manipulate him
C. Evil, Disloyal → Larceny ∴ deserving of a hard time	give him a hard time
D. Out To Get You ∴ fair game	"get" the customer
E. Source of Income ∴ subject to protection	protect him as an economic investment

The importance of these categorizations is their impact on the salesman's actions toward the customer. The fact that the assumptions are sometimes contradictory does nothing to lessen this impact. An innocent is not treated the same as a crook — a potential source of income the same way as an adversary. Yet these five labels are repeatedly applied to any hypothetical customer and form the basis for the salesman's attitude or perspective.

This chapter will examine each of the five assumptions, the "data" the salesmen supply to substantiate the assumptions and the resultant behavior, although many of the behavioral implications will be discussed in the two chapters that follow. It should be noted that these assumptions are of the same general nature as the assumptions the customer makes about the salesman. They serve as functional equivalents with respect to action. As generalizations, they are not always completely accurate or a "true fit"; they are, nevertheless, assumed at the outset and believed until disputed. Not unrelated to each other, they are described separately here for clarity in discussion.

The salesman thinks of the customer as larcenous, greedy, and unpleasant, therefore demanding and aggressive, yet also gullible and innocent. The complexity of these assumptions when seen against the imperative to "sell" is what makes the interaction particularly interesting. No particular assumption is crucial to the interaction save the fact that the customer is the source of income. The various manifestations of the generalizations are recognizable in different salesmen's statements. Their significance lies in the significance of any stereotype; it forms the initial, crucial basis for interaction and can easily structure a relationship regardless of accuracy.

The major source of consternation to the salesman is what he feels is the customer's overwhelming, all-encompassing, pervasive ignorance of his line of work, from product to technique to income.

Unlike the case with other "professionals," this ignorance is a hindrance rather than a help to the salesman. It does not make the client submissive and compliant, but aggressive and unpleasant because the client is unwilling or unable (in the salesman's eyes) to admit his ignorance and place himself in the salesman's hands (primarily because the customer doesn't trust the salesman). If by some chance, the customer does admit his ignorance and surrender himself to the salesman (a highly unlikely possibility) the salesman will usually try to get him a good deal.

Usually, however, the customer's ignorance is not only a source of scorn to the salesman (primarily because of the attempt at concealment), but a source of annoyance. The salesman is not in a position to tell the customer that he, the customer, is stupid; instead, he has to educate him and "turn him around" (Chapter 7) in a manner inoffensive enough to make the sale. The customer's ignorance of both the car and the car business is not what bothers the salesman most although he is derisive about it: "What goes on under the hood is a mystery to most buyers; it takes them four or five months to determine whether or not they got themselves a lemon."

The salesman will admit that he himself is not an automotive genius. But the salesman is most upset by the behavior of the customer resulting from ignorance: the arrogance, the unreasonableness, and the subsequent waste of the salesman's time. From the salesman's point of view, this aggression is based on the customer's notion that he has to act knowledgeably while knowing he's ignorant. He is therefore doubly aggressive.

One salesman summarized an occupation-wide viewpoint when he pinpointed the source of the customer's misinformation and smug, but thin, veneer of assumed knowledge:

You know these consumer magazines really make it hard. They're really way out. For instance, they advertise that you should be able to buy a Ford for fourteen, fifteen hundred dollars plus $100 over cost. That's right, that's what the price to the dealer is, $1500, but what they don't put down is the $70 for freight, or the money for installation, or the $25 for installing the antenna and drilling a hole in the fender and the protective covering, tuning the radio in, putting the carpeting in; it's all in the back seat when the car arrives, putting on the hub caps, washing and polishing the car, installing the cigarette lighter, connecting the speedometer and the saleman's commission. Now $200 over cost is beginning to be reasonable. Unless you're talking about the Maverick and you can't buy that for under $2000, unless it's a year old. I never sold one for that.

The problem (for the salesman) is widespread because the "misinformation" is available to everyone, or as one nostalgic salesman put it:

Any guy who wants to can go the the library and read up and know what to look for and what he should be getting. Then there's got to be a lot of dickering, really the only place left for real horse-trading, but it's not like it used to be.

His disappointment is based on the fact that the dickering is necessary simply to get the "facts" understood before any bargaining can even begin. It's not particularly pleasant for the salesman:

You tell him $1695 and they want it for $1100. They want it for less than it costs, and they'll argue you for hours about it and tell you how you're making $200 on the deal.

This salesman put his finger on one of the reasons for the bitterness with which salesmen view the misinformed customer. Customers are misinformed about exactly how much the salesman makes on the deal. Because the salesman makes about $35 top commission on any used car at the time of sale, his bitterness is understandable. This salesman worked on a "higher-priced" used car lot:

The other thing that gets me is after they sign, they say, what do you care? You made $200 or $300 bucks on the deal. You should be happy. Two or three hundred bucks! And you say, sure, sure, cause if you told them the truth you might lose the sale.

The behavior engendered by the salesman's view of the customer is often quite simple; if the customer thinks he knows what is going on, the salesman can pretend to play along with disastrous results for the unwary customer. The format of the salesman's thinking is a simple "if/then." If the customer is going to act that way, then it is okay for me to act in an equally "unscrupulous" way. The following dialogue was carried on between two salesmen at an affiliated dealership after a third salesman had failed to make a sale with a "know it all" who had returned to the lot three times:

T: (exploding) It's people like that that just ask to get misled. They just ask for it, so you oblige.

J: Sure, you low-ball 'em.

T: There are lots of legal ways to get out of that. Tell 'em it was a one day special, or that you forgot to include transportation charges, or an automatic transmission.

J: Sure, they want to hear the bull shit so you give it to 'em. Even if you level with 'em they'd never believe you, so you might as well. They're sure you're going to cheat them and they'll try to cheat you, put sawdust in the rear end, so when the assistant manager drives 'em everything is nice and quiet; it lasts for about thirty minutes, but that's all they need.

The concept of the innocently misinformed customer comes out a bit the worse for wear here. It is destined for even tougher treatment later on.

Parlaying the customer's ignorance is also occasionally institutionalized; a car is advertised at a ridiculously low figure (in the same manner as a low-ball) for the purpose of ensnaring the customer in his own ignorance (the car couldn't possibly be sold at the offered price) and greed:

. . . Nobody sells the Maverick for $2000. It's just a scheme to get you in. It's stripped down, with no cigarette lighter, or carpet on the floors or hub caps or automatic transmission.

On Washington's birthday, the boss said, "sell one car at dealer's cost from the manufacturer." Actually it was sold before Washington's birthday cause every salesman called up his people and told them to come on in first thing and people gave the salesmen their deposits, but the boss wouldn't take it 'til that day, cause he wanted to be on the up and up about it. The company actually loses money on a deal like that; the boss did it in good faith, it's just that the salesmen beat him to it. Usually the guy who takes the ad down at the newspaper gets the jump on it and comes in before the paper even hits the stands.

In addition to the "if/then" formulation (if the customer thinks this is how much cars cost, then I'll sell one for the much, but just as a come-on because I'm losing money) the quote above also emphasizes that above all, the customer is the source of income to the salesman. As such, he is to be treated accordingly even if it means short-changing the boss.

Interestingly enough, the salesman believes the customer justifies his own behavior toward the salesman in the same way that the salesman justifies his behavior toward the customer:

Every guy who comes in here is sure he's getting cheated, is getting charged $200 too much for the car he buys. And every guy is equally sure that he's getting $200 too little for the car he's selling you.

The ignorant customer can continue to be a source of difficulty to the salesman even after agreement is reached about the car itself. One astonished salesman reported that:

The customer actually thinks that the filter and oil are free at a maintenance check. They forget it isn't even if you tell 'em it isn't.

Another was equally surprised and disgusted by a customer's expectations of the responsibilities of the salesman:

Some of the people who come in here, you wouldn't believe it. You really meet all kinds. Some guy came in yesterday and says, "that's a nice car you sold me, but it hurts my wife's back." This guy comes in and wastes two hours of my time and then last week, he goes next door (to a competitor) . . . he tries to chisel me $200 and we can't make a deal, so he goes next door. This guy with his wife's back, he's a mechanic, and so I says to him, "look, you're the mechanic and you just told me it was a nice car, so what do you want from me?"

In addition to the fact that the "misinformed" customer is almost always misinformed about price including the salesman's specific piece of the pie, the misinformed customer wastes the salesman's time and he thinks that his time is money. The chief time-waster is the "friend" or "expert" who comes in to help the customer.[13] The salesmen are sure that he is every bit as misinformed as the customer is, if not more so. He wastes even more time because he forces the salesman to sell to two. The salesman must also diplomatically discredit all discredit all without hurting any feelings:

Most people don't know very much about cars and neither do I. But one guy came in here with a friend to help him, an expert. The guy started the car and checked the lights. Nothing is less important. You start the car, put it in first, listen to it, to check for front end and rear end trouble, put it in reverse for the same thing, drive it and listen for loose bearings. Smell the oil filter; if it smells like chloroform, the engine's busted; check the oil stick for water and that's about all you can tell much about.

A fellow salesman on another lot thinks similarly:

They think they're expert and they don't know a damn thing. What really gets me is that they think the salesman is here to pass out cookies for the Salvation Army. They don't seem to realize that this is how he makes his living and his time is valuable. This is his bread and butter. They think nothing of wasting his time.

A third salesman has found an easy way of dealing with the time-waster and his unfair demands. He sends him to a professional expert to be reassured:

That's people for you. He'll bitch about how his father got screwed over there and he can't hardly wait to go back and get himself screwed again. I'm not a mechanic. I always say, "tell me what you want done." People give me a deposit, tell me what they want done and I get it done for them and they come back to pick it up and if they decide for some reason or another they don't want it, we give them their deposit back. Some places won't, but we do. What the hell, for 10 bucks or so, you haven't really lost anything, have you? Even if they kept the deposit. That's my strong point. You can take the car anyplace you want to get it appraised, I'll even tell you where and if you don't want it, you don't have to take it. That's the way we do business around here.

It should be emphasized that the terms "ignorant" and "misinformed" have absolutely nothing to do with "conventional" standards of intelligence. In fact, to the contrary, the two seem to exist in inverse proportion to one another, at least in the salesman's mind:

I know this guy, he's had thirteen years of college and he gets screwed more (that's a slang expression among salesmen). This guy, he's a school teacher, a reputable guy. He bought a '63 Ford from Albany Ford and crashed it; then he bought a '65 Ford, still owing payments on his '63 Ford. He decided he didn't like the Ford, so traded it in on a '63 Buick. All this guy does is read, read, read. He sits on his can all summer. He had a library card for twenty-five years for every library within a twenty mile radius. So now, he owes $7300 on his car. This is an example of the value of education in the car business. They took him for everything he had. Then there was something wrong with his TV, so he went to a shop that did repairs near his house and he asks the guy, "do you think I should get a new one?" and the guy tells him sure, and gives him $10 on his old one; then he tells everybody, "I only pay $28 a month for my new TV." The next week, he went by the shop and there was his old TV in the window for $95. Here's a guy who got lots of education with no common sense.

The story goes on and on recounting misadventure after misadventure. The theme is definitely not unusual among the salesmen. "Doctor," "professor," "intellectual" are all used as terms of derision. A pipe smoker is considered to be the most difficult kind of customer to sell. A smart aleck with a slide rule comes in a close second. A customer is considered ignorant and misinformed when he makes unfair demands on the salesman in terms of time, money or both. However, a customer can be considered innocent, naive or childlike to the extent that he is malleable and can be manipulated by the salesman.

Bogdan studied door-to-door salesmen (encyclopedia and vacuum cleaner) as a participant-observer. He reported his research in a paper on the techniques of persuasion by describing both the obvious persuasion of the customer by the salesman and the more subtle technique practiced *on* the salesmen themselves by the instructors — the men who were selling selling.

The night I went out with him (the salesmanager) we drove into this driveway. There was this man standing there working on his garden. Howard (the salesmanager) lifted his hand, waved at the guy and said, "Good evening." The guy got this big smile on his face, raised his hand and waved. Howard looked at me and says, "This asshole is sold, get out the contract." He sold him too.[14]

Used car salesmen seem to be a bit more good-natured about the malleability of their customers, perhaps because their customers come to them rather than the converse. They seem to enjoy this manipulation a great deal more than the encyclopedia salesman; the possibility of "turning a situation around" seems to be relished:

There's this one guy who come in . . . he tells me, "You guys are all alike; when you're selling you want the top dollar, but on a trade-in, you won't give anything." So I says to him, "I tell you how much I want your car; I'll give you $100 on it, then I'll sell it back to you for $75." I could tell right there that I had him. So he says, "What if I bring in somebody who'll buy it for $200?" and I tell him, "Then you make $125 and I get rid of a crapper in the meantime."

Sometimes the salesmen are derisive about the naivete of their customers:

I don't know why they kick the tires, just nervous tension, I guess. People do strange things. I had this guy get underneath a car once, a brand new one on the showroom floor. All the salesmen gathered around asking him things like, "What's under there?" . . . the stupid s.o.b.

More often than not, they appear to be mildly bemused by the strange rather childish behavior of their customers and utilize it to their best advantage: "What you try to do is to get them to answer yes to every question. You ask your question so that every one has YES for an answer." Another salesman on another lot says that his best technique for a gullible customer is to describe a car as having come from a "status location": "That stuff about Belmont might have helped. I don't know. I always try and tell them that a car is from a status location, like 'it's from Belmont.' "

Based on the philosophy of one salesman that:

... for every car there's an ass and there's a seat for every ass; the trick is to get the right ass in the right seat . . .,

a common technique is to "keep up a running monologue" to say anything but just keep talking. This is a rather dominant theme; another man half way across the city reported: "Sometimes you just say anything; it doesn't have to make any sense. You just keep talking . . . cliches, bullshit, anything."

The predominant opinion that the customer will believe anything and can be manipulated by the clever salesman is evident in all the following techniques, each suggested by a different man at different times at different locations. The "presentation of self" becomes significantly simplified when working on the assumption that the audience is not overly bright:

Always tell him that you have a need for his car; tell him you have a desire for it . . . he wants you to (the car he is offering in trade for the one the salesman is selling).

Compliment him on his own car; tell him it's a fine car.

Let him leave with the opinion that he took you, that he worked you.

You're the bum; you make the apologies; you take the blame; you make the mistakes.

You always go out and look at the customer's car even if you don't do the appraising.

When you go out to his car with him, run your hand over the fender; let him know you know that the dent is there, but don't mention it. Get down on your hands and knees like you are really interested. The customer will volunteer information as you walk around; he will assist you. Then he will be willing to take less money on his vehicle. Be complete. Open up the trunk, the speedometer, the hood; have an appraisal sheet and explain to the customer that you want to give him a fair price.

All of these techniques serve a single purpose: to get the customer on the salesman's side, under his control: "If you establish a good relationship, the customer will be willing to give you more money because you are a nice guy."

The efficacy of this technique was attested to by one and all:

Originally, the customer wanted $400 . . . well, I said maybe I could get him $125 with the boss if I really tried; the customer said, "how about $175?" Well, right there, I knew I'd made out.

As previously mentioned, the favorite used car story centers around a man who gets a beautiful blonde as part of his car deal and when he tries to prevail upon her to be a little more receptive to his advances, she cheerfully replies that he's already gotten screwed once in the car deal.

The other side of the gullibility coin seems to be counterfeit; salesmen are thoroughly convinced that the customer is the least reputable of all beings. Bogdan offers two criteria for despicability; both involve taking advantage of the salesman from the salesman's point of view:

We had this buy in Boston (a salesman) . . . he got in with some real bastard. I mean he really was an s.o.b. . . . This guy was really loaded too (had money) . . . It was a fifty or sixty thousand dollar house. He was giving the demonstration and this s.o.b., that's all I can call him, he says all I have to do is give you a list of names and you're going to give me five dollars for each name (the advertising gimmick). This young man says, "Yeh, that's right." The bastard, he said, "Can I have that in writing?" This guy (the salesman) didn't know what was up so he went over to the desk and wrote out "for each name so and so gives me, he will receive five dollars" and he signs his name. This bastard writes down the names of 30 people and says, "OK, when do I get the money?" . . . Now you'll usually run into nice people, you seldom run into a bastard like this . . .[16]

Neither cleverness nor excessive curiosity is considered a virtue in a customer:

This one man, hell of a nice fella, went out on his first call. He got into this place . . . It was the house of a G.E. engineer. Let me tell you, he really gave the demonstrator a hard time . . . asked all questions about the motor . . .[17]

Car salesmen, as might be predicted, share many of the same views about the trustworthiness of their customers. Some of this apprehension undoubtedly stems from the fact that the customer is almost always interested in selling his old car and the salesman is well aware of the techniques of selling a used car. On the other hand, the salesmen believe, as does a spokesman in Sutherland's work, *The Thief,* that: " . . . it would not be so easy to stay honest here in the United States because so few other people would keep me company in honesty."[18]

There is general agreement in the book that conning requires some help on the part of a greedy or scheming participant. The same kind of consensus that the customer is no paragon of virtue occurs among a cross section of used car salesmen.

As far as the customer is concerned, you're not a thief 'til you get caught.

Hell, everybody has a little larceny in their heart; a thief is someone who has a percentage of larceny, but five percent is not a thief.

The majority of the people lie.

The customers are all liars; they'll try and cheat you; they all lie anyway. You're no different than anybody else, you lie too . . .

There is no lack of specificity in their complaints either: "Guys will swap tires and take out the radio between the appraisal and the sale." Another is slightly more benign about the situation:

They'll probably cheat you; if he wrapped [crashed] it [the appraised car] between the deal, *he's* probably getting the insurance. Tell him, it's at his expense, "you got to pay for it" and he'll probably be willing to pay.

But the final infamy is not that the customer will "undoubtedly" "lie to you, cheat you, slit your throat and low-ball you," but he has no appreciation, loyalty or gratitude after all the salesmen go through for him.

Jesus Christ, you sweat with them getting them credit and they're just as meek as hell 'til you get the financing arranged, but then once it's arranged, all of a sudden they figure they can buy anything they want and they get real cocky. This guy came in and wanted me to tighten the mirror and get new tires. Well, hell, I'd just tightened the mirror and you saw that big mitt of his, he yanks on it real hard and it needs to be tightened again and the boss says he'll get him a new tire. Christ, they get cocky.

Across the city another complains: "He wants his God damned car washed and I had a deal getting it through at all (getting the deal approved and financed)."
    A final justification for any shenanigans on the salesman's part, if needed, comes from the widespread belief that the customer is trying to "get" the salesman.

Every guy that comes in here has it in his mind that he's going to beat you. Let's say Jack was coming to buy a car from me, he'd be trying to beat me.

A rather unbelievable confirmation of this fact came from one of the men who related the extent to which people will go to "win":

You may not believe this, but in 1959, a woman came in here and gave me $50, right out of her pocket; she took it out and counted it out to me, to bargain with her husband, but not to let him know it. So I could cut my price by $50. He had a bad heart, and he was old and didn't get out much and he wanted to beat me, but she said, "don't make it easy for him, but let him win." Fifty dollars. I'll give you the woman's name and you can talk to her if you like. She's a real nice lady.

The will to win is not often so pleasantly expressed; the salesmen continually reminded me and themselves that the customer is selling too and can be pretty unscrupulous:

You know where we learn most of the dirty tricks? From our customers. We learn from them. Each one of them comes in with something a little different, trying to cheat you. They're all experts and they bring their friends in.

There is also a slightly more pragmatic reason for dealing harshly with a customer which leads neatly into the final consideration, customer as income source rather than adversary:

If you're the first man a guy talks to, you'll never see him again; if you're the second, he'll have your price beat by the third, but if you're the fourth and you figure he's just pricing, you offer him a price $400 below the factory price which is ridiculous because new car prices are all the same, but that way, you'll insure his coming back and you take him off the market. He'll go check your price out and when nobody else meets it, he'll be back and quote your price and then you say, "Now let's sit down and be reasonable."

The interaction is not without occasional sympathy. As noted earlier in the chapter, salesmen tend to keep their customers informed on "special deals." They go to bat for them with the dealership if need be. They'll even lower the price a little if they can, if they like the customer, although the opposite is also true:

Do we ever give anybody a good deal on a price? Sure, a young couple comes in and we'll give 'em a little better deal or sometimes one of those bearded long-haired types comes in and we give 'em a high price, take it or leave it. They're not our kind of people. Most of 'em we'll bargain with.

The financial plight of the customer is not completely unrecognized and unappreciated:

The average salary in this country is $7200. Mr. $7200 a year is afraid he'll get a lemon; he's probably already overextended, so he's afraid about bills.

A special protectiveness is also evident occasionally:

Most of the cars here are worth their price tags, but there are some here that I wouldn't touch because in spite of the warranty and everything, you just don't trust 'em for your customer. It's not worth it to have 'em on your neck. Every guy here feels that way about certain of the cars.

So, for whatever the reason, a salesman perceives a customer, real or abstracted in a certain way. This perception forms the basis for his interaction with any particular customer and customers in general. By and large, the philosophy of *caveat emptor* applies, as described by Hughes.[19] It applies not only out of a tradition of the marketplace, where the buyer is assumed to be aware and informed, but because he is thought to be treacherous, aggressive, unpleasant, demanding, unfair, and unscrupulous as well. Part of this philosophy is based on the knowledge the salesman has of the customers' techniques of selling. He is wary of the customer who is trying to unload his own car on the salesman using many of the same techniques. Yet, in spite of all these factors, sales must be and are made, and that involves the present, the missing piece of the story. The salesman's view of the customer is complex and multidimensional; he must take into account not only all the factors described in this chapter, but his own expectations as to how a salesman should act.

5

Selling Yourself for Fun and Profit

This chapter will deal with the salesman's self-image — how he views himself — who he is, what he is doing, and how it should be done. These factors determine his interactions with the customer specifying how much the salesman is willing to bend, what factors are crucial to his self-image (or "face" as Goffman would define it) and what he can let the customer "get away with."

Used car salesmen see themselves as both part and apart of the undifferentiated world of salesmen. Hughes noted this factor in dealing with men and their work; salesmen consider themselves a part of a larger fraternity: "Hear a salesman who has just been asked what he does reply, 'I am in saleswork,' or 'I am in promotional work,' not, 'I sell skillets'."[1] A used car salesman paraphrased the sentiment very nicely when he stated: ". . . whether you're selling refrigerators or TVs or houses or vacuum cleaners or cars or I don't care what, the first thing you got to sell is yourself and the product will be sold."

Part of the reason why salesmen see themselves as salesmen rather than men who sell a specific product is this idea of "selling yourself." If this is indeed what is involved, then the product becomes nearly irrelevant. The idea is reinforced by the fact that many of the used car salesmen held other selling jobs on the side or had "sold" some other product at some other time.[2] Well over half of the men interviewed had a background of selling, with the average number of years being slightly over nine years. A number were involved concurrently in selling real estate, vacuum cleaners, or plate glass, and saw selling cars as part of a continuous pattern:

I used to sell real estate, then I bummed around for a couple of years, went broke, needed a job, came to Boston, went to an agency, wanted something where I could have my own car and expenses and they sent me here . . . it's very unusual for them to have an opening . . . I want to get back to real estate, but this is ok. I've been here four months and I'll stay on 'til the first of the year (another six months).

As will be seen later, the "free" car is a major inducement for salesmen to sell cars. It is not particularly surprising that the men do not see their selling job as significantly different from any other selling business with recommended techniques of selling being used universally. For instance, the car salesman gets the customer used to the sales order form by leaving it out on the table when he is talking with the customer while the vacuum cleaner salesman: ". . . dumps dirt on the order form to get the female accustomed with the form . . . it's in her hand."[3]

The salesmen recommend techniques to one another that are used in selling other products; one suggested using the gambit of a color TV salesman:

You can do like the color TV salesman. He says, "We'll call after a week and see if you like the TV, no obligation of course," and after the week, he'll call to see if the TV is adjusted 'OK', with no attempt to close the sale. Then he'll call a week later to close. Now that's selling.

Letting the customer take the car home is an approved technique, although one salesman admitted that one guy took a car home to show his wife . . . in Ohio. It took him three months to get the car back.

As already mentioned, salesmen commonly express the sentiment that it doesn't make any difference what the product is, you have got to sell yourself before you can sell anything, even the proverbial popsicle in Alaska.

Car salesmen talk about selling, often not used cars, but just selling. Yet they cannot be considered members of a profession by any current definition of a profession. They do not refrain from advertising; other businesses, not to mention the public at large, certainly do not consider them as engaging in their line of work from an "admirable, painstaking sense of responsibility and pride in service rather than an interest in the opportunity for personal profit," as Carr-Saunders would require before they be considered "professionals."[4] In fact, to the contrary, the public view of the men's work is that they are definitely out for the "fast buck."

They also lack most of the earmarks of increasing specialization: transferability of skill, a proliferation of objective standards of work, the spread of tenure arrangements and licensing, not to mention certification, which also separate the amateurs from the professionals, at least in the sociological annals.[5] Luckily, they can be considered as happily non-professional.

With tenure unsure, standards nonexistent and little possibility of increasing specialization, why sell? The draw, in general, is quite simple. When asked why they spend their days selling used cars, most of the men replied that it was (1) easy, (2) lucrative, (3) easy, (4) lucrative, and (5) didn't pin you to a desk. The fact that the job is both easy and lucrative was repeated time and again:[6] "Where else can you easily make $25,000 a year without investing a cent of your own money, absolutely no capital yourself." The salesmen see themselves as making an easy and quick buck: "This is a lazy man's business. You just sit around. Go get a cup of coffee when things are slow. Make a call occasionally."

Selling has always been thought of as a job in which a man could make "good money." The specific lure of selling cars as opposed to selling anything else would seem to be dependent on a single item; the fringe benefit of a new car every year, although one salesman felt that used car salesmen were being "duped" — he, along with the rest of his colleagues, was succumbing to the "American dream" in the same way that he hoped to convince his potential customers:[7]

You get a new car every year. Big deal. What they don't realize is that if they were working, they could buy and OWN their own car. I think some of 'em stick with it just for the car, big deal.

This air of not so gentle cynicism is pervasive in men who are not particularly cynical about their customers or their house but direct their cynicism toward themselves, their own gullibility and their own "something for nothing" (lots of money for precious little work) philosophy. "Take the money and run" is a common theme with the younger men, cheerfully assured that they can beat the "system," that *they* can make out. The older men are sourly convinced that they can't, that no one can:

There's no future in this racket. There's no place to go. I call it a racket. If I was a young guy, I would get out of this. Hustle a little. When you get older, you don't feel much like hustling, but if I was their age . . . I'd go sell for one of the big companies where there's some future. There you can move up. Here you got to wear a tie, no sport shirts. Big deal. Here you got to deal with stiffs.

There seems to be an almost Willy Loman[8] sadness in the men who have bought the system, allowed themselves to be sold what it is they are selling, the car and all its charms. As one laments:

I don't see why these young guys stay. There's no future in it for them. Some of them even have a college education. Now what do you need a college education for in this business? I can out sell all of them and I never went to no college. What you need here is experience and how do you get that? By selling, that's how. These guys, they have to look at the book, the one that comes out twice a month that gives a national average price for every car, but you got to know the cap, the top on every car, without even looking. These guys, they all got to look at the book. Sometimes Freddie comes up to test me and says, "how much for that car," and I tell him and then he tells me all the things that are wrong and I say to him, "if you'd told me that in the first place, I would have given you a better figure." These guys think they're so smart, but they're not, not really. No future in this business. There's a lot of collusion here, too. Freddie gives his brother all his deals and the boss does, too, cause he wants to make Freddie happy . . . collusion . . . (Freddie is the sales manager who has to okay all deals before they become official).

As could be predicted, part of the salesmen's definition of themselves stems from what they perceive others think of them and part from what they do.

One of the first things any used car salesman will confide is that he feels himself to be initially on the defensive with the customer and many of his actions can be attributed to this feeling. Selling yourself is that much more difficult if you are not seen as desirable to begin with. This point will be discussed in greater detail in Chapter 6, but suffice it to say, at this point, that a salesman's dealings with the public are something less than straightforward and he is more than cognizant of it. The fact that the men refer to their business as a racket should probably be taken with a grain of salt, although they happily admit to engaging in "playful shenanigans":

... to sell the quiet ride of the car, we set Mr. Jones in the car and talk soothingly to him and tell him how quiet and peaceful the ride is ... meanwhile you slowly roll up the window and when it's all rolled up, just move your lips ...

and

... say, "Mr. Jones, this car is quite safe because you sit high off the road and can see very well. I'll go around in front and get down on my knees so I'll be the height of a child and you can see how easily I can be seen." ... then go around in front of the car and just crouch down a little bit ...

But he sees these "tricks" as no more insidious than those that "everybody" uses, as detailed by Vance Packard, for instance, in his view of the advertising business.[9] The salesmen are in agreement with Ned Polsky, when he points out that it is hard to tell the good guys from the bad guys without a scorecard, in his study of *Hustlers, Beats and Others:*[10]

... conning is only a matter of degree, in that all of us are concerned in many ways to manipulate others' impressions of us, and so one can, if one wishes, take the view that every man is at bottom a con man. This form of "disenchantment of the world" is central to Herman Melville's *The Confidence Man* (one of the bitterest novels in all of American literature) and to the sociological writings of Erving Goffman. Its principal corrollary is the view expressed by hustlers, by other career criminals, and by Thorstein Veblen that all businessmen are thieves.[11]

And not only businessmen either:

"When we get to Ocean Grove, the President will probably want to work the crowd," one of Richard Nixon's press aides had said. Work the crowd? That's underworld slang gone respectable if you ever heard it. Interesting thought: The President as pickpocket. Of votes.[12]

If "everybody is doing it," why, then, is the used car salesman singled out for derision? While admitting that he is: " ... selling the sizzle – not the steak – that's what it all boils down to!" he feels that his behavior is more than justified by the suspicious and devious customer. In fact, that customer *wants* the salesmen to "con" him. A blurb distributed by Sears, Roebuck and Company in *The Advertiser's Digest* pleads, "don't sell me things," and signed by "your customer":

Don't sell me clothes. Sell me neat appearance ... style ... attractiveness.

Don't sell me shoes. Sell me foot comfort and the pleasure of walking in the open air.

Don't sell me candy. Sell me happiness and the pleasure of taste.

Don't sell me furniture. Sell me a home that has comfort, cleanliness, contentment.

Don't sell me books. Sell me pleasant hours and the profits of knowledge.

Don't sell me toys. Sell me playthings to make my children happy.

Don't sell me tools. Sell me the pleasure and profit of making fine things.

Don't sell me refrigerators. Sell me the health and better flavor of fresh-kept food.

Don't sell me tires. Sell me freedom from worry and low cost per mile.

Don't sell me plows. Sell me green fields of waving wheat.

Don't sell me things. Sell me ideals . . . feelings . . . self-respect . . . home life . . . happiness.

Please don't sell me *things*![13]

The point of these statements is not necessarily that the customer does want the "treatment" but that the salesman can believe that the customer does. Sutherland discusses the same concept in slightly different terms:

The statement that if there was no larceny in a man and if he were not trying to get something for nothing and rob a fellow man, it would be impossible to beat him at any real con racket is unqualifiedly true. This remark is often made by professionals. "These suckers ought to be trimmed." It is a hard thing to say, but they are a dishonest lot and the worst double-crossers in the world. A confidence game will fail absolutely unless the sucker has got larceny in his soul.[14]

While it is a mistake to consider the car salesman a thief, some of the aspects of the con are present in his behavior and he is more than willing to admit this although he sees nothing dishonest, peculiar or immoral about it. Part of the reason he feels that he is playing a relatively harmless game and that it's "no big deal" is that he sees the customer as either playing the same game or wanting to play the same game; two con men trying to outcon one another with the best man winning. The salesman has no doubts that he is the superior combattant and that it is The salesman has no doubts that he is the superior combatant and that it is the customer's own fault for tangling with him.[15]

To thrive on this kind of existence, the salesman must obviously be aggressive, gregarious, and "lean and hungry" as one of the men said. Other occupations require similar characteristics:

A professional confidence man wrote: Not all persons can be good con men. They generally must have a winning personality, shrewdness, agility, like the good things of life and be too lazy to work for them and have great egotism. They must first of all, be good actors. The whole con game is a matter of acting. If they cannot put on this veneer of culture, they cannot make it go. A confidence man must live by his wits.[16]

Many of these characteristics are not unfamiliar. The comparison becomes even more appropriate if what Sutherland calls acting, the salesmen call selling, although presumably, their sell does not have to be as hard as that of the professional con man. The salesmen are seldom involved in selling absolutely nothing for something, even in the case of the worst clunker. They are almost always operating well within the law and do not have to fear the sudden intervention of the police.

The whole idea of the con has its use and its limitations, which will be seen even more clearly in later chapters, but as is always the case in human dealings, appropriate behavior is quite dependent on the context in which it occurs. "Conning" the boss or the customer is quite all right; stealing a customer from another dealer is equally permissable, but a rigid code of ethics is adhered to between salesmen of the same agency.

The degree to which other dealerships can be victimized is a matter of self-preservation; preserving both self-image and income. In terms of image, it is okay to chisel another dealer since "some used car salesmen act in an unethical manner, although it isn't me, and if this other chap is unethical, then it's okay to steal his customer." Thus considering themselves a large happy fraternity of used car salesmen has some built-in problems for the men themselves.[17] Used car salesmen do indeed have a bad press and it realistically must have come from somewhere, so while seeing themselves as part of the wider group of "men who sell," they must differentiate among themselves and the "unscrupulous" other for their own self-preservation.

The men differentiate among themselves as to who sells what kind of car from what kind of dealership (see Chapter 2). This differentiation could be partially explained in terms of competition based on the laws of supply and demand.[18, 19, 20] There are a large number of used cars and a theoretically small number of car buyers, so conflict arises between car salesmen. Another way of explaining the competition between different kinds of used car salesmen (i.e., ones associated with different model cars or dealerships) stems from the negative values associated with used car salesmen. Salesmen are quick to point out the difference between themselves and their kind of operation as contrasted with other used car salesmen and their less scrupulous, less honest kind of operation. The greatest distinction made by the men is among affiliated (new car associated) and unaffiliated dealerships:

(An unaffiliated dealer describing an affiliated, multi-man operation.)
... if you work a big place, when a customer came in you could say that this was Mr. Murphy's day off and then you could go and hide or something, but if you're it and there's no place to hide, nobody to shift to, you'll be a hell of a lot more square with the guy when you sell him. So an operation like mine is much more honest and cause I don't pay anybody else, I got a lower overhead, so I can sell cheaper than an affiliated dealership with all those salesmen to support ... I don't make promises I can't keep cause the guy will be back the next day on my back, there's no dodge, nobody to shift to.

(An affiliated dealer talking.)
Well, ninety percent of what you hear about used car salesmen is true. They're in it to make a buck and they'll tell the customer anything to make a buck, so I'll

tell you, the best advice is to buy your car from a new car lot, i.e., a man who sells new cars too, an affiliated dealership. They have a reputation to protect, and they have the service and the warranty and they'll stand behind what they say. A lot of places, they just work on commission and the guy will do anything to make a fast buck and it's sort of like vacuum salesmen or any other kind of salesmen, they just do piece work. They get paid on the number of units that they sell, just like in the old shops where the women sew up seams on pants and they get paid 35¢ for each pair of pants sewn, $1.75 by the place, but if she sews eight an hour, that's $2.40. They'll pay her the minimum $1.75, no matter how many she sews, but they sure won't keep her around long and that's just like it is here.

(Another unaffiliated.)

When you've got a lot of salesmen in a place, then they got to wait their turn, it's called waiting for ups and when it's a guy's turn, if he doesn't make his sale, then he's got to wait 'til all of the other five guys have had their turn before he gets another chance. So they'll tell you anything just to keep you. So you've got guys making wild promises that they can't keep, but I'm the only one over there and I'm the owner and I don't have any salesmen.

It is worthy of note that although the salesmen differentiate among themselves with respect to dealership, price of the car, domestic or imported product, there are a number of sociological issues that emphasize their similarity rather than their differences. First, the similarity of their sentiments toward one another concerning who is honest and who is not. The reader is left to try and judge which kind of salesman (affiliated or unaffiliated) was talking about which kind of dealer in the quotes presented. Second, salesmen move easily between different kinds of dealerships, whether they be domestic or foreign car, luxury or economy priced, when they decide to move to a different employer. One of the more compelling pieces of evidence for this ease of movement lies in their common language. As Whorf and others have noted, language tends to structure thinking and thus behavior. The glossary printed at the back of this book is solid evidence of the communality of the men's language and hence their world. While no salesman would necessarily use all of the words listed, all would know what any of them meant. Thus, the distinction between salesmen is a distinction undiscernable to the public and irrelevant behaviorally and thus sociologically. It would seem to have the same value to the public or to the researcher that the distinction between a doctor who was a member of the AMA and one who wasn't or one who got his degree at a state university or Harvard. The distinction is of some importance to doctors, but of little to patients.

To a certain extent, this competition, essentially for a good name when the name is primarily bad, is part in earnest and part in fun. The salesmen are willing to ruefully accept part of the onus of being used car salesmen to the extent that it implies that something is being put over on the poor dumb customer, as evidenced in the used car salesman joke, as repeated by a gleeful salesman:

This fella went into a showroom and they had these three cars on a special, one for 1900, one for 2100 and one for 2500 and beside each of the cars was a model and beside the $2500 car was this beautiful, blonde, buxom girl and so the guy bought the 2500 job and the model came along with him and so they go home and she fixes him dinner and he says, "well, gee, thank you. I really appreciate it." She says, "Think nothing of it; it's part of the deal." So to thank her, he takes her out bowling and buys her dinner and tells her to order anything on the menu she wants and she says that's very nice of him, but he doesn't really have to be so nice to her because it's all part of the deal. Finally as they're driving home in the car, he looks at this beautiful blonde chick who's so good to him and he pulls over to the side of the road and stops the car and puts his arms around her and whispers in her ear. She turns to him and says, "Oh, no, sir. You got *that* when you bought the car."

The follow-up to the story is that both the men present at the time swore that they knew of instances "before the attorney general moved in" where dealerships had given away call girls for the night with their used cars.

The salesmen are also willing to talk about the mechanics of the occupation if they are ascribing it to another kind of dealership:

I'll tell you where he gets his cars. There's an auction up at Concord. Say a car has been sitting on a lot for a year; a dealer puts the car up for bid and it goes to the highest bidder if the price is right . . . keep that confidential. Don't tell him I told you or my boss; I'd get fired. (This last was delivered in a hushed tone of voice and as far as I could tell was utterly sincere, not a put-on.) The cars aren't stolen and a guy can really get a buy on it. A car that was bought for 1700, he can get it for 1000, spend 200 to fix it up and make 3, 4, 500 on it.

The auction is especially good for high mileage cars; the guy that buys it isn't afraid to turn back the speedometer whereas we won't touch it (the speedometer). I sold two high mileage cars last week, but I had to give a deal on 'em. A small dealer, for instance, he can pay his rent if he's having a rough time by selling cars to the auction. But really, don't tell my boss, I'll get fired.

Because there is no love lost between competing dealerships, stealing from a competitor is not only acceptable, but commendable. (It is altogether possible that the stealing is justified by the competition; which came first is hard to ascertain and which serves as cause and which serves as effect. At any rate, conning another dealer is considered okay if you can get away with it.):

This morning there was somebody over on Clyde's lot who called up before to ask me about a car and I saw them and motioned them over and they came over and they said they thought that they were on our lot, but I said, "No, there's the boundary," and they said, "Then how come you motioned me over," and I just laughed and finally sold a Comet; made 25 on the car and an extra 20 on the insurance, made at least 45.

When the shoe is on the other foot, indignation is expressed over the possibility that one "knowledgeable" tried to con another "knowledgeable":

My girl bought a used VW, my girl, hell, she's my wife now. Anyhow she got the VW with a 13,000 mile warranty on it. But the muffler was ruined, so I took it back and said, "What's this about the muffler," and they said, "Who are you?" and I flipped out one of my cards and he says, "Oh, well, no problem." You don't try to snow another dealer. I said I'll be back in an hour and he said we can't and I said you can if you want to and then I took the car over to VW to get the warranty reinstated and the same thing happened. You don't bull another dealer.

The salesmen utilize differences among salesmen in order to expedite sales with their customers:

Let me educate you about the guy down the street who sells for a buck and a quarter over. He depends on appraisal and trade. Now if he has a good used car trade, a car comes in that is worth a thousand, he can go to 1100 because he knows he can mark it 1595 and sell it for 1500. Another guy sells it for 950 cause it's just a wholesale piece for him. I can reach for it cause I've got a good used car business going here.

Salesmen are cautioned not to downgrade another dealership or the integrity of another salesman in front of a customer because it just confirms the customer's worst fears about used car salesmen, although apparently the temptation is occasionally too much to resist.

Although they are allowed to be competitive with outside salesmen, the name of the game within the dealership is strictly cooperation:

We work just as hard for each other's customers as we do for our own sales.

Last month Henry was short two for his bonus and I had mine cleared, so the last Saturday of the month, I wrote mine up for him so he'd make his bonus. This month, I'm short, but he's out sick. Too bad, he could do the same for me.

In an affiliated dealership, there is even cooperation between new and used car salesmen:

Well, like it is now, there are three guys over here and four over there and it's okay. But over there, if a guy comes in the new part, then one of those guys will bring him through to sell him a used car and if the customer comes through the other side, then one of us will take him in and sell him a used car and let's face it, there are only two doors to come in.

Occasionally, the lack of permissable competition grates on the salesmen who have been around for awhile:

Hell, if a guy in the shop sends in a customer and somebody sells him, damned if the guy in the shop won't go in and ask the boss for the commission.

The reason that cooperation is the byword within the dealership is straightforward and quite pragmatic:

Before, we used to fight over the ups and it was a real mess, guys arguing on the floor over a customer. Now we just take turns on the ups and if a guy comes in, we ask him if he's spoken to anyone else and if he says he has, then we write up the sale in that guy's name and he does the same for us. It's a lot smoother that way.

Selling takes on a pattern determining whose turn it is, who is next, and if a walk-in is somebody else's former customer. Taking turns on ups alleviates any competition per se on the showroom floor and salesmen cooperate with one another by making the sale for a colleague and writing it up in the colleague's name. They will also support each other by turning over a unit at the end of the month if another salesman is short for the bonus, but he has made his own. Trouble with a customer is often handled jointly by a salesman pretending to be the house and rescuing the harried partner from his predicament. Using this technique (described later) the customer can often be lulled into submission.

Yet, as is true in many situations, competitors can find common ground on which to unite against a common enemy, in this case, the house:

All this stuff I'm telling you about commissions and bonuses and how it all works, you put it in your book so other guys will know about it and get their bosses to come across with the dough.

On this note, we turn to the house in order to further supplement the "I" that has been begun in this chapter. In addition to the chapter concerning the salesman's relationship with the customer, enough of the basic "I" should be differentiated to enable some understanding of the salesman's actions in the bargain. This chapter should not be considered alone, but taken as a part, the first and most generalized part of the "I" that is the salesman as actor coupled with the salesman and the customer as "me" as reactors.

If life was as simple as a game, the next discussion could be of the sale — customer and salesman could decide to do business or not — but thre is another significant component to this situation. The salesman and customer must come to terms with one another, but both must also receive the approval of the house. Because the salesman realizes this ahead of time, his actions must take the house into consideration. In addition, the house is a separate obstacle as well. The next chapter describes the house in both contexts. The following chapter describes the final trade-offs tantamount to the bargain.

6

A House Is Not a Home

Just as self-image is based on "who I am," "who I am" is to a large part based on "what I do," so that this latter conceptualization is as important to understanding action as is the former and is every bit as much of both the "I" and the "me" that Mead describes.[1]

Selling used cars is a job, but, as is the case in any occupation, self-concepts, expectations, and actions are quite dependent on that job. This is especially true when it is remembered that, on the average, nearly 45 percent of an American man's waking hours are spent "at work."[2] The significance of an occupation can be empirically documented by the frequency with which strangers "locate" one another in society by questioning one another on what it is they "do." Thus, who you are is largely determined by what you do and what you do is dependent on who you do it for and who you do it to. The consideration of who it is done for and who it is done to will be the subject of this and the following chapter in order to further specify the "I" and "me" of a used car salesman relevant to his interactions with his customer. The format for this chapter will consist of a discussion of the place of "I" and "me" within a working relationship, a discussion of working relationships that can be generally classified as "brokerage," and a brief look at employer-employee relationships, again on a general level. The specific features characteristic of the used car occupation will then be delineated with the same eye toward creating a background against which action occurs.

The whole idea of attempting to describe those factors that are relevant to action is at once both presumptuous in its simplicity and challenging in its complexity. The purpose here is not to describe individual motivation (a task more appropriately left to the psychologist) but to describe sociological "universals" (at least in terms of used car salesmen) that can offer insight into an incredibly complicated yet vital human capacity, the ability to compromise in a dynamic, ongoing sense. The presumption then becomes necessary if the process is to be understood, and so it is hazarded here.

As to the complexity, to describe human relationships in such a way seems at once inadequate and unnecessary. However, this chapter, if nothing else, should underline just such a statement of complexity. The salesman's relationship with the dealership (the house) will be presented on a number of levels. On the first level, the salesman and house will be shown as having natural and predictable complaints with one another. One is employer and one is employee, one seeks to maximize profits for the dealership he owns, while the other seeks to maximize his own salary which results in a higher overhead, thereby reducing the owner's profit. Their demands are clearly incompatible.

At the same time, in spite of their basic opposition to one another's self-serving outlook, the salesman will admit to being in a relatively good set-up and the house will admit that the salesman often has a rough time with the customer.

Disregarding actual grievances with the house, there are structural reasons why it is reasonable, advantageous, and even parsimonious for the hostility that salesmen presumably bear toward the customer to be displaced, in a relatively harmless fashion, to the house. However, any of the relationships are susceptible to change and the alliances between customer, salesman, and house are constantly shifting.

On a symbolic level, analysis need presuppose no actual hostility, but can rely solely on the efficacy of establishing a "bad guy" for the salesman to defeat in the presence of the customer and to be the "fall guy" in the case of the customer's displeasure, thereby leaving the salesman innocent of wrongdoing and free from taint of complicity toward the customer. The distrust of the customer as described in Chapter 3 makes this kind of analysis relevant.

Yet, after all is said and done, very real feelings of hostility do exist toward the house and are expressed by the salesmen in "private." Complex seems a hopelessly ineffectual term.

Mead, who seems to thrive on the complexity of human interrelationships, agilely describes the inherent conflict between an employer and an employee; on the one hand, an employee as part of the team, while on the other hand, possessed of goals not necessarily compatible with those espoused by the management:[3]

In the baseball game, there are competing individuals who want to get into the limelight, but this can only be attained by playing the game. Those conditions do make a certain sort of action necessary, but inside of them there can be all sorts of jealously competing individuals who may wreck the team. There seems to be abundant opportunity for disintegration in the organization essential to the team. This is so to a much larger degree in the economic process. There has to be distribution, markets, mediums of exchange; but within that field all kinds of competition and disorganizations are possible since there is an "I" as well as a "me" in every case.[4]

The analogy of the team is probably most useful in describing relationships where it's "us against them," but, as has already been implied, it's difficult to tell which side is which in the used car game. Nevertheless, the discrepancy between "I" and "me" is well taken here. In the narrowest sense, the house can be seen as the significant other (although there are other significant others) who exerts a form of societal constraint on the salesman, the "me" as opposed to the "I." At this point, suffice it to say that a conflict between "I" and "me" is neither unusual or unexpected in the economic process.

Within the economic process (the simple distribution of resources, whether goods or services) the brokerage relationship is especially prone to this type of conflict since an individual acts as an agent for another and thus does not have the final authority over the outcome of the situation. Simmel is perhaps the best-known chronicler of this type of relationship, but describes situations in which either:

> ... the third element is at such a distance from the other two that there exist no properly sociological interactions which concern all three elements alike ... (but) rather ... configurations of two.[5]

or

> ... two parties are hostile toward one another and therefore compete for the favor of a third element; or they compete for the favor of the third element and therefore are hostile toward one another.[6]

Neither are applicable to the brokerage arrangement on the used car lot in which, at times, all three parties are simultaneously involved and explicitly or tacitly influence the course of the interaction.

Freilich,[7] in his discussion of natural triads, expands on the Simmelian scheme by defining the three parties involved as the high-status friend, the high-status authority, and the low-status authority. While allowing for three-person simultaneous interaction, his model does not allow for either high-status individual to ally himself with the low-status individual against his high-status colleague or for the roles to shift at some point during the interaction. While these factors just mentioned are not necessarily limitations when dealing with kinship systems as Freilich does, they are not as viable when applied to used car salesmen. In fact, because of the shifting alliances, the classification of high and low status, not to mention authority or friend, becomes if not impossible, at least meaningless.

Even if the brokerage relationship does not seem to follow "natural" formations in this case, the "natural" kinds of hostilities that can be expected to occur between employer and employee[8, 9, 10] are all present here in spades, additionally underscored by the fact that the salesman is acting as broker for the house, an intermediary between the customer and the dealership that employs him for the purpose of selling cars.[11]

As previously mentioned, this kind of arrangement, that of an individual acting on behalf of another, is not uncommon in our society, as evidenced by the vacuum cleaner salesman,[12] the encyclopedia salesman,[13] the stock broker[14] in the specific sense or in the larger sense as performed by the welfare worker,[15] the nurse,[16] or the bureaucrat.[17] Because of the lack of control inherent in a brokerage relationship, all of these situations can be expected to be ones fraught with at least potential conflict. However, because of the unusual degree of ignorance concerning relevant issues crucial to his dealings with the customer, the used car salesman has any conflict that might be inherent in the relationship intensified.

He doesn't know the condition, price, or value of his product, what income he will derive from particular sales, or what the house will let him promise the customer in the way of repairs, service, or extras. In addition to these unknowns, he has no standard spiel as does the encyclopedia or vacuum cleaner salesman, and most used car dealers function more independently than either of these other salesmen. Yet it is the salesman who deals directly with the customer and must ultimately determine a workable compromise.[18]

The house, or the backer, is not unique to the used car trade. Here, as in real estate or gambling operations, it is the term used to describe the party with the greatest financial interest and investment in the dealings, holding final veto power over all transactions.[19]

The relationship between the house and a salesman can be typified by Hughes' description of the real estate salesmen in *Men and Their Work:*

The salesman is the casual of the real estate business. His services are enlisted by ads which assure the prospect that no experience is necessary. According to the realtor [comparable to the house] the salesman is the lowest order of the real estate man. He came into the business because he could not get a job elsewhere. He stays only long enough to get an advance draft on commissions, and will not govern his occupational conduct in the interests of his employer or the real estate business in general. Every salesman complains of mistreatment by his former employer and of "dirty deals" given him by his fellow-salesmen. He is the Ishmael of the business; like the waitress, he accuses his fellows of having stolen his tips, and proceeds to steal theirs. He considers the formulated codes of business as checks upon his enterprise.[20]

This, it should be remembered, is the salesman from the house's point of view.

Yet, even assuming that the feelings of house toward salesman are as bitter as this, the situation need not be disrupted or destroyed. To the contrary, Simmel positions conflict as a positive, functional factor in many relationships and as a continuing part of the combatants' self-image:

A certain amount of discord, inner divergence and outer controversy is organically tied up with the very elements that ultimately hold the group together; it cannot be separated from the unity of the sociological structure. This is true not only in cases of evident marital failure but also in marriages characterized by a *modus vivendi* which is bearable or at least borne. Such marriages are not "less" marriages by the amount of conflict they contain; rather, out of so many elements, among which there is that inseparable quantity of conflict, they have developed into the definite and characteristic units which they are. Secondly, the positive and integrating role of antagonism is shown in structures which stand out by the sharpness and carefully preserved purity of their social divisions and gradations. Thus, the Hindu social system rests not only on the hierarchy, but also directly on the mutual repulsion of the castes. Hostilities not only prevent boundaries within the group from gradually disappearing, so that these hostilities are often consciously cultivated to guarantee existing conditions. Beyond this, they also are of direct sociological fertility: often they provide classes and individuals with reciprocal positions which they would not find, or not find in the same way, if the causes of hostility were not accompanied by the *feeling* and the expression of hostility — even if the same objective causes of hostility were in operation.[21]

Not only does conflict serve to differentiate between "we" and "them" and thus serve the dual purpose of role definition and group solidarity, but it allows a socially acceptable pressure valve, a means by which feelings can be expressed in a relatively undestructive way. So, although he probably knew only an occasional used Daimler or Mercedes dealer, Simmel couldn't have been more pithy about the house and its tenants.[22]

One of the surprising factors about the research was that in spite of the widespread and obvious distrust between salesman and customer, very little bitterness or hostility was ever expressed by the salesman concerning the customer. Simmel, in a functionalistic vein, may have provided the reason for the absence of hostility between the two. Perhaps the lack of overt hostility towards the customer is due to the fact that this hostility is displaced towards the house in a less destructive way in terms of the system as a whole.[23]

A customer, even an unusually surly one, is always a potential customer and source of referral, so acting hostile toward him at any point is self-defeating for the salesman. On the other hand, the house is an ever-present annoyance of perhaps less magnitude, but of a more enduring quality. The house is always the same house, while the customer continually changes, and while the customer may indirectly control the amount of money the salesman makes, the house controls it directly. An antagonized customer means a lost sale, while an antagonized boss means little if the salesman continues to produce, which entails not alienating the customer.

The pressure valve theory can be seen most clearly in the following quote; the hostility can actually be seen shifting from customer to house. A customer had requested a number of services to be performed on the car he had just bought to which the salesman had docilely replied, "I'll do what I can!" His reaction after the customer left was quite different:

He wants it washed and the lights fixed and the battery secured (mimicing): "If I went over a bump, it would knock the thing to pieces." Christ, it's a used car and they [the customer] want you to make it like a new one. I freeze my fanny off all day and you see the kind of bull I have to take. I've been moving cars around all day; the mechanic comes over and says the boss wants me to move 'em around and I tell him I'm not his God damn boy. I'm a salesman and he can move 'em himself.[24]

Being unpleasant to the customer when he was listing his demands could have resulted in a lost sale, so the salesman translated his anger to the house in the person of the mechanic who was transmitting the house's message.

Functionally, the grievances between house and salesman fall into three categories: disputes over money with the salesman seeing the house as money grubbing with respect to his salary; the intransigence of the house with respect to the customer and his demands; and the unscrupulous nature of the house as compared to the salesman's own nature. This unscrupulousness is often tinged (in the salesman's mind) with a pervasive stupidity.

Still, the most common source of disagreement is the price paid for the car itself:

Well, I can write up anything I want and send it over and see what the boss says. If a guy offers me 200 for a car, I can send it over, but if the guy is only 100 off, I write it up and send it over and see what happens.

Of course, writing up an order and having it refused by the house is embarrassing to the salesman, so his lack of control over the situation is not particularly pleasant.[25] Arriving at a price is not a straightforward proposition between the house and the salesman, just as it is not simple between the customer and the salesman:

The only person harder to convince than the customer is the house . . . to get the house to sign-off the car . . . they always want more money. "Make him go a little higher" is all they ever think about.

Not only does the house have the final sign-off ability, but because the salesman is acting only as an agent, he can make the decision, but only to an unspecified limit; he lacks control over the situation with the subsequent results of hostility as described in Chapter 2. The house endeavors to keep the salesman ignorant of both the price of a particular car and the salesman's commission on it. While related, price and commission are not directly dependent on one another.

The house goes to great pains to keep the salesman uninformed of the intake price of a particular vehicle. He thinks the salesman will make a better deal with the customer if he does not know what the profit margin is on the car. Although there is a certain rationale to this policy, as stated in classical decision making theory by Edwards:

. . . if one member of a bargaining pair knew the costs, prices and profits of both while the other knew only his own costs, prices and profits, then the member with more information was at a disadvantage because he more quickly arrived at the equitable offer and consequently was at a disadvantage in subsequent bargaining.[26]

it does not make for cordial relations between salesman and house. Few individuals could be expected to relish the feeling that they are powerless in a situation, especially in front of an audience.

It is obvious that the house is not convinced that the salesman has its best interest at heart. Part of this distrust stems from the system of recompense for the salesman. In some dealerships, a minimal salary is paid, usually around $50 a week, but it is not uncommon for no base salary to be paid. The rest of the salesman's income is derived from commissions on the cars he sells. Two salesmen discuss the system:

At some dealers you get a salary, fifty bucks a week; some you don't get any. At Caddy and Olds dealers, you work straight commission, no salary. There's more money in that. Most places you get 25% on new cars and used. (Twenty-five percent of the difference between a trade-in and the selling price of the car.) Carl, what do we get here, actual figure?

This place you get four. Other places, four, five, sometimes even six percent. [Four] is the cap (top commission) here or $35 whichever comes first. Some places you get a straight share of the profit at the end of the month or a percentage of a hundred, but most places don't do it that way anymore. Here there's a ten dollar minimum on any car (the percentage has to be greater than ten dollars to the salesman). The house sells the back lot to the junkies (junk car dealers). Sometimes they'll sell five or six for $50 apiece, but then the salesman doesn't get anything, so there's a ten dollar minimum.

To the salesman the difference between selling a car for $100 or $1500 is a maximum of twenty dollars — quite often it is considerably less than that if his top salary commission figure has already been reached.

The complex arrangement by which salary is determined (which led one of the salesmen quoted above to be unsure about the exact commission his own house paid) depends more on how many cars are sold during the month than on how high a profit the salesman makes for the house. The salesman is thus torn between maximizing his gains on a particular car and maximizing the number of cars he is able to sell. One salesman "told all" displaying not only his knowledge of the system, but his attitude toward his house:

The boss told me not to tell you everything, but I'll tell you what you want to know. This here is the list. They come out during the slow months, not during June, July, September. One won't come out again 'til November. In the fall, the new cars come out, but in the summer, people want a car for vacation. In New England, it's better in the winter, cause people smash up their cars and get to figuring how much it will cost to have them repaired and so they decide, what the hell and get another one. Here's the list:

Cars Sold	Bonus per Car
6	$ 2
7-10	$ 5
11-16	$10
17-19	$12
20 plus	$15

(Car must retail for more than $200 to be eligible.)

(Laughing) See that 200 business at the end? That's cause I caught 'em last month and sold a fifty dollar piece of junk that we'd gotten from one of the junkies and they had to pay me $10 on it.

This revelation came from a salesman at a different dealership than the one in the quotation where the two salesmen discuss commissions. The ten dollar minimum figure specified by the house becomes more understandable.

the quotation where the two salesmen discuss commissions. The ten dollar minimum figure specified by the house becomes more understandable.

The fiscal situation becomes even more complicated by the fact that certain cars on the lot come complete with financial incentives to the salesman:

... Here's a car's been around a year and they have a sales meeting and they announce a bonus and that car's gone in three days. Tell all the salesmen they get a $50 bonus cause everybody who comes in you show that car no matter what they say they're interested in and sooner or later you find somebody who likes it.

Thus, the salesman views any car in terms of profit margin vs. top commission allowable vs. number of cars sold for the month (lowering the price on a car increases the probability of a sale) in addition to the incentives on a particular car. He deals with all of these variables while also considering his relationship to the house and the customer.

And although the uncertainty in which he is kept about the price and commission on a car is calculated to result in maximum profit for the house, the salesman's resentment of the situation may cause the tactic to fail. As one disgruntled salesman noted:

I never ask for more than a car is listed for. Some places they do and they [the house] give the salesman $25 for every $100 he sells over, but I don't do that (increase the asking price). Why soak the customer for another $100 even if it means $25 for you?

The house is not unaware of this tendency on the part of the salesman. He knows the salesman sometimes sides with the customer against him even if the salesman is penalizing himself in the bargain. The house is not entirely "straight" with the salesman, not only because he feels it is the way to increase his own profits, but because as Hughes pointed out, he does not hold the salesman in particularly high regard. He considers him lazy (with which the salesmen *privately* concur) and is aware that a salesman can occasionally commit the house to doing something the house does not wish to do. As a result of these reservations, the house limits what the salesman is allowed to do and to promise. The issue centers around money, but is much more pervasive than that. The house believes the salesman's lack of monetary motivation and loyalty spills over into the salesman's attitude about working in general. One manager (the house, in that he doesn't work on commission) comments on a salesman's absence, purportedly due to illness:

Yeah, I think he exaggerates a little. People can come in if they want to. They can talk themselves into feeling much sicker than they are.

Often this skepticism is more specific, sometimes bordering on accusation;

the house is lamenting the "irresponsible" attitude of its salesmen:

Whatever I sign, we gotta do. Like once I just asked the guy [salesman] if he'd checked everything and he said he had, so I didn't check him and he'd forgotten to add transportation and we were a couple of hundred dollars short and we had to make good.

As might be predicted, the house displays a limited amount of sympathy for the salesman's plight; after all, it is the house who stands to lose big and who has the greatest investment; the salesmen can always move on to greener pastures:

The salesman's price can't be too low. He can't close a deal without my signature. If he's already named a price he has to go back and tell the customer that he's made a mistake.

The effect of having to backtrack with a customer has already been discussed. But obviously, the house cannot always be against the salesman; it certainly would not be in the best interests of the boss to overly antagonize the man on whom his bread and butter depends. The house at least admits to understanding some of the hardships of the salesman:

Each of the men is on the defensive when a customer comes up. He has got to sell himself, make the customer like him and trust him because the customer expects not to.

Yet in spite of this understanding, the house persists in keeping the salesman uninformed. Being in the dark so much concerning the product he is selling does not endear the house to the salesman. He correctly assumes that he is not trusted by the house and thus finds himself in an uncomfortable position:

I can never tell what the margin is — how far I can come down cause I didn't take the car in and so I write up anything and then go back and forth between the house and the customer making the boss come down a little and the customer go up.

The overt manifestation of the distrust and dislike in the form of hostility smoulders around the price of a car but becomes an open flame when the subject is money out of the salesman's pocket whether it is a commission or petty cash:

I must have spent a buck on this phone yesterday, what with calling HFC (the friendly local finance company) three or four times, the kid at home, then his wife, then him at work, then his wife back, then HFC again. (The kid being a hot prospect for a car.) I haven't been reimbursed for phone money; I asked him (the boss) for the money once and I expected a five, but he gave me two dimes. It does cut down on the trying. You figure to hell with it if you don't have the dimes. It's not worth the trouble to walk across the street for change. I guess some guy was making long distance phone calls, so the boss put this pay one in, but I ain't about to keep paying for my own phone bills. The boss CLAIMS that somebody was making long distance phone calls.

Sometimes the grievances are more imagined than real:

A guy came in last night that had been to see me and I thought sure as hell he'd steal the deal, but I'll be damned he (the boss) wrote it up with my name on it. At this rate, I'll run out of the God damn cars to sell.

or more real than imagined:

Well, the boss gives all his business to Fred or Tom (the managers) and everybody else gives all their business to Tom's brother cause Tom is the manager. I'm going to work for a Jewish man again; he'll take care of you. Tom's mad at me cause of the sale I made on Friday to the "professor." He'd talked to his brother once (Tom's) but he talked to me first and had talked to me about four times, so I told him I didn't care what he (Tom) wanted, I was going to make that sale, whether he wanted me to or not. Come on, I'll show you. See this (order form). This is my handwriting, this is Tom's. See what it says, "No repairs done before delivery." Now how would you feel if you saw this on your form and I had told you that I would tighten up the transmission. So I just voided the whole form and took it over across the street to the boss (the owner, in this case) and had him sign.

It often seems to be the "little" things that add fuel to the fire: "Do we get paid if we're sick? That's a laugh . . . we don't get paid when we're well . . . sick pay . . . ha, ha. That's a laugh."

or things that have absolutely nothing to do with work:

I went over and got a beer; the boss'd kill me if he knew. He thinks I drink the milk (picking up a carton on the window sill) . . . thinks I'm a nice guy . . . heh, heh, little does he know.

This hostility is sometimes expressed in a way that attempts to belie the control the house attempts to exert over the salesman in terms of his drinking habits as described above or his "secondary," non-policy making role in the organization:

(Lamenting the dearth of available used cars for him to sell): I got real smart . . . I dropped a hint to the sales manager, to make him feel like a bigshot. I whisper in his ear . . . figure out how much money you can make if you park the new cars somewheres else and just stock the used ones . . . he'll figure it out, tell the boss and . . . hee, hee, you just wait and see.

The salesman attempts to not only control the house but to "get" the house, either by conning the house, selling a piece of junk for commission or giving the customer a break, but also to "get" the house, to win, to beat the boss at his own game. But getting the house has definite boundaries. Destroying or running the house out of business at one extreme or even cutting the profits of the house to the extent that it might substantially jeopardize the livelihood of the salesman and his job would be foolish, biting the proverbial hand that feeds, even if it feeds none too gently. So, while some express hostility openly:

This place is cheap. The place I worked before, that guy was a peach, learned everything I know from him. Just up the street at the foreign car place . . . what a prince of a fellow. I would make a good sale, make a big profit, he would say to me, fella, you make money, I'll make money. Just like that, what a guy. I'd make a good deal, he'd say, fella, go down buy yourself a suit, or a sportcoat, charge it to me. What a fellow. I got all my wardrobe on bonuses. What a guy, a little Jew, he loved it, he could make $200 a day, just buying and selling and trading a car, back and forth from dealer to dealer. What a man. But then he died and his son took over and it just wasn't the same, he was bad to work for. Everybody would quit after two months, so he used to give my sales to the new salesmen so they would stay on for awhile and one day I told him I'd had it up to here and left and came down here, but this outfit's cheap, cheap. The old man, not only would he give me the bonus at the time, but at the end of the month, when he was totalling the sales again, he'd say, fella, you did real well for me on that one, here's a hundred and would take it right out of his pocket and give it to me.

most express a preference for working where they're working:

The guys here are nice, honest guys . . . the guy next door (another dealership) won't go any over for you. The guy next door is really cheap, won't give you anything. Even on a bonus car that's been around a year he won't give you nothing.

and recognize a "good" thing when they see it: "Hell, I'm in business for myself with no investment, no risk." And, as implied above, there is a certain amount of loyalty expressed, the feelings of preference for "my" house to another. Although salesmen do move around quite frequently,[27] the often expressed goal is to "find a good house and stay there" — an admission to the possibility that there is such a thing as a good house.

Up to this point, I have discussed the salesman's view of the house and his relationship to it as employer versus employee — how much latitude do I have — how much money do I get. But the salesman is also aware of the house's symbolic value to the customer. It, therefore, has a very real practical value to the salesman in his dealings with a suspicious public. The house is the scapegoat, the forces of evil, the bad guys, especially when contrasted with the customer's friend, the salesman. The following examples from my field notes are so similar as to have been uttered by the same man, yet each came from a different salesman in actual conversation with a customer:

. . . I'm giving you a good price now — my boss, he'll probably yell at me — but I want to sell you a car and then I want to sell you another one in a couple of years; so I gotta see you get taken care of. Maybe if I do a good job you'll even send me a friend sometime. This is how I figure to do business – sound reasonable?

I'll write up these kids, but when the boss sees it, he'll say, "Where's the 500?" (deposit). But I'd rather try and get refused than not try at all.

(Laughing) Look, we already knocked off a hundred; you're working on your second hundred. I've been slicing all week . . . what the hell. Last week, the boss called me and said, "How come you're giving away all my cars? You trying to run me out of business. I believe in giving a good deal, but hell . . ." And I said, look boss, when I sell only one a day, damn right I'm going to make a good deal and he said, "OK, but don't run me out of business, don't give everything away."

Notice that when something good occurs, a hundred dollars knocked off the price, it's WE that did it, but when there's something more to be done to the car, it's *me* that's going to get it done for you or at least try, while *they* will oppose *me* who is on *your* side. And if the customer requests an improbable task, it's "I'll check with the boss – I'll see what I can do for you."

Stephen Miller noted the same technique among the used car salesmen he studied. As he stated:

The salesmen now suggests he will have to and well might act on the customer's behalf to convince the sales manager to accept the deal on the customer's terms. ("I know the salesmanager is going to jump all over me when I go in there but we've come to an agreement . . . let me go in there and work on him and see if I can get that car at your price.")[28]

Given this technique, once can visualize how catastrophic a rejection on the part of the house is to the image (both self and customer's) of the salesman. Yet the house will not infrequently reject a deal.

With all the possibilities for bad feeling between salesman and customer, it is not surprising that when the shifting alliances that Mead predicts do occur, they are the direct result of an unusually obstreperous customer who can cause the salesman and the house to unite:

One day a customer came in here and called me a liar and was getting ugly and the boss up and threw him out and told him not to bother coming back.

Another salesman related that it took an actual threat of physical violence by one customer before his house stepped in and bodily removed the offensive customer from the premises.

Yet in spite of the symbolic, pragmatic possibilities of the house being a useful symbol to the salesman as a boogieman with which to confront the customer, very real feelings of hostility do exist between the house and salesman, occasionally taken lightly:

Sometimes you know a guy is at rock bottom, so you go across the street and con the boss. You tell him the crank shaft is split or sounds awful, and he says no, it's not, and you say, trust me boss, it is, and then you come back here and give the guy the lower price.

and sometimes not so lightly:

The boss had a rule, no money, no keys. This lady came in. She was crying. I took her home, brought her back after I called the boss and asked him to make an exception just this once and he said, no chance. After we got back, the customer said, "I hope your boss doesn't make 5¢ – but you were nice – I'll send in referrals, it's the only way I can say thanks for taking me home." The boss was a real s.o.b. about it.

Thus, while hostility is a significant factor in a salesman's dealings with his employer, the relationship is symbiotic and, as such, is kept within boundaries; the house will protect the salesman against a customer and neither the house's antipathy toward the salesman nor the salesman's dislike for the house keeps either from using the other and functioning adequately and appropriately within the relationship.

Because the relationship is one of employer-employee, a certain amount of hostility could be predicted. The fact that the relationship is a brokerage one to boot increases the opportunity for conflict. The unusual nature of the brokerage, with so many unknown variables, makes the situation significant in understanding subsequent action. The house's utility as symbol to the customer will come into focus more sharply in the concluding chapters on the bargaining itself. The next chapter deals with the customer as significant other, the other "me." It is the final chapter on the perspective of the salesman, a perspective that molds interaction with his customer.

7 Shifting Gears

There can be no doubt that most customers see the used car salesman as something less than a paragon of virtue, as far as the salesman is concerned. Stephen J. Miller documents the fact that even new car salesman, who enjoy a far higher reputation, feel themselves to be on the defensive: "A majority of automobile salesmen admit that their customers regard them as 'con men', who attempt to 'put one over' on the buyer."[1] One used car salesman phrased his dilemma quite eloquently: "They come up to me and say, 'Okay, Jesse James, you can take off your guns now' . . . how do you think that makes me feel?"

However it might make the salesman feel personally, occupationally he knows that he can expect this kind of attitude, yet his success as a salesman is predicated on his ability to sell, so sell he must and to the very man who distrusts him from the outset. How he accomplishes this initial contact that must necessarily precede any sales is the subject of this chapter.

In simplest form, the salesman who is initially on the defensive must be able to switch to the offensive (no pun intended) in order to be able to sell. The steps by which he accomplishes this are:

1. Change distrust to trust;
2. Change dislike to like.

in order to be able to:

3. Assume control;
4. Find out what the customer wants;
5. Practice a selling technique;
6. SELL.

This chapter will deal with the value of setting, front and facade to the salesman in establishing a climate of trust. Because the customer does not trust him initially, the creation of such a climate is crucial.

A by-product of the efforts to create a comforting setting is that by doing so, the salesman has assumed control for the interaction. He has gone from a defensive position to one of controlling not only the interaction, but appearances.

He first reeducates the customer as to why he is different from the kind of used car salesmen he was expecting to encounter. He establishes a groundwork for trust. Part of this trust, as Simmel has pointed out, is the establishment of intimacy, that nothing is being concealed. This apparent openness gives the salesman another means of control.

Once control is gained, the salesman has only to determine what the customer has on his mind in order to be able to greatly influence the outcome of the encounter. In other words, he will be able to sell the customer a car. The final step of this procedure, prior to selling a car, requires the salesman to bind the customer to him. To accomplish this, he creates a feeling of indebtedness on the part of the customer which will carry through to the final dickering. Trust has been created as has the vehicle for its maintenance. The technique of this accomplishment follows.

In a sense, what the salesman must do is not unique to his situation as car salesman. Bogdan discusses the establishment of a "front" by both vacuum cleaner salesmen and encyclopedia salesmen in which the negative feelings the customer has toward door-to-door salesmen are made irrelevant by the salesman's assumption of a facade different from what he actually is.[2]

This same concept of "front" or facade is discussed in *The Big Con*[3] and by Sutherland in *The Professional Thief.*[4] In both of these instances the man goes to his customer in functionally the same way as the door-to-door salesman. Although this offers the man the advantage of surprise over his "customer," he must deal with the customer on the customer's "home turf," which, as Miller points out, is a distinct advantage to the customer.[5]

The hustler in the poolroom has the advantage of being in familiar territory and thus has the added control that setting can offer. He also has a certain element of surprise working in his favor since he could conceivably be something other than a hustler and still have occasion to be in a poolhall. On the other hand, as Polsky points out, hustling is quite often a "one shot" affair, so a "front" need only be constructed, not maintained.[6] Goffman adds the dimension of maintenance or even reconstruction of a front in order to "cool out the mark,"[7] but even here, the cool out or soothing need only be temporary, sufficient to avert confrontation or capture.

The salesman must not only construct, but maintain a pliable enough "front" to sustain him through a lengthy interaction and potentially ensure a repeat sale or a referral. He must accomplish all of this without the advantage of surprise or initial deceit. The customer knows who the salesman is the moment he enters the lot. This initial phase of the sale is not only vital, but predictably complicated and delicate.

Goffman's concept of "face" is extremely useful (more so than "front" or setting) because it is pliable enough to allow for long-range, sustained use required by the used car salesman. He defines "face" in such a way as to bring the idea of a mask to mind:

The term *face* may be defined as the positive social value a person effectively claims for himself by the line others assume he has taken during a particular contact. Face is an image of self delineated in terms of approved social attributes – albeit an image that others may share, as when a person makes a good showing for his profession or religion by making a good showing for himself.[8]

The salesman establishes an image that he feels is conducive to making a sale, one which the customer can trust. By doing this, the salesman becomes the stage manager, the director of the scene; he gains control.

Miller calls this initial stage "contact" and ascribes the gain of control as fundamental to it:[9] "The salesman desires to keep control, in fact achieve mastery of his relationship with the customer."[10]

This search for control is most probably not limited to salesmen, service professions (as discussed by Becker[11] and Freidson[12]) or any other occupation, but characteristic of human interaction in general. This is especially true if behavior is viewed from the standpoint of psychoanalytic theory following Freud, Adler, Horney, and others.

Control is the objective, but the first step is simple appearance; Goffman notes:

When an individual appears in the presence of others, there will usually be some reason for him to mobilize his activity so that it will convey an impression which it is in his interest to convey.[13]

In this case, there is no doubt as to the reason an impression must be conveyed. It must be not only an impression, but a counterimpression; one that simultaneously counteracts the preconceived image while erecting a second, more favorable one. Bogdan cites an example:

The reason for the use of the false front by the companies is that they believe the public is leary of the salesman and imputes traits of aggressiveness and foul play to him. Presenting a front which corresponds to that of the salesman would thus start the salesman off in the interaction with a strike against him in his attempt to persuade. The client could be on the defensive and cautious in his dealings with him.[14]

One obvious method of presenting a favorable image is by looking a reputable part, or at least *not* looking the disreputable part:

The instructor in the encyclopedia training course makes suggestions to the trainees regarding their appearance and the importance of having it in keeping with the front they are presenting. They are told not to wear white socks, side burns or mustaches because, "they don't go with the image . . . you'll come off as a con man." Being well groomed in a suit or dark sports jacket is recommended.[15]

In the same way, used car salesmen are told to wear a sports coat and a tie to maintain a neat appearance. They are urged to have nothing more on their desks than: "a telephone, a calendar, a blotter and an ash tray" and to keep their drawers "neat."

Nevertheless, the strength of the negative image is never far away. As one salesman reported:

The customer wants to believe you, but we're the bums, he's afraid of us and other things that I can't mention. So you have to relax him, bring him down to your level, don't be afriad to explain to him.

Another salesman felt similarly:

People come into this dealership with a fixation in mind — components, price, car. Their brains are filled with garbage about us that isn't even true, and you have to sell him. This is salesmanship; he's prefixed, thinks he knows, but he doesn't really.

As discussed in a previous chapter, the customer's view of the salesman is in part harsh because of what he thinks he (the customer) knows about the selling price of the car. The assumed profit of the salesman does nothing to endear him to the customer: "Every customer thinks you make $200 every deal. It's obvious where they get the idea, the consumer magazine." The point still remains that whatever the source of the image and the bad feelings, the situation must be altered, for as one salesman stated: "If you don't get him (the customer) in the right frame of mind, you won't sell cars. You might sell some, but not many."

How is this alteration to be accomplished? One method is to re-educate the customer, tell him the facts, explain the "you are a horse of a different color." A salesman explains how he deals with the customer who "knows" how much the salesman will make in commission:

People come in and say, "you've got a 25% mark-up on that car." They want to be educated. After all, buying a car is a high risk decision. So you tell him flat, there's no 25% mark-up. Then you tell him that there's a 7-10% tax on $4000 worth of car which is $400 and pre-delivery costs $100 and transportation another $100 which totals to between five and six hundred bucks and that's no mark-up at all yet. You're not telling him a lie either. Once this is in his mind, the 25% shatters; you're only talking about 17%. So then you ask him, what do you think is a fair mark-up? Ten or twelve percent. And let me tell you, you're more than willing to sell at 12%. Macy's sells at 7% and they're the biggest discount store in the United States.

This bit of explanation applies to the finances on a new car, but the same general technique can be applied to a used car. Educate the customer, and dispel his preconceived notions.

A second salesman offered another compelling reason for the salesman to try to educate the customer: "If he leaves with unanswered questions, he won't buy."

One of the factors about which the customer must be educated and his questions answered is the difference between this salesman (himself) and all of the unscrupulous other fellows. One such approach uses the historical perspective. The history of used cars is carefully traced with references to shoddy men who conned a less knowledgeable public. Cars were in greater demand and lesser supply. Another is for the salesman to carefully disassociate himself from affiliated dealerships (if he works for an unaffiliated dealership) or the converse. Salesmen are careful not to use "jargon" with the customer because it closely allies them with a shoddy image and makes the customer fearful. Bogdan notes the same advice among door-to-door salesmen:

Don't say deal! People don't like to hear that. They think you're trying to put something over on them. We don't want people to think that we're wheelers and dealers . . . We don't have any deals, remember that fellars . . . We have wonderful programs, a terrific machine, but we don't have any deals.[16]

The advice not to use words like "deal" is more an admonition not to remind the customer of the negative connotations of the salesman; the assumption that he is out to "get" the unwary customer and not to be trusted. Simmel underlines the significance of dealing with a party who is not trusted. He points out the importance and the pervasiveness of trust in day-to-day human interaction:

. . . Our modern life is based to a much larger extent than is usually realized upon the faith in the honesty of the other . . . We base our gravest decisions on a complex system of conceptions, most of which presuppose the confidence that we will not be betrayed . . .[17]

Trust and expectation are inextricably linked and the semantic issue of whether if one expects to be cheated and is in fact cheated he can consider himself to be betrayed becomes less relevant with the inclusion of Simmel's definition of the lie:

The lie consists in the fact that the liar hides his true idea from the other. Its specific nature is not exhaustively characterized by the fact that the person lied-to has a false conception about the topic or object; this the lie shares with common error. What is specific is that he is kept deceived about the private opinion of the *liar*.[18]

The crucial factor is not so much that an untruth is told as that the truth cannot be ascertained. This concentration on the absence of veracity rather than the presence of falsehood removes the issue from the realm of value judgment and Simmel suggests that this is exactly the case:

The ethically negative value of the lie must not blind us to its sociologically quite positive significance for the formation of certain concrete relations. In regard to the elementary sociological fact at issue here — the restriction of the knowledge of the one about the other — it must be remembered that the lie is only one among all possible means.[19]

Concealment is then the problem. If used car salesmen can be considered students of human nature in the same way that anyone who deals with people can be so described, then it is not unreasonable to assume that they, too, are aware of the difficulty with implied concealment. (Whether or not their approach is Simmelian, there can be no doubt that their solution would certainly please the theoretician.) The salesman attempts to counteract the effects of implied concealment and subterfuge by the antidote of intimacy, of complete openness, the antithesis of concealment. The cheerful slap on the back, first name basis approach of the salesman is well known, but Bogdan points out that even more direct tactics are employed:

The salesman tells the client about his personal life, about his wife and children, and attempts to elicit conversation from the client about his personal life. The rationale behind the creation of intimacy is that it is conducive to building trust and places the client under personal obligation to be cooperative.[20]

A part of this intimacy can be based on the salesman revealing information about himself. He can also seem to include the customer as a "member of his team."

The alliance between the salesman and the customer against the house has already been discussed; Bogdan describes the same phenomenon:

In some parts of the presentation the salesman pits himself and the client against a common enemy. In both companies' scripts the salesman and the client are joined together in combat against the advertising industry.[21]

On a less specific basis, the salesman wants to establish a general air of confidence and caring about the customer:

Part of the salesman's strategy is to present himself as someone who is concerned about the best interests of the client. Rather than creating a situation in which the salesman appears to be trying to get the client to do something the trainees are told to handle the interaction so that a partnership is established between the client and himself. They are then both working together for the good of the client. The salesman is showing the client how to solve his problems and how to do something about his concerns.[22]

Assuming that the salesman is successful in his attempt to establish a degree of intimacy or at least to deflect strong notions of concealment, he should now be well on the way to asserting control over the situation. He becomes instrumental in establishing the present tone of the relationship. He can even suggest procedures by which the interaction can be continued. He can begin on the long road to the sale. One of the assumptions that allows the salesman to function in a moderately guileless manner is that he still sees himself as different than the customer, as described in Chapter 6. As Bogdan says:

The clients are abiding or asked to abide by the rules of fairness which the salesman helps them to define in the situation. The salesman is using different standards than the client in determing his behavior and action.[23]

Some of the ways by which the salesman can exert control are simple, some a good deal more complex, but all are designed to move the customer toward a sale: "The trainees are advised to speak faster in the touchy spots and slower in the more easily accepted sections."[24]

Car salesmen, as previously discussed, keep up a running, calm, reassuring patter in order to constantly be in control. Yet all of these techniques pall before the major technique of control. Salesmen are influenced by the actions and reactions of the customer, but basically, they know what it is they are doing, what they are going to say and what comes next:

The salesman is in a position which affords him a good deal of control in his interaction with the client . . . control is an important conscious strategy in sales. The trainee is told that because he has given the presentation a large number of times and because he has memorized the script, he will know what he is going to do in the presence of the client and be at ease. The trainees are told that the client is often ill at ease and does not know how to act. One instructor told the students that although they were the strangers in the home of the client, the client was ill at ease and thus was in a sense the stranger and guest at the presentation even though he was in his own home. They are told that they should direct the show by putting the clients at ease and by arranging the setting so that it is advantageous to the salesman in his effort to make a sale.[25]

The instructor in Bogdan's described course was even more specific:

Now notice, you've just gotten into the house and already you're the stage director. You've got control. You're placing people where you want them, you're setting the stage so it's advantageous to you.[26]

The used car salesman will direct the customer in the same way, into his office, to a specific car, to a chair. His advantage, like the door-to-door salesman, lies in knowing what comes next although his patter isn't usually as "canned" as the door-to-door man:

Knowing more or less precisely what he is going to say to the client, the salesman has confidence and control and thus an advantage over the client in the situation.[27]

The first effective use of control must be to find out what it is the customer is seeking. This makes the salesman's task much simpler, even if he doesn't have what the customer wants. Until he specifically knows, he is at a distinct disadvantage. The customer knows something that the salesman doesn't know and something crucial at that. One salesman offers his sure-fire technique for eliciting information: "Let the customer do the talking and he'll tell you what he wants every time." Another amplifies: "Be silent, they can't stand silence, they'll spill their guts to you." Although seeming to contradict the idea of keeping up a constant patter, when information is needed the salesmen listen. The patter is used as filler between questions. It is used as a soothing background lullaby to keep the customer's attention while allowing for control. The stage of eliciting information can be handled only after control has been obtained. The salesmen utilize two categories of technique to gain the information they need, indirect and direct. The simplest way to get an answer to a question is to ask the customer a direct question. An equally effective way of "finding out" is by observation of clues, a more indirect method. This art of analysis is conducted to find out as much about the customer as possible, including whether or not he is really a likely prospect:

Sizing up refers to the process by which the salesman collects information and makes judgments about the clients in regard to their buying potential. Through sizing up, the salesman makes evaluations as to the likelihood of a sale evolving from interaction with the client . . .[28]

This information is bound to influence the subsequent actions of the salesman:

First thing you got to do with a customer is find out if he's legitimate. You talk to him and you find out if he's a tire kicker or a shopper and you find out in his mind, what I call qualify him, whether he's serious or not.

Finding out whether a customer is a "live one" or not is only part of the battle. A "live one" can be as good as dead if the salesman is using the wrong approach or selling the wrong way. As one of the salesmen said, "You don't try and sell a guy with four kids and a dog a Mustang as a family car." Door-to-door salesmen have an advantage in gleaning clues in that they are at the customer's home:

The trainees are told that toys and children on the lawn are positive signs for the encyclopedia salesman in that clients by (buy) the product for their children. Houses which are run down or extremely modest should be avoided they are told in that this indicates that the buying power of the client is probably low. While trainees are not told not to call on clients with expensive homes these do appear to be avoided by new salesmen.[29]

The used car salesman is not left completely without clues. The customer's car if quite often a valuable source of information containing miscellaneous sports gear, children's toys, vacation stickers, ski racks, and the like. All give the salesman a clue as to what kind of car the customer wants and what kind of man he is. It can also furnish subject matter for intimate chats. The customer himself is the single most important data bank. There is the way he looks, although one salesman cautions against overly facile conclusions:

This young fellow with long hair and holes in his sweater came into the showroom asking about our performance cars. Well, everybody shied away from him and finally he got to me. I talked to him, listened and showed him one of our Shelby Cobras. He bought it and paid $8,000 for it in cash — that's right — *cash*! And he's still wearing the same sweater with the holes, but now he's driving a Shelby from our dealership.

In addition to tacit information, the customer can also be probed by direct, yet subtle questioning as students practiced in selling door to door:

Instructor: This is a nice section of town. Fine house you have her Mr. Jones. Are you the owner?

Student: No.

Instructor: Oh, I see; you're leasing it then.

Student: That's right.

Instructor: It certainly is a very fine place. Mr. Jones, I have an old friend by that name, really a nice fellar. He's an engineer. That wouldn't happen to be your line of work would it?

Student: No, I'm a salesman.

Instructor: Oh, is that right. With a local firm?

Student: That's right.

Instructor: Well, that's a demanding line of work. They must keep you pretty busy.

Student: That's right.

Instructor: I noticed some tricycles on the back lawn. Reminds me of my own place, how many little ones do you have . . .[30]

The student salesman learns how to ask leading questions that a reluctant customer might not otherwise answer. In this way, the salesman can glean the kind of information that allows him to make his "pitch," as Stephen J. Miller calls it,[31] uniquely suited to his customer. A used car salesman details just such an instance:

. . . The way I figured Chambers he needed a reason to trade. A lot of people are like that. They're not really traders. They're indecisive. They need a *reason* to buy. I let him "walk" on our first meeting because I sized him up that way. My plan was to get him to believe in me. To get him to like the car, and then to throw out a little bait . . . a reason to buy *now*! Frankly, I didn't have a buyer for his car. But it was a very saleable car and I knew I'd have no trouble finding a buyer. I also sized him up as a man who was not a shopper. My clue here was when he said he *wanted* to get three thousand (for his car). He didn't say he *could* get three thousand, or had been *offered* three thousand. I also knew he was well fixed . . . money wasn't that important. He wanted to play games. So I played games. But it was an honest game. I played it straight. And in the end I did him a big favor. I made him happy with his deal.

In order to be effective the salesman must find out what the customer wants, in the largest sense:

Hell, for every guy that comes in here I have to find out how much assistance he needs to help him get the best buy, even though sometimes there's a conflict between extra features and his pocketbook.

Another salesman expressed the process as nearly mystical:

A salesman has got to unconsciously weigh each factor in the total scheme in order to assist his customer in the best buy.

The best buy is best for the customer and best for the salesman, keeping both happy. The final "massage" of the customer before the sale is crucial, with technique all important. Distrust has been turned aside, confidence is rampant, intimacy is on the rise, and information is at the salesman's disposal. It is now time to start "selling" as never before. The first and most widely recommended technique for dealing with a customer at this stage is to "yes" him: "Get him to say yes, yes, yes. See this front end styling, isn't it great? Don't you think so, sir?" Salesmen are told that the response to every question should be yes, so the customer is in a "positive" frame of mind. The customer by now should be "brought into the act." By asking him to respond, just that is accomplished. He is shown around the car including each of the "six selling point positions" each one of which highlights a specific part of the car:

Go to all six points of the car. Get him to say yes, yes, yes. Show him the visibility of the car. Put him in the driver's seat and say, "See how easily you can see me, I'm on my knees." Of course, you only scootch down, but he's involved in the act and saying yes. That's selling and they'll believe you. You're creating the desire to buy, the desire to own with just a little bit of play acting. Put him in the driver's seat, move the seat back if he's a tall man. Tell him, "See how quiet it is" as he rolls up the window. When he's got the window all rolled to the top, just move your lips.

"Yessing" seems to be a generic sales technique.[32] Othe procedures are uniquely involved with a car. The most obvious is simply to take a customer off the market by removing his car from the market. A salesman explains:

Offer to have the guy's car appraised or repaired at cost for him. This will do two things. First, it will take the car off the market which means he can't drive around to look at other cars and he doesn't have his own car for a trade-in appraisal. The second thing is, he'll feel indebted toward you and that's good.

The used car salesman is desirous of creating an indebtedness for the same reason any other salesman is: the customer is slightly more under his control because

... once you create an obligation, you've got him. He'll feel guilty if he doesn't deal with you, like he's a crook or a thief. He'll also think you're a nice guy.

There are other techniques to foster the good guy image:

Do you want the car? That's the first thing to decide. If you really want it, then we can decide later how to pay for it. I don't want you buying something you don't really want. Now, if you decide you really want it, then we can go to bat for you and see what we can do, but you first have to decide if you really want it . . . then we can put in a call to Harriet (at the finance company) and see what she says. You tell her to call us up tomorrow and we'll tell her all about it and see what we can do. Talk to your wife, see what she says. Tell her you want it and what can she say. We can handle the wife for you. If you really want it. You have her call us tomorrow and we'll see about going to bat for you, you just don't worry about that part of it, you just decide whether or not you want this car. You'll have it for a long time and that's the most important thing.

Now the salesman can move in for the kill. He's the totally helpful, nice man who has only the customer's best interest at heart. He is aware of the customer's financial problems (reference to the finance company), and even his marital situation, ". . . we'll take care of the wife for you." This method above is fairly straightforward; others are slightly more ingenious. A pint of ice cream is given to the customer on a hot day so he has to rush home right away or it will melt; he's removed from the market and obligated simultaneously. The puppy dog sell allows a man to take the car home to show it off: "Have you ever tried to return a puppy dog, especially after the kids and the neighbors have seen it?"

Indebtedness can become more literal when the salesman puts his own $20 bill as a loan on the sales order for the customer. The $20 goes right back in the pocket when the customer leaves, but the salesman has established a bond, literally and figuratively.

Melodrama also has its place. Salesmen never talk about accidents, only safety features and only when absolutely necessary. But a fable now and then, especially when a couple is reluctant to shell out the amount of money involved, is often quite effective:

Sometimes I tell my customer a little story. If they're hesitating, I might tell them about the couple that was in only last week and decided not to buy, and the husband was killed two days later. It bleeds the customer a little, but people just love stories. They'll listen, too. Insurance people do this and they're only selling a hunk of paper, I'm selling something they can see, sit in, drive.

Money is also the basis for another selling technique. Options can be sold like cigarettes, on the basis of how many cents a day:

Sell options on a monthly basis. Three cents a day like. Figure out the cost of all your options that way. That way, it costs less than a pack of cigarettes and people are willing to spend nickels and dimes without thinking.

The most important single factor is still caring about the customer, convincing him that *he* is important. A number of techniques are suggested, all by different men, to accomplish the same end:

Don't leave a customer alone. He'll be hurt and it gives him too much time to think.

A customer will be impressed if you ignore a phone call for him.

If the customer is not satisfied, tell him, you don't usually do this sort of thing, but in his case you'll make an exception and try to arrange something with the manager for him. Then "turn" the customer to another salesman that you give a title to who will reconfirm what you've been saying. Turn him to anybody 'til he crawls out on his knees. Even the guy who does the financing, if he happens to be around, will do.

If everything is going all right at this stage, the salesman can prepare the customer for business, signing a sales order slip. Yet, even this must be done cautiously. No price has yet been discussed, but it is time for the customer to begin thinking in terms of signing:

Have your order pad out, so the customer gets acquainted with it because sooner or later he has to sign it if you're going to make a sale. So you might as well be prepared to work right on the form.

If the salesman has achieved this point, he is definitely to the homestretch. But there are a number of things that could have gone wrong in spite of technique, confidence, and the salesman's best efforts. Possibly the most troublesome single problem for the salesman is that someone else has very likely quoted his customer either less money on the car that he is interested in or more money on the customer's own car as part of a trade-in. The problem is much less with a used car than a new one, but is still a major obstacle to a completed transaction.

If you're the first man a guy talks to, you'll never see him again, if you're the second, he'll have your price beat by the third, but if you're the fourth and you figure he's just pricing, you offer him a price $400 below the factory price which is ridiculous because new car prices are all the same. But that way, you'll ensure his coming back and you take him off the market. He'll go check your price out and when nobody else meets it, he'll be back and quote your price and then you say, "Now let's sit down and be reasonable."

The technique of combating over-appraising a trade-in would work similarly. Both must be combated if the sale is to be consummated. The key word is education. All the trust and confidence and niceness that the salesman can summon must be brought to bear here. A salesman describes how he handles "low-balling":

First of all you show him that the other guy's price has got to be too low. If there's still a question in the customer's mind, you've got to follow it up. Don't tell him he's been low-balled. Tell him that that price must have been on a car that was not equipped with extras like the one you're showing him. Tell him he probably had an arm chair estimator on his trade-in; someone from Hiawatha appraisal who only looks from afar. Tell him transportation costs vary. Get him involved, explain what's going to happen when he goes back to the dealer. Say, "why do you think my price is high?" but don't let him answer. You don't really know what he's thinking, so don't be foolish. Ask the shopper what he plans on spending, what figure he has in mind. Tell him you'll do anything you can to put him in a car. Tell him to be realistic, say, "that's what you *want* to spend, how much *can* you spend?" Let the guy talk, don't cut him off too soon, even though you're proud of your gift of gab. If he's really convinced on the low-ball, try switching him to a slightly higher priced car, so you can give him more on the car in terms of trade-in on his jalopy.

To the salesman, even the low-ball cannot prevent him from a sale. The dickering is yet to be done, which will be discussed in the next chapter, but convincing the customer to buy now can be done without any reference to price:

This is done by presenting the opportunity to buy this product . . . as a "now or never" proposition . . . or by offering some added bonus to the client for purchasing the product the night of the demonstration.[33]

For the door-to-door salesman, the game is nearly over; for the used car salesman, the best is yet to come, the dickering over price. Presumably, the customer is now firmly in the hands of the salesman. The customer came in suspicious, with all sorts of misinformation, but he came in to buy a car. He needed help, he was susceptible and to a certain extent, he definitely deserves what he gets. He is definitely not favorably disposed toward the salesman. On the other hand, the salesman is there to sell and to do so, he must overcome an unfavorable disposition on the part of the customer and convince the customer to buy from him. He must soothe the customer, find out what he wants, and figure out how to give it to him. He says "trust me as a person because I'm a nice guy, I'm interested in you, I'm on your side and I know what I'm talking about, I'm an expert on cars. Because of all this, you can trust what I say about this car. There is no reason not to buy from me and many reasons why you should buy from me." The salesman has now firmly established, from his point of view at least, exactly what kind of a guy he is. All that remains is to dicker about the price.

8 The Bargain

The purpose of this final chapter is the traditional two-fold. First, as all final chapters must by convention summarize, it presents a model of the bargain based on information in the previous chapters.

To do this, data specifically relevant to the concept of the bargain are introduced which then allows the bargain to be described in terms of who, what, when, where, and how; the used car game; and the middleman's perspective.

Second, further avenues of research and the potential ramifications are briefly discussed.

As a part of the first purpose, this chapter will evaluate those theoretists and their studies that directly relate to bargaining with emphasis on the basic, everyday quality of the bargain as an emergent process in a situation where more than one solution is possible.

Previous chapters have underscored the ambiguity of roles, goals and, hence, relationships. This chapter will detail the mechanics whereby uncertainty is tolerated, trade-offs are effected, and commitment is reached, resulting in a conclusion satisfactory to all.

The first chapter dealt with the "unrecognized" bargain; the chapters that followed showed how a specific group of people bargain. This final chapter will deal specifically with the bargain as a basic unit in human interaction. To this purpose, Schelling is an excellent point of departure since he has been concerned with the bargain in quasi-military situations for more than a decade.

He describes bargaining as "common interest as well as conflict between adversaries." The relevant examples that he lists as applicable tickle the imagination:

... negotiations, war and threats of war, criminal deterence, tacit bargaining, extortion ... in the strategy of conflict there are enlightening similarities between, say, maneuvering in limited war and jockeying in a traffic jam, between deterring the Russians and deterring one's own children, or between the modern balance of terror and the ancient institution of hostages.[1]

It is these similarities which hold particular interest for "enlightening" the bargain. If the bargain is a common format for human behavior and bargains have common characteristics, then the study of the bargaining of used car salesmen has potential implication for human interaction in general.

Other social scientists (Homans,[2] Blau,[3] Miller[4]) have described bargaining behavior as a form of social exchange in which information, services, and similar "social goods" are bandied back and forth.[5]

More specifically, Roth finds bargaining between doctor and patient in a tubercular ward.[6] It is the unit of compromise between what doctor wishes and patient desires with the nurse occasionally acting as broker. Freidson also sees patient and doctor interacting on the basis of what each is willing to give up and what each is unwilling to lose.[7]

Laymen also recognize the utility of the bargain as evidenced daily in headlines dealing with strikes, disarmament talks, treaties and even "Bargaining Goes to College."[8]

The "ordinary haggling of the market-place" is one and the same with the extraordinary haggling at the peace table and requires much the same tactics. Both sides can gain only by a mutually satisfactory agreement. In order for such an agreement to be reached at all, the parties must see in each other both a source of conflict and a potential advantage to resolution. Or as Deutsch states:

1. Both parties perceive that each party would be better off or no worse off because of the agreement than if no agreement were reached . . .

2. Both parties perceive each other to have conflicting preferences or opposed interests with respect to possible agreements.[9]

However, while he is willing to specify the conditions under which bargaining will occur, Deutsch refuses to predict the form of its eventual resolution. This is because he defines the parties involved as perceiving more than one feasible solution. Therefore, a satisfactory resolution can only be arrived at jointly. While this may seem exceptionally straightforward, Schelling emphasizes the complexity of such interaction by detailing the hypothesized thinking of one participant in considering why "I should concede:

(Why should I concede?) Because (I) think (he) will not. "I must concede because he won't. He won't because he thinks I will. He thinks I will because he thinks I think he thinks so . . ."[10]

This reactive or emergent process can be explained thusly:

There is some range of alternative outcomes in which any point is better for both sides than no agreement at all. To insist on any such point is pure bargaining, since one always *would* take less rather than reach no agreement at all, and since one always *can* recede if retreat proves necessary to agreement. Yet, if both parties are aware of the limits to this range, any *outcome* is a point from which at least one party would have been willing to retreat and the other knows it! There is no resting place.[11]

The complication of this description is nothing compared to the complexity of the actual process. The participants are competing with one another, yet dependent upon one another for a successful outcome to their social intercourse.

There are situations in which the ability of one participant to gain his ends is dependent to an important degree on the choices or decisions that the other participant will make. The bargaining may be explicit, as when one offers a concession; or it may be by tacit maneuver, as when one occupies or evacuates strategic territory. It may, as in the ordinary haggling of the market-place, take the *status quo* as its zero point and seek arrangements that yield positive gains to both sides; or it may involve threats of damage, including mutual damage, as in a strike, boycott, or price war, or in extortion.

Viewing conflict behavior as a bargaining process is useful in keeping us from becoming exclusively preoccupied either with the conflict or with the common interest. To characterize the maneuvers and actions of limited war as a bargaining process is to emphasize that, in addition to the divergence of interest over the variable in dispute, there is a powerful common interest in reaching an outcome that is not enormously destructive of values to both sides. A "successful" employees' strike is not one that destroys the employer financially, it may even be one that never takes place.[12]

Schelling further implies that conventional standards of advantage may be extremely misleading in this case and may, in fact, be disadvantageous:

"Bargaining power," "bargaining strength" "bargaining skill" suggest that the advantage goes to the powerful, the strong, or the skillful. It does, of course, if these qualities are defined to mean only that negotiations are won by those who win. But, if the terms imply that it is an advantage to be more intelligent or more skilled in debate or to have more financial resources, more physical strength, more military potency, or more ability to withstand losses, then the term does a disservice. These qualities are by no means universal advantages in bargaining situations; they often have a contrary value.[13]

This is not surprising if it is remembered that the bargain deals with the fine art of feigning, or as Morgan stated:

Bargaining power has also been described as the power to fool and bluff, "the ability to set the best price for yourself and fool the other man into thinking this was your maximum offer."[14]

because someone has got to give in or no agreement can be reached for:

... if, during cooperation, each cooperator is individually oriented to obtain maximum gain at minimum cost to himself (without regard to the gains or costs to the other cooperators) cooperation may be unrewarding for all ...[15]

In addition to the substantive issues involved, agreement is further complicated since the relationship of the participants to one another is ambiguous; they are neither exclusively friend or foe. Schelling calls this situation one of "mixed-motive":

Mixed motive refers not, of course, to an individual's lack of clarity about his own preferences but rather to the ambivalence of his relation to the other player — the mixture of mutual dependence and conflict, of partnership and competition.[16]

The opposition has got to be conned, made to believe that a final agreement must be centered around a point already discussed, that rock bottom has been reached. "Truth" is not nearly as important as what is believed, anticipated or expected to be true. Roth explicitly makes this point:

Most bargaining, I would guess, is a product of not overt demands and pressures, but rather of the *anticipation* by the parties involved of the likely or possible consequences of certain behavior on their part.[17]

This expectation is nurtured by one party or the other giving the appearance of commitment, i.e., of absolute adherence to a point over which control is no longer possible. Therefore, the bargaining process has ended since neither can budge. An appearance must be given so that it seems that:

... the conditions affecting an individual's motivations and opportunities to engage in certain behavior are arranged so as to leave him with no other acceptable alternative except to do what he is committed to do.[18]

Yet, in spite of all of these complicating factors, the bargain would not be such a widely practiced form if it didn't work. The three models that follow offer just such an explanation of not only why, but how a bargain works on three levels; the simplest: who, what, when, why, where, and how; the second, for the used car salesman and the third, for the middleman who deals for others.

A note as to how a researcher finds out *how* adds insight to the models. They were created as a result of a field technique in which the first step was to go into the field to study a situation, watch it and then begin to question the participants. *Who* and *what* to study was defined by simply assessing around whom the action centered. This seemed parsimonious since the object of the study was action, itself, and also since action is a significant clue to control. Focus was chosen on the basis of this action, who seemed to be at the center and who are the satellites. Succinctly, the technique can be summarized as situation, action and focus resulting in a pattern of interaction. Within these three general headings, the previous chapters can be considered in terms of significant other (Chapters 4 and 6), self as other (5), process and interaction (7 and 8) and perspective (3).

While these models give a general picture of the used car game and the wider practice of bargaining itself, human interaction is usually more complex than two-dimensional models can reflect, even when three are considered simultaneously.

Two of the main concepts which appear in the models but which benefit from further explication are commitment and control. Because of their central significance to the bargaining procedure, they add insight and dynamism to the models.

Commitment has a number of uses in the bargain, but it always serves as a binding or limiting device, whether it refers to the bond between salesman and house, customer or price. It signifies an inability or unwillingness to budge.

The salesman has a built in commitment and reminds the customer that such is the case by constantly referring to the house as the final authority on price. "I'll have to check it with the boss; I think it's too low, but I'll see what I can do" gives the salesman the appearance of commitment. By saying that the matter is out of his hands, he is saying that he is no longer able to bargain. Whether or not this is the case is irrelevant; the importance lies in the customer believing that the salesman is committed.

Roth describes the nurse in a TB ward as holding a middleman position similar to that of the salesman.[19] However, the nurse may be less able to "use" the front of being a middleman. Roth does not make it clear how much autonomy the nurse has, although the impression that she is able to convey is far more significant than the actuality. It may well be that the salesman's authority varies from situation to situation, but the customer is unaware of this and it is the customer for whose benefit the ploy is used.

On the other hand, the ignorance of the used car salesman as to the "true" price of the car with which he is dealing gives him access to a "commitment" price that can be made up for the occasion. Edwards suggests this ignorance offers the salesman still another advantage, an ostensible rather than actual commitment:

... if one member of a bargaining pair knew the costs, prices and profits of both, while the other knew only his own costs, prices and profits, then the member with more information was at a disadvantage, because he more quickly arrived at the equitable offer and consequently was at a disadvantage in subsequent bargaining.[20]

i.e., if one member gives in too readily by revealing his fair price, he has nowhere else to go in the negotiations.

The important factor is the management of impression (a la Goffman[21]) rather than actuality. In bargaining, the "facts" can easily cramp the salesman's style. If neither he nor the customer is aware of the "actual" price of the used car, then both are free to bargain and arrive at a mutually satisfactory solution. The first one who can convince the other that rock bottom has been reached has the greatest chance of determining the final price of the car. The salesman can claim that he is only a middleman, representing a larger concern that allows him minimal leeway, while the customer has the possibility of invoking his own minimal resources and tight budget. The action goes something like this:

Figure 8.1 A Bargain

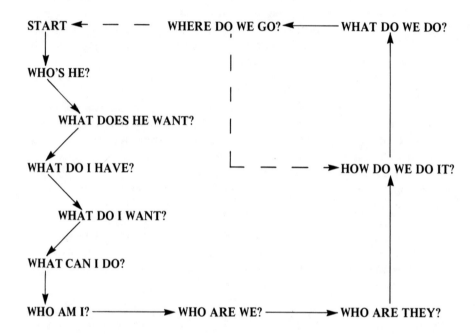

Fig. 8.1 cont'd

CAPTION

A BARGAIN

Social interaction can be expressed in its simplest (albeit sterile) form by the "who, what, why, where, when and how" model used by the journalist. This is not surprising when it is remembered that the journalist is interested in the facts," the bare bones of social interaction of a news story. Of course, facts exist within a point of view as symbolic interaction teaches and these "facts" are all seen from the perspective of the middleman, the used car salesman.

In terms of the salesman's point of view of selling cars, or the used car game, he is first interested in "who," who the customer is. Who he is in this case depends primarily on what does he want. Is he a shopper, a hot prospect, a family man, a difficult personality type. Assuming that I (the salesman) assess the customer as worth any effort, the next step is to analyze in my mind, what do I have (in terms of stock) and consequently, what do I want. (If the customer is analysed as a loser, either a tire kicker or a s.o.b., the game is over for both.)

What I have in terms of merchandise, time, motivational factors, commissions and hours to go in the day all determine what I want. (I would obviously prefer to sell a car rather than not or I would not be standing around.) These factors are weighed in terms of what can I do given what he wants and what I want.

This is a crucial and tricky part of the game because if the two factors are not properly weighed, no deal can be consumated and the game is again over.

Assuming that a balance can and is achieved, I the salesman am now ready to assert who I am to the customer, i.e., the kind of fellow who deserves your trust based on my knowledgability, skill and general honesty. At this point, I first display a commitment to the customer and by doing so, begin the process of committing the customer to me because I am a virtuous human being.

At this point, the bargain takes on the character of we, the two of us against the world. Who we are is defined by who we aren't: we're not the house (they). We're together, on each other's side. Who they are has now been defined.

The crucial part of the bargain has now been reached. We have a basis of trust. *How* we do it is now the chief problem remaining as opposed to *do* we do it? How we do it relies heavily on who we are both individually and jointly, but this has already been established even though it must be constantly reinforced. What we do is now accomplished which leaves only where do we go from here.

Figure 8.2 The Used Car Game

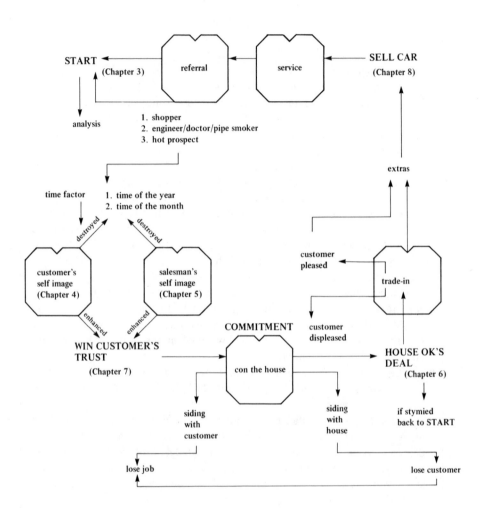

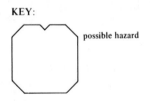

KEY:

possible hazard

Fig. 8.2 cont'd

CAPTION
THE USED CAR GAME

After the initial encounter, the middleman is engaged in the process of analysis; he scopes out the customer, "is he a tire kicker, a looker, a hot prospect"; is he a family man, wealthy, an outdoorsman. What is his reaction to various "pitches" likely to be. During the middleman's analysis, he is aware that the customer is conducting an analysis of his own based partially on the image the salesman attempts to convey. If either party decide not to continue as a result of this analysis, the game is discontinued. If both are convinced by their original analysis that the possibility for successful interaction exists, the next step is a level of sophistication above the first cursory, go or no-go decision.

At this stage, the participants "balance self-images." That is to say the salesman offers the possibilities of what I can do for you and to you. This weighing of each's needs and desires is crucial in that if it is not handled to each's satisfaction, the game is over. Both participants must feel that they have "equal" right to impose their will on the other, that their demands are equally just, fair and IMPORTANT. If this is handled successfully by the salesman, the most hazardous part of the game has been overcome.

It is at this point that the salesman displays his first commitment to the customer by letting him in on who "I am," the kind of guy I am, skilled, cheerful, honest and worth dealing with. If the salesman handles this step successfully, he is not only committed to the customer (his customer), but the customer becomes committed to him in the sense that these virtues "deserve" a reward or at least some consideration.

The salesman can now establish who we are; that it's the two of us against the house and that I'm even willing to go to bat and con the house for you. They are against us, but together we can overcome them and the house will ok our deal. The salesman uses the same technique on the house, of course, its you and me against that wily, undependable, ungrateful, sneaky customer.

Once the salesman has convinced the customer of their "us-ness," all we have to settle on now is the details, your trade-in, my extras (our sidebets and facesaving devices) and what we do now is sell a car.

After the car is sold, the salesman refuses to relinquish "his" customer by guiding him along the path of future service and a possible referral until each is ready to begin the game again.

Parenthetically, the advantage of referrals and repeat business is that the hazardous business of assessing who each is and what we can do can be at least partially circumvented and the entire process can begin at *we*, the majority of the battle having been alleviated and bypassed.

Figure 8.3 Middleman's Bargain

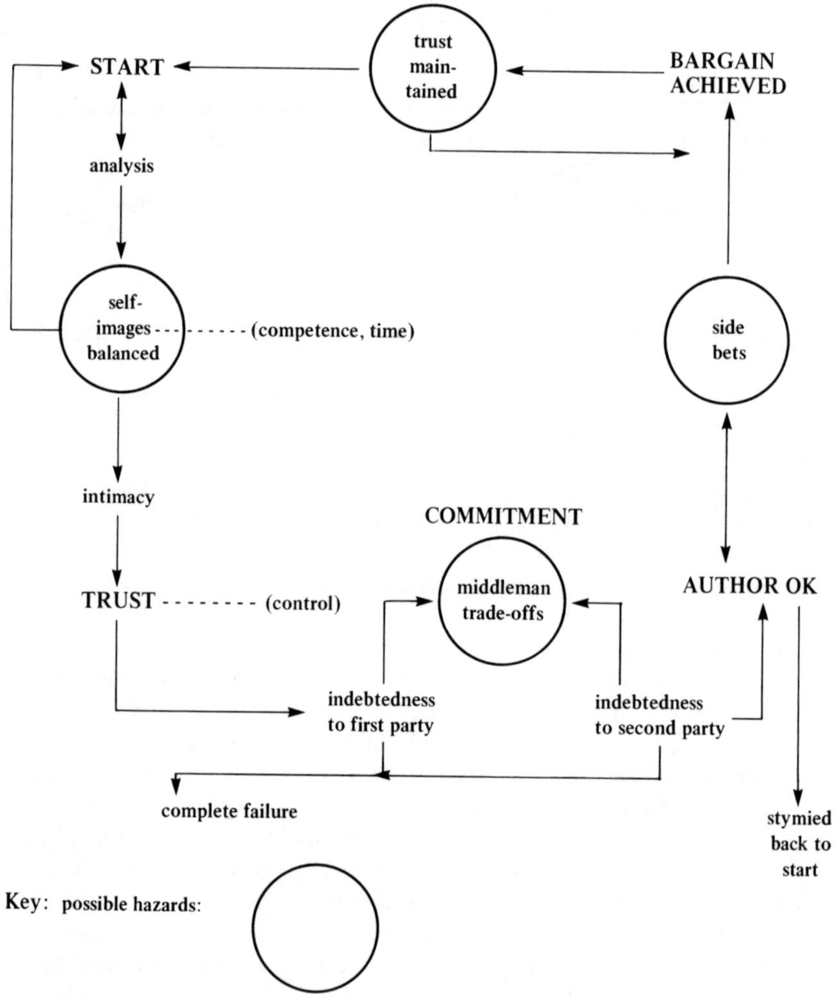

Note: The possibility for complication or failure to consummate a bargain is much greater initially; more steps are involved with many more pitfalls. As trust is actively sought and achieved, "falling-out" becomes less and less likely. However, this trust must be balanced on both sides or too much indebtedness to either party will also result in failure.

8.3 cont'd

CAPTION

MIDDLEMAN'S BARGAIN

The middleman's bargain starts at the beginning with analyzing his prospective "partner" in terms of what he could conceivably want and what he would be willing to do to get it. He retains the option to refuse to play although presumably he is strongly motivated to play unless he is sure that the game will waste his time or end unfavorably for him. (One of the advantages of being a middleman is that if the game is played at all, an unfavorable outcome for him personally is unlikely since he has a backer who stands to win or lose the most.) On the other hand, a "bad" bargain affects his image of himself as a competent bargainer and human being and may also jeopardize his career as a middleman.

The crucial step is always the middleman's ability to balance the goals of his partner and himself without damaging the self-image of either. Having successfully achieved this, he is now able to lay the groundwork for an intimate relationship allowing his partner to identify strongly with him resulting in his partner's trust. This trust allows the middleman maximum control of the situation, although he is now committed to his partner to a certain extent, his partner is committed to him.

Presumably the partner's commitment is the stronger of the two unless he too is a middleman and must experience a dual loyalty. The middleman must give the impression of a stronger if not total commitment to his partner rather than to his backer while maintaining a working relationship with the backer. Assuming he is able to accomplish this rather delicate balance, his backer allows him to continue in the game. The middleman is relatively free to arrive at his own side bets with his partner assuming they do not jeopardize or violate his contract with his backer.

Once the bargain is achieved and realized, all that is left is to maintain the trust that has already been established so that the whole process can be reactivated at some future date without the tedious and dangerous machinations necessary to initially establish trust and control.

(Notice that the middleman has two "partners," a reluctant one whose loyalty is tenuous and undependable and a silent one who occassionally thrusts himself upon the scene. The latter is referred to as a backer above, but is, in reality a sort of partner, as well.)

If each does not know the other's true reservation price there is an initial stage in which each tries to discover the other's and misrepresent his own, as in ordinary bargaining. But the process of discovery and revelation becomes quickly merged with the process of creating and discovering commitments; the commitments permanently change, for all practical purposes, the "true" reservation prices. If one party has, and the other has not, the belief in a binding ceremony, the latter pursues the "ordinary" bargaining technique of *asserting* his reservation price, while the former proceeds to *make* his.[22]

The idea of commitment becomes a controlling one during the bargaining process, but only if communicated, for it is for the "other's" benefit that a commitment exists at all. If the commitment is not clear, it might as well not exist as illustrated by the following example:

If my neighbor's fruit tree overhangs my yard and I pick exactly all the fruit on my side of the line, my neighbor can probably discern what my "proposal" is, and has a good idea of what he has acquiesced in for the future if he does not retaliate. But if, instead, I pick that same amount of fruit from both sides of the line haphazardly or pick some amount that is related, say, to the size of my family, he is less likely to perceive just what I have in mind. (He may also be more obliged to resist or retaliate if I pick only *part* of the fruit on my side of the line than if I pick it all, since I have failed to demarcate the limit of my intentions.)[23]

Schelling goes on to describe a number of bargaining situations and the purpose of commitment in each one. He summarizes his examples (as well as any other bargaining situations) thusly:

These examples have certain characteristics in common. First, they clearly depend not only on incurring a commitment, but on communicating it persuasively to the other party. Second, it is by no means easy to establish the commitment, nor is it entirely clear to either of the parties concerned just how strong the commitment is. Third, similar activity may be available to the parties on both sides. Fourth, the possibility of commitment, though perhaps available to both sides, is by no means equally available; the ability of a democratic government to get itself tied by public opinion may be different from the ability of a totalitarian government to incur such a commitment. Fifth, they all run the risk of establishing an immovable position that goes beyond the ability of the other to concede and thereby provoke the likelihood of stalemate or breakdown.[24]

As mentioned, commitment offers the double-edged sword of control, but loss of flexibility, for once "commitment" has been reached, communicated, and understood, there is no longer room for compromise or credibility would be lost. The salesman can hedge his bet slightly by invoking the presence of the house, "the boss has the final say," but even this admission substantially weakens his bargaining position.

Whether or not he chooses to imply his helplessness, the salesman does indeed have some say in the matter of price on any particular car for two reasons; the "margin" is often established by the house on the basis of an "assumed" price on any given car:

How do I know how much I can bargain? Well, see the house doesn't tell us how much they actually paid for the car, so we ask around on the lot to see if we can find the guy who took it in trade and after awhile you get so you can tell how much the company appraiser gave 'em for it.

Another salesman reports that salesmen, if they so desire, can give someone a "good deal" on a car:

Sure a young couple comes in and we'll give 'em a little better deal or sometimes one of those bearded long-haired types comes in and we give 'em a high price, take it or leave it. They're not our kind of people.

Most dealerships publish a monthly list of used cars on hand and their suggested asking price, although the list, by its very nature is often incomplete and out of date. However, even here, the salesman assumes quite a lot of leeway:

Observer: Do you follow the listings as far as price?

George: You add on $100 to $150 so you have a high point to bargain from

Observer: Does anyone ever accept that high price?

George: Sure, and then you split the difference with the house.

A fourth salesman explains why the prices on any particular used car were not posted on the car as is sometimes the custom. With respect to a "sticker price":

Some do, some don't (post the price), but if the dealer puts up a price (on the car) that price might be more or less than the customer wants to pay, so this way you can find out a little better. Besides, that price is just a starting point anyway.

A salesman at the only lot of the six that I visited that had prices posted on the windshields of the used cars said the same thing. The number on the windshield was "only a starting point" and he often as not told a customer to "just forget that number anyhow, it's for the suckers."

In spite of the apparent latitude within which the salesman can and does function, he is not without certain encumberances in his dealings, just as is the customer. The ultimate selling price of any car is determined by the house, although the salesman does have a certain degree of control over this:

I never know how much I could come down (from the suggested price) because I didn't take the car in, so I write up anything and then I go back and forth between the two of them making the boss come down a little and the customer go up.

In addition to the case cited in another chapter when the salesman related his action when he felt that customer had reached rock bottom:

I go across the street and con the boss a little. I tell him there's a hairline fracture in the crankshaft and we should let the poor bastard have it cheap anyhow.

Occasionally the salesman can exert "complete" control by bypassing the house and thereby becoming the primary rather than the middleman. He does this by making a deal between two customers on their respective trade-ins and pocketing the commission without letting on to the house. As might be expected, the practice is frowned on by the house, but does occasionally occur and with the same old bargaining techniques:

Salesman: Hell, this guy here fixes up cars. You buy it off of him (another customer) for fifty bucks, I'll put it on the lot and sell it for 200 and it will only cost you 25. You make 175 for a few hours' work. How about it, Pop, and you make fifty bucks.[25]

This is the exception rather than the rule, so control is a rather peripatetic commodity. However one facet of the control, i.e., knowledge of the actual "price" of the car is usually unknown to the salesman. However, this is not necessarily a disadvantage from a bargaining point of view. The price can vary amazingly depending on the dealer's inventory, the time of the month, the time of the year, the boss' mood. While a salesman can only make a certain fixed maximum commission on a car regardless of how good a deal he makes for the house, his value as a salesman and his monthly "bonus" are often influenced by the kind of deals he's made during the month. Also the salesmen feel that knowing the exact price the house would settle for in every case would take some of the fun out of the whole process. When asked if he didn't mind being kept in the dark as to the price of a car he was trying to sell, a salesman replied:

I guess I don't want to know. It would be harder to deal if you knew that the house bought it for $800 and was going to make $1000 profit.

Once control has been tentatively established (even though it will continually shift) and once the salesman has ascertained what the customer wants, the next part of the game is the trade-off between what the customer wants and what the salesman has and therefore wants to sell. An incentive to sell is attached to some cars because they have a bonus attached:

... sometimes the house has a bonus car. After it's been around for awhile, they want to unload it, so they give you a special cash bonus if you sell it and the funny thing is, it can sit around for months and some day a guy will come in and it's just what he's been looking all over for and you make out.

Yet every salesman I met was adamant in explaining that there were certain cars on the lot that he would simply not touch, wouldn't sell to a customer of his, because, "it's not worth the aggravation to have the guy on your back all the time about the car you sold him that he doesn't like."

Conversely, a customer may come in with a specific car in mind that the salesman does not have. The salesman has two possible courses of action; he can take the customer's name and phone number and say that he has "one coming the latter part of the week and I'll call you" or he can try and change the customer's mind about what it is he "really" wants. The second alternative is the more attractive to the salesman since it keeps the customer on the premises, thus giving him an opportunity to make a sale. On the other hand, this switch becomes one more part of the bargain itself, but it is apparently worth the added effort as one salesman reports: "If you don't have what they want, then you suggest something else. I do it and I sell more cars than any other guy here."

Here is the technique as practiced by another salesman in action with a customer:

Four doors? Hard top sedan? An Oldsmobile? That one right behind you's got four doors. I also have a Fury in good shape, late model; and a nice little Falcon. The Fury is quite comparable to the Olds and I should have an Olds or two coming in in the next few days.

While the salesman was unsuccessful at this particular time, the customer did come back a week later to buy the Fury from the salesman.

"Turning" a customer from one make or model car on which he has his heart set is not an unusual problem and does add another dimension to the bargaining process. It is similar to trying to sell a man who wants apples for a pie, lemons for a drink. But the most common factors to be bargained for between salesman and customer are price, options or extras, and service.

In its simplest form, the salesman has to figure out how to get the customer to buy at the salesman's price and still be happy about it. Sometimes it appears as a nearly insurmountable problem: "His damn car is worth about fifty bucks and I got to figure out how to give him $295 on it." Although it is often surmounted this way:

If a guy thinks his car is worth 300 and it's worth 100, then you add another 100 onto the price of the car you're selling him and then you can offer him 200 for his car even though it's only worth 100.

At other times, the transactions seem to go like clockwork:

Salesman: The station wagon is selling for 2995 with air (conditioning) and has only 12,000 miles on it. That's 300 under list; a really good car.

Customer: How much will you give me on my car?

Salesman: I figure about 1600.

Customer: Well, I figure that the change in year '68 to '69 is worth $600 and the air is worth $400; that's a 1000. So if you give me 1600 on my car, I'll go another 1000. But you tell your boss if another Fury comes in like that one you sold that you showed me, don't hold me to a thousand. You go ahead and see what you can do, but don't you commit me. Course, the wife sort of likes the wagon, but you see what you can do and I'll check back with you in a couple of days.

Salesman: (aside) Last time he was in he wanted 1900 on his car, so that means that he's come down three hundred dollars, so he's really beginning to move in and he'd probably buy that wagon at my price the next time he comes in.

This transaction highlights a number of points. First, like many negotiations, buying a used car is infrequently accomplished in one encounter. The used car game is often played in more than one sitting. If the salesman had his preference, he would sell on the spot because his time is valuable and he has no assurance that the customer will return. The salesman is quite willing to admit, as discussed in the last chapter, that high pressuring a customer can lose him a sale, so he often has to be content to establish the ground rules and begin his initial bargaining to be continued later "when" the customer returns.

Although the salesman used jargon in the instance cited above, he was quite specific about the pricing of the car. The customer was able to follow along on his points which meant that he accepted the salesman's pricing in general, even though there might be some dickering about the final sum. As the salesman pointed out, the customer was slowly but surely moving toward his price. The car was sold at the end of the week for fifty dollars less than the "salesman's price."

In this example, the salesman had done an unusually good job of favorably impressing the customer to the extent that the customer was siding with the salesman against the house. His manner was, in the words of the salesman, "very friendly and rather conspiratorial with the salesman, it's me and you against the boss, buddy, kind of thing."

A knowledgable customer can make the salesman's job easier as above and in this instance as well:

Customer: How much will you give me off if I take the GTX as is?

Salesman: How much were you thinking about?

Customer: Fifteen hundred. It's got a crack in the windshield and that would be expensive to fix.

Salesman: Let me look and see. Well, it says 1695 here (on the monthly list sheet). Yeah, I think I could let you have it for around 1500 give or take.

The bargaining doesn't stop even when the sale has been "completed" and the customer is awaiting the actions of the finance company. Many customers come to "visit" their soon-to-be car:

Customer: I'll be down to get it first thing Saturday morning. When I've got the cash right in my hand, then he'll knock another hundred bucks off, just wait and see.

Salesman: Hell, I already knocked a hundred off, but what the hell, if you can convince the boss, I'll back you. I'll tell him it's really not worth it and you can slip me another ten and we'll see if it works.

The customer has about as much chance of pulling off that deal as the proverbial snowball. Once a deal has been signed off, only the dealership can change anything and they are reluctant to do it unless somebody has made a mathematical error heretofore undetected. As might be expected, raising the price at the time the customer comes to pick up his "new" car is not guaranteed to cement customer relations.

But bargaining is not only over price. As discussed before, a customer must leave happy, thinking he's won. Schelling points out a technique to insure this state of affairs:

Perhaps two adversaries who look forward to some large negotiated settlement would do well to keep avenues open for negotiation of minor issues. If for example, the number of loose ends in dispute between East and West should narrow down so much that nothing remains to be negotiated but the "ultimate issue" (some final, permanent disposition of all territories and armaments) the possibility of even opening negotiations on the latter might be jeopardized. Or, if the minor issues are not disposed of, but become so attached to the "big" issue that willingness to negotiate on them would be construed as over-eagerness on the whole settlement, the possibility of preparatory bargains might disappear.[26,27]

Price is the "big issue" in the deal, so smaller matters are left open for negotiation. As one salesman explained:

Keep something in reserve. Something free. Be willing to give up five bucks worth of floor mats on a three hundred dollar deal; just pull them right out of inventory. It will help the customer to make a decision in your favor.

Another notes:

Let the customer leave with the feeling he won. Be specific about price, even if you have to double code (selling something on the sales sheet twice) later. Never talk up from a price, it's better to include everything. If you have to double code you can always be apologetic, go and see the sales manager and he can say, "you're right, we already included that." You can be apologetic and the customer will leave happy.

Selling an option or an extra at a reduced rate or "free" can often clinch a difficult sale for the salesman:

Customer: The tires are bald on this one.

Salesman: (grinning) You wouldn't buy them like that now would you? We'd change the tires for you. Now you just let me run up and get you the key and we'll take it for a little spin.

The other commodity with which the salesman can bargain as a "minor" issue is the more intangible product of service, either preparatory to the final pick-up of the car, during the warranty, or for the life of the car.

A salesman often refers to the service his dealership offers as an advantage worth quite a lot of money, thereby making the actual price of the car even lower. Most customer's bad experiences with service departments seem to be borne out by the effectiveness of selling a car on the basis of service. One salesman describes how he leaves the customer with a happy feeling by handling service problems for the customer:

I make an appointment for the customer if there's an emergency. That way he feels like I did everything I could. He's proud of me and he buys from me and sends his friends in to buy from me.

Another salesman relates how he takes his customer in and introduces him to the service manager and tells the customer that if the customer ever needs help that he will be more than glad to oblige.

The success of this kind of approach was demonstrated by a customer who told me he always bought from a particular salesman because once in a pinch, this salesman had called around and found a spare part for the man's recently acquired car when he was frantically trying to leave for vacation.

The concept of service to the car underlines the point that selling a used car is not a "one shot deal." The salesman's livelihood is extremely dependent on the return and referral of a satisfied, happy customer and it is here that the concept of commitment takes on an added dimension.

The commitment must cover not only the initial and present bargain but also the less specified one, the future and enduring one of customer and salesman. The customer must see the salesman as a nice guy not only for purposes of the sale, but for the future as well, so commitment during the bargaining process must take on long-term significance. A salesman is one who will perform extraordinary services for the customer:

Call me Friday or come by Saturday. I'll wait for you Friday if you call before six. Normally, we don't work late on Friday, but if you'll let me know . . .

or another salesman:

. . . if you'll call Friday before six, I can have the car all washed and ready for you. I'll also have a Plymouth Valiant four-door sedan, any color you like.

A salesman will "personally" perform for the customer, but most important, the salesman is on the customer's side; he is interested in the customer's well-being. Here, a salesman called a prospective customer on the phone to inquire as to the customer's luck with the finance company:

How are you making out on the co-sign? What the hell, it's just a small loan, just get a co-signer and you'll be okay. Another guy was in looking at it (your car), but I figure first come, first serve, I want you to have it, so try real hard. I have to write up a second order for this other fellow on the car, but I'll hold it 'til 3 or 4 (o'clock) for you. Call HFC (a finance company), get him out to look at the car. I want you to get the car. I'm just being honest with you; it's a good wagon, you're a young couple. You need a break more than anybody else, so try real hard. Okay, so long.

(aside) They probably don't believe me . . . (shrugged shoulders) . . . but it's true.

The customer may not believe him, but it works. He does sell cars and customers do leave happy and in spite of neither participant trusting one another or liking each other (at least initially), used cars are bought and sold. Bargains are made and kept; lasting convenants are reached and do endure through time; relationships are formed. What clue can these interactions offer to diplomats, school administrators, parents, marriage partners that they all seem to miss? What do used car salesmen know that enables them to operate while others seem paralyzed by circumstances?

Used car salesmen are effective because they are "professionals", i.e., they are practiced, reasonable, and motivated. More specifically, the men involved in used car transactions are professional bargainers. They practice it as a part of their livelihood and seem to enjoy both a sense of proficiency and a sense of pleasure in its practice. They are competent and confident and, as such, are knowledgeable as to what is reasonable in terms of what they can offer, what they are willing to receive, and what they are willing to concede.

Nothing dooms negotiations more quickly than unreasonable demands,[28] empty threats, and other tactics that do little more than undermine confidence and credibility.

Car salesman have a genuine need to be successful in what they do since their economic viability is dependent on it. As such, there seems to be a certain amount of ego involvement in what they are doing; doing a good job, a successful job is important as well as lucrative. Their actions must of necessity assume a somewhat "professional" air since the relationship they are attempting to establish must endure through time.

Finally, perhaps most remarkably, in the midst of a situation where cynicism and bitterness would be predicted, in which trust is nearly nonexistant, where little is sure, concrete or established, used car salesmen display a sense of humor which is completely unexpected, a sense of fun that makes unpleasant situations anecdotal and hurt feelings salvageable.

Used car salesmen bargain in the classic sense and, as such, they follow all the rules, however unconsciously, of leaving themselves and their "partners" face-saving devices, "outs," compromises, and small victories. Their philosophy seems to be a cheerful willingness to lose a battle to win a war. Perhaps it is this philosophy more than any other factor that enables them as a group to succeed where others attempting solution by negotiation so often fail. They personalize the involvement while allowing for protection of both their own and another's feelings. In a nutshell:

Bargainers are more likely to reach an agreement the more resources they have available for recognizing or inventing potential bargaining agreements and for communication to one another once a potential agreement has been recognized or invented.[29]

Communication never breaks down and the number of potential bargaining agreements seem nearly infinite, either actual or invented. How can a man who will give another man a quart of ice cream on a hot summer's day so that the man will have to go home and talk to his wife about a potential car in their future ever fail at anything he sets his mind to? No solution is too farfetched, no technique too human.

If this study was intended as a description of exclusively how used car salesmen bargain, then no more would need to be said. It is not. It is intended as the basis for a systematic study of the concept of bargain. For this reason, it is necessary to look beyond this study to see what can be learned in terms of a general model of bargaining behavior and what remains to be studied.

The bargain has been presented as a basic unit of social interaction, used by, but not defined by a variety of social scientists. In the interest of clarity and discipline, the concept has been explored with the intent of establishing the groundwork of a systematic exploration of the subject which could eventually lead to an understanding permitting social action and intervention.

The used car salesman has been the focus and perspective of the study since the bargain is an everyday part of his life and livelihood and through his actions, its basic components can be isolated and studied.

How the salesman establishes a climate of trust to replace the customer's distrust centers around the salesman's ability to create a positive self-image, analyze the desires of the customer in a very detailed way, create a feeling of intimacy, establish control, and engender indebtedness.

Expectation, trust, control, and competence all come together when the salesman accomplishes this "shifting of gears" in order to perform successfully, to sell and he does it all seemingly without effort.

In this final chapter, three models have been presented that describe and explain what a bargain is and how it works from the viewpoint of a middleman. The main purpose of this study has been to explicate a bargain; what is it, how does it work, when does it work. The particular success of the bargain in the situation described (the *why* does it work) can be traced to the used car salesman himself.

Any study that is concerned with bargaining behavior must focus on trust, competence, and control. Trust is necessary as a basis where the outcome is unpredictable and the stakes are unspecified. This trust must be generated as the participants in the interaction simultaneously compete while cooperating. The necessity of their bargain must serve as the basis for trust.

Each of the parties concerned must feel some sense of competence, that he is capable of giving a good account of himself and will not be shown to be ignorant or a fool. Part of the trust that is established must contain such a guarantee for both parties.

Each party must feel that he can exert some control, either over the final outcome or the behavior of his adversary; without this sense of control, neither trust nor competence can be fostered. As was continuously emphasized in the body of the study, these elements do not necessarily have to exist, but must appear to exist.

As a part of establishing these three most basic elements, commitment (which is the endpoint of trust), reasonableness (which is the fruit of competence), and control, side bargains are used. A commitment must be communicated in order to be effective. It is a statement of the boundary conditions of the interaction. The advantage goes to the party who can first offer a convincing commitment because he then exerts some control over the eventual outcome. Backing down from a commitment is nearly impossible, so care must be exercised in offering the appearance of a reasonable commitment. In fact, reasonableness is an image to be constantly sought by both parties. It is the enduring basis of the necessary trust.

Reasonableness can be served by side bargains that allow for face saving and pressure release. Skirmishes can be lost while the war is being won.

The idea of face saving is fundamental to the bargain. As human beings, we all act before an audience even when it is only our conception of self. This idea of audience is known as the significant other. A participant can never appear to have lost. Everyone must appear to win.

A man more skilled in the intricacies of bargaining than we Westerners summarizes the complexity of the process, and parenthetically all human behavior as well:

Bargaining can be seen as an attribute of the free market systems of economic exchange; it regulates prices in societies where suspicion and uncertainty of the value of commodities dominate . . . through manipulation, the bargainer tries to eliminate suspicion and establish an atmosphere of trust leading to a client relationship.[30]

If all human behavior is seen as compromises between those who have and those who want, "systems of economic exchange" takes on global proportion.

This study is a beginning, a description of process from a single perspective. The whole area of the difference between negotiation and bargain, of negotiations between equals remains untapped. How is the crieria for bargaining arrived at? What is it that constitutes equality. How are conditions equalized?

What is the affect of a third party? How does time affect bargaining? Can parties to a bargain be studied independently and simultaneously? What are the possibilities for intervention? All of these questions remain unanswered, but tantalizing. Surely further research is indicated.

Not only is the bargain a complex model, but there are methodological techniques that could potentially allow for simultaneous studies of both parties, bargaining over time, multiparty bargains.

In addition, distinctions between various forms of multiparty relationships are ripe for investigation. How does a three-party brokerage relationship function? What is an intermediary? How valid is the concept of middleman? Where is the middle and who defines it? Is impartiality a meaningful concept?

Some of these questions can and will be answered in the process of studying the bargain. Others warrant their own investigation. If social scientists are to be of use to themselves and society at large in the coming years of complexity, conflict, and confusion, overlooked, hastily defined or undefined concepts must be reassessed and evaluated with an eye toward their purposeful application in a troubled world.

The used car game has been detailed. From this specific application, a more generalized model of the bargain can be derived. As noted time and again, this study is only *one* sociology of the bargain, seen from a single perspective. There are other sociologies which can and should be described.

Appendix I Glossary

The value of the understanding of a subgroup's jargon in social research is a hotly disputed item. The extremes range from the classical Whorfian hypothesis that language determines thought to the opinion of Ned Polsky that:

... the presence or absence of special language referring to deviance is conclusive evidence for nothing except the presence or absence of such special language.[1]

In fact, the very use of the term jargon is not without peril, for while one student of language traditionally defines it as a term:

... applied to the special terminology in use in any given walk of life. Every trade, profession and business has its own special vocabulary, more or less unintelligible to people not in that line, which may run into the hundreds or even thousands of words, expressions and special meanings. . [2]

while Roger Brown derisively defines jargon as:

... any unfamiliar term created to name a concept that is already familiar and has a familiar name.[3]

Ben Johnson left no doubt as to his feelings on the importance of vocabulary when he poetically mused: "Language shows a man; speak that I may see thee!" and Sutherland reflects similar sentiments when he describes "language as a means of identification" for the thief,[4] the password by which friend and foe can be quickly perceived.

But the purpose of this appendix is not to arbitrate between philosophic differences among schools of linguistics but to present a glimpse into a viewpoint that can be gained in no other way, the used car salesman's perspective as seen via his language. As Polsky points out, vocabulary alone is not sufficent to elicit this view for the simple reason that all is not reflected in language:

Once you know the special language, there is a sense in which you should try to forget it. You cannot accurately assess any aspect of a deviant's lifestyle or subculture through his argot alone, although many investigators mistakenly try ... Such attempts result in many errors, because there is often a good deal of cultural lag between the argot and the reality.

One cannot, for instance, assume that every important role in a deviant subculture is represented by a special term.[5]

Note, however, that even Polsky suggests that the "special language" should

113

be learned, even if only to be forgotten. And it is certainly undeniable that vocabulary does add color, insight, and spice to the study of any subgroup, deviant or not.

Additionally, if Whorf is correct in his analysis of the importance of language, then no study of a subgroup is complete without such an analysis; that a linguistic reality does exist in which each language embodies and perpetuates a particular world view. The speakers of a language are partners to an agreement to perceive and think of the world in a certain way.[6]

The fact that proponents of one extreme or the other tend to base their theories on different kinds of data (Whorf et al. tended to study non-European Indian tribes while Polsky, Brown, etc., assess language in American subgroups) would tend to indicate a middle road for an acceptable place for the study of language. On this basis, the following glossary is presented, to be taken with a grain of salt as a part, important but only partial, of the clue to the perspective of the used car salesman taken in conjunction with the rest of the study neither to be overemphasized nor belittled, but understood and enjoyed.

Appearance Recondition — to make a car *look* better as opposed to run better.

Bath (as in taking a . . .) — selling a car at a loss, usually because it's been around for awhile.

Bird Dog — a salesman's contact or "stringer" who sends in customers and receives a commission on that basis. One salesman explains how the system works:

I solicit Bird Dogs from among people who are in public places — in jobs where they have contact with a lot of people. One of my better Bird Dogs works at U.S. Steel, in the plant. A tavern is the worst place in the world for setting up a Bird Dog. At least I've found it so. When a guy is drinking he'll promise to buy a Continental the next day — but it's not really him talking. One of my best B.D. is a body man. You have to select them carefully. I have one who is a church worker. You'd be surprised how people will work for a twenty-five dollar bill. I've got one man in particular in mind. He's good for an average of anywhere from 5 to 7 prospects a month. And I'm able to close 3 or 4 or them. He works in an office in a big company. Uses just people he has contact with on a daily basis — that's all. He drives a Ford that I sold him. It's sharp — he keeps it looking good. As soon as anybody mentions the car, he mentions me. Keeps a stack of my cards on him all the time.

A bird dog is often registered with the house rather than the salesman, especially if the house has anything to say about it, since that way, he can still be of use to the dealership even if the salesman leaves. Also that way the house is sure that the salesman isn't padding the account (in the instance where the house pays the commission to the b.d.) and the house can use the expense as deductible for tax purposes. At some agencies the salesman assumes the cost of the bird dog figuring philosophically: "I wouldn't have the cost if there was no b.d. — but then I wouldn't have the referral either, so even if I have to share, I'm ahead of the game."

Blood Bank — a finance company.

Blow Out — sell to a wholesaler.

Blue Book — listing of retail and wholesale value of a used car, used in appraisal; the salesman's bible; sometimes called the red book.

Bonus Car — one that's been around for awhile to which a cash bonus is attached; the salesman then tries to "sway" a customer toward it. (See Chapter 5.)

Bucks — hundred dollar increments; e.g., two bucks = $200.

Buster — a low commission.

Cap — top commission on a car.

Car Classification — There are four car classifications: sharp, clean, fair, and rough. They are used in appraising a trade-in. The general rule is that a car must be able to be upgraded at least one classification to be of much use to the dealer either by appearance reconditioning or a performance upgrading. A SHARP car has no rust, dents or scratches, has the original paint job and can be considered "like new" with no rips and no wear in the interior. Tires have to have more than 50% of their mileage left, even wear, matched with no recaps. The engine must be clean, wiring not cracked or worn. Trunk clean and free of rips or signs of unusual wear. Basically, the car must need no repairs and be ready for retail sale. A CLEAN car has flecks of surface rust, small dents or scratches. The paint job must be either the original or an excellent repaint job with a small number of rock chips, scratches or discoloration spots caused by rusted metal. The interior needs cleaning with some wear of upholstery and floor mats evident. The tires have more than 50% of their mileage left with even wear; they must match or have excellent recaps. The engine must be clean, slight wear and cracks in wiring evident. Trunk needs cleaning but is in good condition. Mechanically, it needs minor repairs such as a general tune-up. A FAIR car has several spots of surface rust, dents or scratches, with marred metal. The paint evidences general fading, chips, scratches or rust discoloration. Needs spot painting. The interior needs a thorough cleaning with tinting or dying needs on the floor carpeting and upholstery repair. The tires have 25-50% of mileage remaining, don't match, or have 50% mileage remaining on recaps. The engine isn't clean; there are signs of oil leakage; wiring cracked, trunk needs thorough cleaning. Floor mats need to be replaced. Mechanically it needs repairs such as new brake linings, new springs and replacement of universal joints. A ROUGH car has general rusting of body, rust holes in the metal, large dents, scratches and marred metal; it needs complete repainting with a thorough cleaning of the interior, a replacement of the upholstery, floor carpeting or kick panels. The tires are shot with 25% or less of their mileage remaining, uneven wear and unmatched. The engine is very dirty with signs of excessive oil leakage, wiring cracked and worn, trunk showing signs of rough usage. There are major mechanical defects such as the engine, transmission, etc. (Partial source, Ford Marketing Institute.)

Clean Deal – no trade-in, no financing. The salesman always kisses him goodbye (really digs this kind of customer).

Cleaned – (as in to get . . . on a deal) – get rooked, scalped, cheated.

Closing – completing a sale.

Cold Spearing – calling through the telephone book in an attempt to find prospects; no "in," hence no "hot" prospects; a sort of last resort when there's absolutely nothing better to do.

Cold Canvas – same as cold spearing; prospecting without a lead.

Courtesy Discount – a fictional price; a technique for allowing a customer a better deal if he balks; often used in low-balling, or as a way of reneging on a commitment without losing face.

Close Deal – minimal profit.

Crapper – a bad car, rat, rough car, etc.

Cream Puff – good car, easy to sell, nothing necessary to make salable; an exceptionally rare occurrence.

Demo – demonstration; taking the customer out for a drive, as opposed to taking him for a ride.

D. D. – dealer development: things the house has to do to get a car ready to sell.

Dog – a really bad car.

Double Coding – salesman sells something twice on the sales sheet in order to make up for a mistake or a close deal.

Double Hocking Through the Mouth – same as a downstroke; financing twice.

Downstroke – financing for the down payment, borrowing twice; strictly illegal, but can be accomplished if both loans are phoned in on the same day after noon, so the deal has been consummated by the time the bank and the finance company have time to check; same as double hocking through the mouth.

Finner – five dollars.

Five Hundred Club – association for salesmen who have sold 500 units; sort of a professional honor society.

Floor Time – time actually spent selling cars on the lot or in the showroom as opposed to time spent phoning or reading or eating or in meetings or just fooling around.

Good Deal – a happy customer, "could be $500 above the list . . . "

Hiawatha Appraisal – hand shading eyes, focused on distant object, the customer's car; fowned upon, lacks the personal trust the customer likes in having his car appraised; likes the salesman to go out and look at it and touch it and get inside, etc.

Goose — (dove) a customer who can be pushed around.

Grind, Grind 'Em Down — to talk a customer out of more money.

Hawk — an individual who is hard to sell.

Hand Job — a tire-kicker who wastes a lot of the salesman's time.

High Ball — . . . . on trade; give an unusually, unrealistically high trade-in figure with the express purpose of bringing the customer back. Similar in nature to a low-ball.

House — dealership, management (see Chapter 5).

In — an entree to a customer, achieved by knowing what he already owns for instance.

Iron — a lousy used car.

Iron Monger — a used car dealer who deals in iron and quite often does it for purposes of speculation.

Knock the Clock — turn back the speedometer (odometer); against the law, among other things.

Jesse James — derogatory way of referring to used car salesmen.

List — retail selling price, often posted on the window of a new car; also the "asking" price of a used car; the starting figure, hence the expression, "nobody pays list."

Live One — a good potential customer; a "hot" prospect.

Loaded — lots of optional equipment.

Looker — same as a shopper; someone without an obvious, immediate intention to buy.

Low Ball — unusually low price for a car; strictly used to lure a shopper back (see Chapter 6).

Lush — customer that's easy to sell. Notice that the term is equally as derogatory as one used for an extremely difficult customer; the fun is with the customer who's in the middle, neither extreme.

Make Out — to do well on a deal.

Mark-Up — percentage of base price of the car added to reach list price; a constant source of friction between salesman, customer and dealer (see text).

Mickey Mouse — same as downstroke, etc.; essentially financing the down payment by going through two sources; the lag time involved prevents either from knowing that the car has been bought with no down payment.

Mini-Deal — used as an alternative to low-balling; giving a price spread instead for minimum profit.

Monger — used to describe either the car, a problem car, hairy canary, or the man who deals in them.

Mouse House — finance company.

Music and Air — radio and air conditioning.

Odd Change Type of Close — a type of closing used by the salesman in which he acts like he's coming down to pennies, that he's working that close, i.e., $23.39. A technique used to impress the customer with how close things really are.

Old Enough to Vote — car that's been around for awhile.

On the Money — a car that was taken in after appraisal at the same figure that the wholesaler will pay for it; you gave the customer what the wholesaler gave you.

Order — commitment to buy a car, signed by the customer.

Pig Farm — used car lot with lousy cars; often fly-by-night.

Prospecting — searching out customers.

Pump In — dealer whose customer lives in some other area and buys from him, even though Betty Furness suggests that a primary criteria for buying from any particular dealer is his proximity to your house, since "any car needs a lot of service, so you'll be spending a lot of time there."

Pump Out — dealer whose customer doesn't buy in his own area where he lives; see above.

Puppy Dog Selling — a sales technique whereby the salesman allows the customer to take the car home with him for awhile, based on the assumption that a car, like a puppy, "grows" on you and the wife and the kids and neighbors, so "how can you take it back" and voila, a sale.

Pushover — a lush; a customer that's easy to sell.

Put — (as in to . . . a customer on a car) — get a customer interested in a specific car; to create a desire for a specific car.

Put the Guy On Paper — to write up an order as a form of commitment, i.e., the customer feels committed by the form itself.

Qualify — used in two different ways: (1) to separate the buyers from the shoppers; (2) to qualify self, i.e., give the customer the "proper" introduction to the salesman.

Rat — a wreck, full of cancer; a bad car.

Reach — to offer more than wholesale for a used car on trade-in if the salesman thinks he can sell it quickly and profitably and make up the loss.

Repeat – a customer who returns to buy another car; the backbone of a salesman's income.

Sell Up – to go to a higher priced car.

Sharp – to undercut another salesman; considered unethical.

Shim – a slightly shady wholesaler.

Shop – used in two ways: (1) a customer who shops is one who is out pricing and must be convinced to buy; (2) a salesman who shops takes a trade-in around and finds a dealer or a buyer for it himself rather than just keeping it on the lot. "Shopping" allows the salesman to give a higher trade-in price and can also cement goodwill if he knows of someone who is looking for that particular car.

Shopper – customer who is visiting various dealers trying to find the lowest price; one who has no immediate intention of buying; see above.[7]

Six Position Technique – a selling technique widely practiced by salesmen that urges them to stand at six specified points around the car and to "sell" the features at each point, i.e., interior, brakes, front end, etc.

Skate – to steal a customer from a fellow salesman or to switch deals on a customer; basically to act unethically toward either.

Skins – bald tires.

Sled – a bad car; a "yech."

Spread – margin; often the difference between the asking price and what the dealer will sell it for if necessary; the leeway from the salesman's point of view; does not necessarily correspond to the leeway from the house's point of view.

Steal – to get a car for nothing or next to it: "it's worth 500, you figure you'll get it for 300 – you offer the guy 100 and the dumb cluck takes it."

Sticker – list price; retail selling price pasted on the window.

Stiff – either a looker or someone hard to finance; a pain in the neck either way.

Stretch – to go as far as possible monetarily to get a customer; to give the best deal possible by offering a lot on a trade-in, of discounting the price of the car, etc.

Stripped – no options.

Thin Deal – minimal profit.

Tie 'Em in Close – obligate a customer, get him to feel committed; sometimes accomplished by the salesman offering to put $20 down for the customer himself when the customer says he does not have any money. (The money is quickly removed from the order form the moment the customer leaves the lot.)

Tin Can — junk, bad car, shit box, piece of junk, piece of iron.

Tissue, Tissue Paper, Paper — a close deal, minimum profit; (salesmen advise against using the term in front of the customer "because the customer thinks of the bathroom when you say it.")

Top-Hatter — high selling salesman.

Turn — to refer a customer to another salesman on the floor under the guise of the manager who will then reconfirm whatever the salesman has been saying; "turn 'em to anybody 'til he crawls out on his knees."

U.I.O. — units in operation; the number of cars, etc., a dealer has contracted for.

Up — an opportunity to sell a walk-in; salesmen take turns on ups.

Upgrade — to improve the saleability of a car enough to promote it to the next level: (1) sharp, (2) clean, (3) fair, (4) rough. (See Car Classification)

Walk-In — a cold, unqualified customer who drops into the showroom or onto the lot for which salesmen take turns in trying to sell.

Walk-Outs — people who come in and look and leave without buying; a black mark against an aggressive, ambitious salesman.

Warranty — completely dependent on the good will of the dealership.

Salesmen comment:

Some dealers say they'll fix anything under $1000, others say you own it after delivery. Some say $800. Some have a 50-50 iron clad warranty and that means nothing. That means you have a 50-50 chance of getting it over the curb, like on a thirty day, 50-50 deal. Affiliated dealerships with their own service departments, it doesn't cost them anything; they build the bill up high enough so that the customer is really paying for everything. They figure, "I'm going to make ten bucks, so get ahead."

Read this (the warranty). This was printed up by a common stationery company. It's your average used car warranty. It means nothing. It says if the car is misused, tampered with or was serviced anyplace outside the repair shop, it's no good; it has to be brought to the dealer's. Look at that listing (warranty does not apply on tires, glass, battery, electrical system, paint, upholstery, transmission seal leaks or mileage, or to any vehicle which shall have been repaired or altered outside the undersigned dealer's shop, nor which has been subject to misuse, negligence or accident) of the things it doesn't cover. You tell me, what else could possibly go wrong with a car. You know what we say, 30 days or 30 seconds whichever shall come first. Look, if somebody's within reason, not fresh or nasty, but within reason, I'll take good care of him. A guy came in a bought a car for 595 and he came in with a broken speedometer cable. I fixed it for him; I'm creating good will for nothing. It's a chance you take if he never comes back. But there's always the kind of customer that the more you do for him, the more he wants. In that case you tell him, look dear, you bought a used car, not a new one.

Wash-Out — to get completely rid of a stock number. A number is given out when a car comes in; if something is traded for that car in the deal, it is given the same number, so when the number is finally gone, there's only cash remaining.

Work — (as in to ... the customer) — to "cheat" the customer; bargain him down, get him down to where you want him.

Wrap a Car — to crash it, often between appraisal and trade-in.

Yech — an unmentionably bad car.[8]

Appendix II Game Theory

The title of this study is "The Used Car Game," yet very little has been said about games at all. I would like to rectify this omission at this time and give some hint as to why it was not brought in as an integral part of the study.

Game theory has recently enjoyed a rather overwhelming popularity as an appropriate paradigm for human action. Sources as diverse as Spiro Agnew and Charles A. Reich have been accused of playing "nasty little word games"[1] and describing an entire society in terms of a game board,[2] respectively.

Erma Bombeck talks about a new game for adults called "Garage Sale" in which there are very specific rules with the object being to "sell the contents of the garage with the first one who can get his car back in the garage the winner."[3] Games of Interaction are offered by an enterprising California company with prices beginning at $10. "Crisis", in which the affairs of six fictional nations are manged, competes with "Sunshine", a game of race identity and urban neighborhoods. The Great Depression can be simulated with "Panic", and "Star-Power" allows participants to build a three-tiered society through the distribution of wealth. "Napoli," a congressional game, "Mission," or Vietnam for fun and profit, and "Sitte", a game of urban crisis, rounded out the fun.[4] There is no doubt that seldom has an idea had such an impact in slightly more than twenty-five years; it smacks of making mathematics relevant. But all is not well as this chapter will discuss; game theory has not made the transition from mathematics to social science without problem. The format of the chapter will be to discuss the history of game theory, its mutation from the exact science of mathematics to the inexact science of human behavior, the harm suffered in the transition. The reparability of this harm will be assessed as well as the ramifications of such a model to the specific study of used car salesmen and the more generalized field of social research as a whole.

As mentioned above, the actual mathematical study of game theory is little more than twenty-five years old, for although Von Neumann's work was first published in 1928, it did not receive widespread distribution until 1944. At that time, it was ushered in bv some reviewers enthusiastically as "one of the major scientific achievements of the first half of the twentieth century."[5] It was nearly ten years before any other definitive work was done on the subject, partially because the whole concept was accepted as an interesting idea with formidable mathematical know-how required to manipulate the concept. In 1954, J. D. Williams published a folksy, appealing discussion of the basic two-person zero-sum game which was hard for a nonmathematician to appreciate fully and still a simplification of Von Neumann's thesis.[6] Rapoport, Luce, and Raiffa got into the act within the next five or six years, again attempting to make the concept accessible to the layman and its applicability widespread. Rapoport discussed Fights, Games and Debates[7] as well as the basic two-person game,[8] while Luce and Raiffa attempted emphasis on social science applications of the new theory.[9]

Nash[10,11,12] expanded the concept in mathematical directions by discussing balance points, or the Nash-point, and Harsanyi[13,14] expounded on the logical points of the theory, but the social scientists received their real impetus from Thomas Schelling, who decided that conflict, both sociological and political, could be discussed in terms of game theory.[15,16]

From Schelling, it became only a short hop, skip, and a jump to Berne,[17] Garfinkle,[18] Deutsch,[19,20,21,22] and even Goffman.[23] The question is, what was dislodged during the jump?

Even before its new found plasticity, there were claims and counterclaims as to the efficacy, applicability or even utility of game theory in general. As already noted, Von Neumann was received as a latter day Newton by some, or even a male Curie:

Game theory is an intellectual X-ray. It reveals skeletal structure of those social systems where decisions interact, and it reveals, therefore, the essential structure of both conflict and cooperation.[24]

Other critics were a little less generous in their praise, in fact nearly cautious. Williams writes in the *Compleat Strategyst:*

It is probably clear, then, that games do contain some of the basic elements that are present in almost any interesting conflict situation. Does it follow that we can learn useful things by beginning a study with them? Not necessarily. It may be that military, economic, and social situations are just basically too complicated to be approached through game concepts. This possibility gains credence from the fact that the body of Game doctrine now in existence is not even able to cope with full-blown real games; rather, we are restricted at present to very simple real games, and to watered-down versions of complicated ones, such as Poker.[25]

I have now arrived at the point of most social scientists utilizing game theory for their own purposes; I have appropriated it without explaining it, assuming that everybody knows what a game is. As will be seen shortly, not even those exacting fellows, mathematicians, could all agree on what they meant when they used the concept. For instance all can agree that game theory is concerned with decision making, although decision making is expanded to strategy by Schelling, a rather more complex idea:

Lying, after all is suggestive of game theory. It involves at least two people, a liar and somebody who is lied to; it transmits information, the credibility and veracity of which are important; it influences some choice another is to make that the liar anticipates; the choice to lie or not to lie is part of the liar's choice of strategy; the possibility of a lie presumably occurs to the second party, and may be judged against some a priori expectations; and the payoff configurations are rich in possibilities, since a lie can be told for the good of the victim, the truth can be told to pave the way for a later lie, and a lie can be even told with the intention that it not be believed.[26]

The basic elements of classical theory are here, two people, information transmittal and choice, but it must be remembered that Schelling is the link between the theoretical mathematical model and the social science applications. Notice the shift in emphasis between the above and a more classical discussion of game theory by Anatol Rapoport; he stresses outcome, consequences, lack of ambiguity. Obviously these commodities are extremely difficult if not impossible to specify when dealing with actual human situations. For example, game theory is defined as "the branch of mathematics concerned with the formal aspect of rational decision."[27] Rapoport quickly explains that in this instance formal means without content, i.e., without regard to the kind of decision in the same way that arithmetic is concerned with the relationships between numbers, not apples, pears, farmers or cars. The ambiguity present in human relationships was purposely avoided by defining a game as a situation in which "certain outcomes can be unambiguously defined and where the consequences of joint choice can be precisely specified."[28] These and only these conditions define a game. The specificity of any outcome is the result of all choices possible having one and only one known consequence and the chooser having a predictable set of preferences so priorities can be clearly ascertained. Thus, there is no need for a reliance on rules; the outcome is specified by the choices. If an outcome is uncertain or under risk, the problem becomes one of the probability theory, not game theory. (It is of some interest that probability theory was Pascal's response to a number of very pragmatic inquiries by the Chevalier de Mere, a gambling friend, while Von Neumann's work apparently had no such practical base.)

Again, let me stress that mathematical game theory demands by definition that the outcome of a game must be unambiguous or it cannot rightfully be called a game according to the most basic of all requisites. Obviously, this kind of theory is wholly unsuited to all but the most theoretical discussions of human behavior if that. We shall see just how unsuited.

The beginning of the problem can be seen in Rapoport's attempts to relate game theory to "life;" obviously his first sentence was adopted and the meaning of his statement about the unsuitability of the theory was completely lost on students of social behavior, who have "spawned more games than Parker Brothers . . . by the break-up of phenomenon into categories":[29]

. . . game theory has its roots in certain problems abstracted from life situations. The situations are those which involve the necessity of making decisions when the outcome will be affected by two or more decision-makers. Typically the decision-makers' preferences are not in agreement with each other. In short, game theory deals with decisions in conflict situations.

A key word in what has just been said is *abstracted*. It implies that only the essential aspects of a situation are discussed in game theory rather than the entire situation with its peculiarities, ambiguities, and subleties. If however, the game theoretician is asked "What *are* the essential aspects of decisions in conflict situations?" his only honest answer can be "Those which I have abstracted." To claim more would be similar to maintaining that the essential aspect of all circular objects is their circularity. This may be so for the geometer but not for someone who distinguishes coins from buttons and phonograph records from camera apertures.[30]

Surely social scientists are in the business of distinguishing coins from buttons and phonograph records from camera aperatures at least in human terms. Notice how this statement echoes the warnings of Williams, who notes that only the simplest of all *games* can be dissected through this kind of analysis let alone other less specified forms of human behavior, and Rapoport's earlier discourse of the inability of game theory to deal with "content," to answer the question of "is there a best move" rather than "what is the best move."

Yet, the trend of the early sixties persists, possibly because as the games the mathematicians were discussing were becoming more lifelike, it was assumed that life was becoming more gamelike. The first mutation had to disfigure the theory completely. The emphasis had to shift from outcome to rules since outcome could seldom be predicted and rules could always be specified, especially after the fact. The fact that this mutation did irreparable damage to the theory seems to have gone unnoticed, yet as "Dennis the Menace" noted: "Cards are like everything else in life. Rules spoil all the fun!"[31] Certainly insofar as game theory is concerned, I'm with him.

Even with this monumental shift in emphasis, game theory has got its problems which even novelists seem sensitized to:

The difficulty with trying to govern by games theory is that some people don't want to play. What is worse, some people don't even know they are in a game. It is the job of the mathematicians, systems analysts and directors at a government-sponsored foundation involved in Project Nomad to get everybody into their game — or at least reduce to a minimum the chances of irrational, unpredictable moves by non-players, mostly the poor and angry urban masses.[32]

Of course in either the mathematical sense of the everyday sense, you can't have a game in which people don't want to play, or act irrationally (remembering that game theory is the study of rational decision making) and the possibility of influential forces or non-players is strictly not possible.

How, then, could this disfiguration come to pass. Schon offers a generic answer that is rather disheartening:

... we glimpse certain regularities in the life of metaphors: a "Law of maximum expansion" (metaphors will cover as much as they can) to complement a "law of least change" (metaphors will change as little as they can).[33]

A more famous figure foresaw the problem:

When I use a word, declared that famed sematicist, Humpty Dumpty, it means just what I choose it to mean. He mitigated this tyrannical attitude by explaining that when he made a word do a lot of work, he always paid it extra.[34]

Game theory must really be quite wealthy by now. But there is the problem not only of overuse or stretching, but downright misuse. For example:

... The word oxygen means what it means, and neither Humpty Dumpty nor Spiro Agnew can alter that. When a new micro-organism swims into the biologist's ken, he does not reach back into folklore and call it a "small dragon"; ... he concocts a word never known before on land or sea, and therefore relatively free of confusing associations.[35]

On this basis, it can be argued that mathematicians had no right to use a word that meant "sport of any kind, fun, amusement or diversion, a contest ...,"[36] but they did and a double wrong does not clear up the matter; not only did the mathematicians muddy the meaning, but social scientists have doubly muddled it by bastardizing both meanings to suit their own purposes.

Schelling, again as the link between the two disciplines, is aware of the theory's shortcoming thus far in explaining action, but seems unable to take the next step of asking why:

On the strategy of pure conflict — the zero-sum games — game theory has yielded important insight and advice. But on the strategy of action where conflict is mixed with mutual dependence — the nonzero-sum games involved in wars and threats of war, strikes, negotiations, criminal deterrence, class war, race war, price war, and blackmail; maneuvering in a bureaucracy or in a traffic jam; and the coercion of one's own children — traditional game theory has not yielded comparable insight or advice. These are the "games" in which, though the element of conflict provides the dramatic interest, mutual dependence is part of the logical structure and demands some kind of collaboration or mutual accommodation — tacit, if not explicit — even if only in the avoidance of mutual disaster. These are also games in which, though secrecy may play a strategic role, there is some essential need for the signaling of intentions and the meeting of minds. Finally, they are games in which what one player *can* do to avert mutual damage affects what another player *will* do to avert it, so that it is not always an advantage to possess initiative, knowledge or freedom of choice.[37]

Still, he inadvertently answers his own misgivings, even if dooming the use of the tool he chooses. (Contrast his statement with Rapoport's on the place of abstraction in game theory.):

... there is a danger in too much abstractness: we change the character of the game when we drastically alter the amount of contextual detail that it contains or when we eliminate such complicating factors as the players' uncertainties about each other's value systems. It is often contextual detail that can guide the players to the discovery of a stable or, at least, mutually non-destructive outcome. In terms of an earlier example, the ability of Holmes and Moriarty to get off at the same station may depend on the presence of something in the problem other than its formal structure. It may be something on the train or something in the station, something in their common background, or something that they hear over the loudspeaker when the train stops; and though it may be difficult to derive scientific generalizations about what it is that serves their need for coordination, we have to recognize that the *kinds* of things that determine the outcome are what a highly abstract analysis may treat as irrelevant detail. . . . whenever the facilities for communication are short of perfect, where there is inherent uncertainty about each other's value systems or choices of strategies, and especially when an outcome must be reached by a sequence of moves or maneuvers . . . that some *essential* part of the study of mixed-motive games is necessarily empirical. This is not to say just that it is an empirical question how people do actually perform in mixed-motive games, especially games too complicated for intellectual mastery. It is a stronger statement: that the principles relevant to *successful* play, the *strategic* principles, the propositions of a *normative* theory, cannot be derived by purely analytical means from a priori considerations.

In a zero-sum game the analyst is really dealing with only a single center of consciousness, a single source of decision. True, there are two players, each with his own consciousness; but mini-max strategy converts the situation into one involving two essentially unilateral decisions. No spark of recognition needs to jump between the two players; no meeting of minds is required; no hints have to be conveyed; no impressions, images or understandings have to be compared. No social perception is involved. But in the mixed-motive game, two or more centers of consciousness are dependent on each other in an essential way. Something has to be communicated; at least some spark of recognition must pass between the players. There is generally a necessity for some social activity, however rudimentary or tacit it may be; and both players are dependent to some degree on the success of their social perception and interaction. Even two completely isolated individuals, who play with each other in absolute silence and without even knowing each other's identity, must tacitly reach some meeting of minds.

There is, consequently, no way that an analyst can reproduce the whole decision process either introspectively or by an axiomatic method. There is no way to build a model for the interaction of two or more decision units, with the behavior and expectations of those decision units being derived by purely formal deduction.[38]

This quote was used in its excruciating completeness to clearly underline the limitations of game theory as defined by a man competent to discuss the theory from both the standpoint of mathematics and action. The term Schelling uses will be defined in this chapter when relevant, the point being to understand the reservations that a proponent of the theory holds. The fact that the theory is unable to successfully delineate two-person interaction does not begin to hint at the difficulty of handling situations involving three of more participants, such as the one described in earlier chapters.

As mentioned before, when the theory made the transition (however unsmooth) from a field in which outcomes could be specified to one in which they couldn't, rules became central. In the following pages, social scientists will grapple with their version of game theory that relies not only upon rules but trust, predictability, competence and motivation commodities irrelevant to the original theory. A final analysis will be offered on the success of their efforts following by a vaguely theoretical, although sketchily mathematical, section on formal game theory.

In discussion behavioral game theory, as mentioned, its most salient feature is its reliance upon rules, specifically rules that are understood and acknowledged by both or all persons involved in the game, or as Garfinkle states, the tacit assumption of game players is that:

1. a set of rules exists

2. both players are aware of the rules

3. both players are playing by the rules (i.e., feel equally constrained by them).[39]

These three assumptions are treated as "constitutive expectancies." Garfinkle attaches the greatest significance to them since individuals' ". . . treatment of interpersonal environments . . . are governed by constitutive expectancies (insofar as) they trust each other."[40] Trust is thus considered a "compliance . . . to constitutive order of events; the condition for grasping the events of games . . . and daily life."[41]

This emphasis on daily life is echoed by Caillois and Goffman. Caillois comments that in daily life, games are seen as part of recreation and "in principle devoid of important repercussions upon the solidity and continuity of collective and institutional life."[42]

In commenting on Caillois' statement, Goffman notes that:

Games can be fun to play, and fun alone is the approved reason for playing them. The individual, in contrast to his treatment of "serious" activity, claims a right to complain about a game that does not pay its way in immediate pleasure and, whether the game is pleasurable or not, to plead a slight excuse, such as an indisposition of mood, for not participating.[43]

"I don't feel like it" is seldom considered to be a valid excuse for not playing the "games" social scientists describe.

Children play games for "real" according to people who have studied them, but even then, they play on "their own terms" that have nothing to do with the reasons adults play or work or interact for that matter,[44] and it is adults that most of sociology studies.

In Garfinkle's model, rules serve as the reassuring landmarks on which a participant can base his own actions and on which he expects his fellow players to base theirs. Since the rules are apparent to both players, each can trust the other to comply since both are playing the game and:

A game is an ongoing series of complementary ulterior transactions progressing to a well-defined, predictable outcome. Descriptively it is a recurring set of transactions, often repetitious, superficially plausible, with a concealed motivation; or more colloquially, a series of moves with a snare, or "gimmick." Games are clearly differentiated from procedures, rituals, and pastimes by two chief characteristics: 1. their ulterior quality and 2. the payoff. Procedures may be successful, rituals effective, and pastimes profitable, but all of them are by definition candid; they may involve contest, but not conflict and the ending may be sensational, but it is not dramatic. Every game, on the other hand, is basically dishonest, and the outcome has a dramatic, as distinct from merely exciting quality.[45]

A number of factors would seem to be inconsistent at this point. First, ascertaining whether or not participants are playing by the same rules is no mean feat. Even in the simplest game, participants may be trying for very disparate goals which would, of course, imply that at least the outcome and probably the playing would assume very different forms. The best example I can think of was witnessed one evening when a young couple had come to our home for the evening and had brought along their Monopoly set. We all sat down to play Monopoly. It soon became clear that while two of us were playing Monopoly, our guests were playing Humiliate the Spouse to the extent that a basically offensive game (win as much as possible) was played defensively (make your opponent lose as much as possible). We were no more all playing Monopoly than the man in the moon. Turns were lost track of, two hundred dollars was not collected, and the game was never completed. The discrepancy between the players' view of the rules is straightforward here. Imagine how much more complicated and impossible it is to ascertain the rules, not to mention compliance, in the Used Car Game, the Diplomacy Game, the Frigid Bitch[46] Game or the Life Game. Yet in order to justifiably label an interaction a game, these conditions must be met. The application of the rules equally to both players is an unmeasureable commodity. The only indication ever given is the extreme example of cheating, when a rule is not only broken, but blatantly so. How is the observer, let alone the player, to tell if a rule is quietly being bent?

In Berne's definition of a game as progressing to a well-defined, predictable outcome, there would seem no room for excitement, let alone drama since the outcome is already explicitly known by the participants before the game begins (see his "Games People Play").

As to concealed motivation, it would seem that the motivation is to win, the prize is what is in question. A masochist may win by losing, but he is still winning – at his own game.

The rule book becomes even more muddled for Berne's players with the allowance of unconscious games played by innocent people. Obviously, Berne isn't having any of the Freudian, psychoanalytic game.

Garfinkle attempts to restore some sanity to the issue by defining game players as people who: ". . . take for granted the basic rules of the game as a definition of his situation and that means of course as a definition of his relationship to others."[47]

Presumably, the reason participants are willing to abide by the rules is that they favor neither side, they are neutral and objective. If this were not the case, a player could break a rule with impunity as would be seen as having control over the rules and in Garfinkle's and Berne's mind at least, would force the less powerful player to refrain from playing. The explanation of why this is not the case has consumed a great many of the previous pages. Equality is a luxury when a participant needs what his more powerful adversary wants.

Undaunted, Garfinkle notes that in order to play, both players must feel that each "like his partner, is a competent member of the same community."[48]

Rules are seen as objective since they are felt to exist before the players and will continue to exist after them and can therefore not be seen as under the control of one or the other. Reassuringly, the experimenter has been: "... unable to find any game that permits the time of occurence, duration and phasing of moves to be defined entirely as a matter of the player's preference."[49]

If a player is able to assume equality under the rules and similar competency on the part of both players, he is able to predict the outcome (which has already been defined as a part of the definition of game) then he can assume his own competency as well.

Garfinkle attempted to induce distrust by instructing his students to break one or more of the rules and then record the reactions of the friends and families of his students who were used as unsuspecting guinea pigs. As an afterthought, he notes that confusion will result once rules are broken if the player can't leave the field, so that his theory is expected to hold only as long as the players wish to play and so certify by remaining within the field.

Again, the motivation of the players has been ignored. Garfinkle's students trifled with trivial situations, around the house, at the dinner table and the "goat's" most common reaction was simply to withdraw which, while showing the effects of rule breaking, is not a "lifelike" situation.

Deutsch takes cognizance of this factor in predicting that:

An individual may be said to have trust in the occurence of an event if he expects its occurence and his expectation leads to behavior which he perceives to have greater negative motivational consequences if the expectation is not confirmed than positive motivational consequences if it is confirmed. (Note: A positive motivational consequence is one in which the welfare of the individual is either increased or at least not decreased.)[50]

Conversely:

An individual may be said to be suspicious of the occurence of an event if the disconfirmation of the expectation of the event's occurence is preferred to its confirmation and if the expectation of its occurence leads to behavior which is intended to reduce its negative motivational consequences.[51]

What Deutsch is stating is the basis of used car trade: if you didn't want or need that car so badly (or think you do which amounts to the same thing) you'd never put up with or even associate with used car salesmen.

Given such a cheerful situation, it can further be predicted that if the two players know one another and trust one another, they will communicate with one another, whereas if they don't, they're very likely to conceal their motives.

This evidence of communication or concealment is unquestionably dependent on the player's view of the expectations of his opponent as filtered through his knowledge of his own intended actions. If he intends to cheat, he is very likely to suspect his opponent of cheating with the converse being equally true. This was demonstrably true with the used car salesmen. Their prediction of the customer's behavior was predicated on their own as was the customer's prediction.

Specifically, the development of trust is facilitated by:

1. The opportunity for each person to know what the other person will do before he commits himself irreversibly to a trusting choice. (Does one person ever really know another well enough to commit himself irreversibly?)

2. The opportunity and ability to communicate fully a system for cooperation which defines mutual responsibility and specific procedure for handling violations and returning to the state of equilibrium with minimum disadvantage if a violation occurs. (If the players trusted each other before they began, what is the purpose of computing procedures for violations?)

3. The power to influence other person's outcome, hence reduce any incentive he may have to engage in untrustworthy behavior. (I thought you trusted him.)

4. The presence of a third person whose relationship to the two players is such that each perceives that a loss to the other players is detrimental to his own interests vis-a-vis the third person.[52] (Aha, the nitty-gritty of an arbitor, judge, or body guard . . . amidst all this trust??)

If not previously suspected, the parenthetical comments did not constitute a part of the original text, but were my own addition.

In summary, trust will occur when there are rules so that each player feels that the other will cooperate and has positive feedback to this effect. Lacking this, a trusting situation will occur when either player feels he can force the other to cooperate or it is to everyone's best interest to cooperate with one another against a third party. All of these rules apply only when there is trust to begin with or at least not the least shred of distrust. Or the stakes are trivial enough not to be of much interest. The constraints placed upon the conclusions would seem to severely limit their relevance.

Mutual suspicion will exist when:

. . . each person expects the other to produce a malevolent event in regard to himself and in turn, is ready to produce a malevolent event for the other based upon this expectation.[53]

In a game, though, I fear malevolence need not be threatened, simply victory in order to create suspicion, especially if the means are in question. If this is what Deutsch meant, malevolence is too strong a word, and as such is misleading at best.

Appendix II A includes the specific game on which these conclusions were based and some of the variations attempted. At this point, suffice it to say that the experiments were based on a variation of Tucker's "Prisoner"s Dilemma."[54]

Everyday situations are seemingly not neglected: "In everyday situations, mutual trust is predicated upon the existence of socialized motives or conscious or external authority or arrangements that will provide participants with incentive for adhering to the rules."[55]

Thus mutual trust is based on fear of being found out, fear of punishment or reprisal or guilt. This definition doesn't make mutual trust sound particularly desirable.

The model of the game would seem a particularly inappropriate model for sociological or even psychological enquiry. Its obligatory dependence on rules understood and held in common by all participants is an unwieldy and unprovable hypothesis rendering the model ineffectual at best, inaccurate at worst. The only real proof would be reflected in behavior but the behavior is initially defined as reflective of the shared understanding of the rules. The circularity is obvious.

Even more significantly, the word game has a meaning within our society as best epitomized by its dictionary definition: ". . . sport of any kind; fun . . . an amusement or diversion," etc. It is of limited duration and has an emotional tenure to it unlike the aura surrounding more earnest human behavior. The whole implication of a game is something willingly entered into, for the sheer joy of it, with minimal stakes and maximum enjoyment. Both players can leave at any time, presumably when it stops being fun. Both players are aware that they are playing a game and that the game will end at a certain point.

To apply the label of game to the study of the more serious actions that humans perform seems a facile, misleading, unwise choice that can only result in misinformation since the initial premise is fallacious. Only if game is considered as that which is played by the professional athlete is the model appropriate. It may be appropriate and informative to study games as reflections of more serious behavior, but the converse is simply spurious. The widespread use of the paradigm can only be attributed to either its facility or its attractiveness, certainly not its accuracy.

If social scientists are going to take the time and the trouble to analyze, study, and write about their fellow creatures in order to give human beings a better understanding of what it is that makes them do what they do, they would strive for the most meaningful, elucidating descriptions possible and game theory certainly isn't one of them. The whole concept has set behavioral science back before the turn of the century. To illustrate:

The reader should now be in a position to appreciate the basic difference between mathematical and transactional game analysis. Mathematical game analysis postulates players who are completely rational. Transactional game analysis deals with games which are unrational or even irrational and hence more real.[56]

Mathematics seems pretty real to mathematicians even if not to psychiatrists. Rationality is in the eye of the beholder. Human beings do things for reasons and hence can be called rational at all times. It is only the observer who is allowed to demonstrate that he does not know the purpose for another's action and hence deems it irrational.

Behavioral scientists owe it to those who believe in them to be more careful, more thoughtful and more precise in their models.

Appendix II A

Prisoner's Dilemma is a vehicle in which a player must choose between the concepts of maximum gain or minimum loss. As conceived by Tucker, two men are arrested by the police and placed in separate rooms. Both are suspected of committing a robbery together. The inspector tells both of them that if either confesses and implicates the other that he will receive a reduced prison sentence of only three months while the man he implicates, his friend, will receive a sentence of ten years. If both of them confess and implicate each other, then both will receive prison sentences of eight years apiece. If neither confesses, then they would each receive a year's prison sentence on some "trumped up" charge. Diagramatically:

		Prisoner II	
		No Confession	Confession
Prisoner I	No Confession	1 year each	10 years - prisoner I 3 months - prisoner II
	Confession	3 months - prisoner I 10 years - prisoner II	8 years each

Mathematically, the matrix would look like this:

a_1	b_1	b_2
	$(.9, .9)$	$(0, 1)$
a_2	$(1, 0)$	$(.1, .1)$

Deutsch used a slight variation on Tucker's model; person I was instructed to choose between rows x and y while person II chose between columns A and B. Person I's payoffs are the first numbers in the parenthesis and II's are the second:

	A	B
x	$(9, 9)$	$(-10, 10)$
y	$(10, -10)$	$(-9, -9)$

Variations on the matrix were attempted by Solomon, a student of Deutsch, to introduce a power factor as variable and increase the marginal differences between the choices to increase suspicion or more accurately to increase the

135

advantage of winning which was theorized to increase suspicion. Solomon found that an individual would be more likely to trust his opponent if he believed that the other player had nothing to gain from untrustworthy behavior and if he believed that he was able to exert some control over the other person's outcome.

In slightly more quantitative terms, before any cooperative behavior can take place, mutual trust must be present, but the conditions giving rise to either trust or distrust are often ambiguous, so that the outcome is uncertain in any of three ways:

1. the actual alternatives themselves could be seen as either positive or negative va+ or va— (valence plus or minus).

2. va plus or va minus is perceived as being contingent upon the behavior of another person;

3. va minus is perceived as stronger than va plus.

If our slightly confused player opts to play in spite of his well-justified confusion, he is described as trusting; if he doesn't decide to play, he is labeled distrustful.

In the laboratory, prediction is based upon the assumption that an individual is more likely to choose an ambiguous path to his destination the greater the perceived strength of va plus compared to va minus and the greater is his confidence that va plus will occur rather than va minus.

An individual is most likely to make a suspicious choice if he perceives va minus as strong or if he figures his opponent is not playing fair or if he thinks he can reduce the harmful consequences of his opponent's behavior.

All theories have thus far considered only the player and his view of the game; Deutsch chose to experiment with a factor that Garfinkle assumed, i.e., the perceived intention of the other player. Garfinkle states that a player must see his adversary as cooperative before the game starts, but Deutsch brings up the possibility that distrust can be induced and the game will still go on rather than dissolve as Garfinkle describes. He used Lewin's definition of source focus and strength to describe the components of perceived intention that is the foundation of trust and then further breaks intention down as to kind:

a. intrinsic desire to benefit or harm (benevolent or malevolent)

b. desire to obtain or avoid something from another person contingent upon one's behavior (exchange)

c. desire to obtain or avoid something from other (not alter) contingent on one's behavior (third party intention)

d. desire to obtain or avoid something from oneself and one's own behavior in relation to trust of the other is seen as a condition for this (conscience)

e. desire to obtain the satisfactions that are perceived to be intrinsically related to the experiences involved in producing the behavior (activity)

f. other goals mediated by intended behavior.

Exchange, third party intention, and conscience seem the most appropriate to the study of the salesmen while conscience on the part of both salesman and customer (using the above definitions) is subordinated to activity.

As previously mentioned, the vehicle used to test these theories was a competitive two-person non-zero sum game in which each player was to maximize his own gains and also to beat the other individual. Emphasis was placed on the fact that the players had no bond with one another. (A zero sum game is one in which all gains and all losses sum to zero, so one man's win is another man's loss. So in a nonzero sum game, a win for one is not necessarily an equal and opposite for the opponent.)

The variable in the experiment was the simultaneity of choice and the subsequent knowledge or ignorance of the other player's choice and the ability to change one's own choice. The results were rather startling in that 80 percent of the subjects who were competing with one another chose not to cooperate when they expected the other player to cooperate and 75 percent of these same subjects, i.e., those who were competing with one another, chose to double-cross those who chose to cooperate when they knew of the intended cooperation ahead of time. This sort of shoots the whole idea of game theory to pieces, when players who know the rules will frequently and blissfully cheat their mate whom they know is playing by the rules.

Additionally, even when the players were allowed to communicate, the competitive subjects had motives and expectations that made it extremely difficult to engage in or to expect trustworthy communication. Even when a verbal agreement was reached, one of the pair violated the agreement two-thirds of the time. The competitive players were also found to think more in terms of the other player losing than in themselves winning; they didn't expect the other player to cooperate when they were being uncooperative.

A last pathetic note on these experiments is that once expectations have been disappointed, it is nearly impossible to reconcile the two players because of the "hurt" feelings.

Since the concept of game theory is neither new nor strictly confined to the behavioral sciences, enough time has elapsed since its inception for a disciplined, codified series of constraints to have evolved. These rules are the ones described by Luce as logical constraints in a strictly competitive game, i.e., a zero-sum game, in which one player wins what the other loses:

1. It is never advantageous to inform your opponent of the strategy that you plan to employ;

2. It never benefits the players to communicate prior to the play and to decide upon a joint plan of action;

3. Equilibrium pairs are all equally viable, i.e., each strategy in one of the pairs is best against the same in the other pairs;

4. If x is the maximin strategy and if y is the minimax strategy, the (x, y) is an equilibrium pair and the converse is also true.

In addition to the rules for optimizing, game playing also has a very specific set of terms:

Strategy:	a personal set of rules for playing the game
Minimax:	minimizing the maximum loss (i.e., the least ill effects)
Maximin:	maximizing the minimum effect
Zero-sum game:	one person wins what the other loses, so that all sum to zero

In the hands of a social scientist, Jesse Bernard, game theory takes on a slightly different tone with the emphasis switched to goals. Her system is based on rational behavior, strategy, payoffs, rules, coalitions and solutions:

1. rational behavior: the assumption can be made that both players are attempting to win at the least cost and neither can assume that the world is on their side.

Obviously her theory is capable of dealing with only "rational behavior" which would undoubtedly disappoint Berne; by her definition "rational behavior" is construed as the optimum course with respect to a goal. Obviously such words as rational and optimum require a point of view, a perspective, as to what appears rational to one man may not appear so to another. As I mentioned before, it is my contention that human beings are always rational, i.e., they always do things for reasons, even though the reasons may not be readily apparent, or even very "reasonable" to the observer.

2. strategy: in applying this theory, the assumption is made that one of the players takes the other's predicted behavior into account, including expectations of the other with respect to your own behavior.

This is a classic example of the Meadian point of view of interaction as a series of actions, reactions, reactions to reactions, etc., to the extent that behavior is based both on one's own and other's past behavior and the predicted behavior of the other as well as the predicted expectation of the other's expectation of one's own behavior.

3. pay-off matrix: the idea of maximizing one's own gains while at the same time minimizing the other's.

The following is a diagrammatic representation of the concept with the first figure in the parentheses being A's choice. The point is well made here of the classic example of the relativity of values as cited by Van Nostren and Morgen (pp. 176-77) with the theoretical problem of Professor Moriarity and Sherlock Holmes where if Professor Mariarity catches Sherlock Holmes and kills him he receives plus 100 points, if he misses him, he receives minus 50, although if he fails to meet him at some intermediary point, the game is a draw with neither winning anything.

	A-1	A-2
B-1	(2, -2)	(-1, 1)
B-2	(1, -1)	(-2, 2)

4. rules: construed as the "instructions of what is specifically allowed or demanded" with players having the option to specify modifications and the pay-off.

Here Jesse Bernard differs from classic definitions of game theory, which specify essentially unchangeable, nonnegotiable rules. The point may or may not be significant in that both players must mutually agree to any changes.

5. coalition: other parties introduced into the situation (beyond the requisite two) is easily handled by reducing it again to a two person game either by treating all parties on one side as one amalgamation or distilling the game between any two parties before a second set of players is introduced.

While this may often be the case, as Simmel and I have both demonstrated, thre are situations where three people are all in there pitching at the same time and, in my case at least, there is no way to reduce them any further.

6. solution: as conceptualized in rational behavior, there must be an end-point when it can be specified that one player has won and another has lost.

The major difficulty with this delineation of game theory is that it is applicable only in a quasi-mathematical sense. In a mathematical context, rules are defined, and unchanging but this is not the case in a cultural milieu and similarly, rationality can be assessed given mathematical constraints, but is nearly impossible in human interaction.

Notes

Notes to Chapter 1

1. Webster's New College Dictionary, second edition, p. 70.

2. As discussed in the Preface, behavioral scientists are prone to using words that "everybody knows" and then finding out by a tangled mess of observational studies that "everybody" was not talking about identical concepts.

Because there are words that seem to be commonly understood does not mean they should not be clearly defined in the process of study. If this is done by the researcher, then there can be no protestations later of "I thought you meant something different" and the groundwork has been laid for a neat, orderly "scientific" utilization of a commonsense notion.

This rigor can occasionally reap side benefits. As Becker found in his discussion of commitment (see note 4), a rigorous definition of the concept uncovered a parallel concept of side bet. The point cannot be overemphasized that if "everybody knows what it means" let's say what it means and use it. And let's define it as quickly as possible so the gentle reader is not misled.

3. It should be noted that Thomas Schelling (*Strategy of Conflict,* Harvard University Press, 1960) has directed himself to the bargain as a subject worthy of study, and some of his thoughts are utilized within the framework of this paper. However, he conceptualizes the bargain in terms of losses and gains and subsequent predictable strategy as is consistent with his aims as an economist. As he notes on p. 21, he is interested in the "distributional" aspects rather than the "efficiency" of the bargain. His analysis is based on specifiable gains and losses with an emphasis on logic and tactics, not dynamics; he is dependent on rules rather than process. His work serves as an invaluable guideline for any study of the dynamics of the bargain and offers insight into another method of the attempt to study human behavior.

4. H.S. Becker, "On Commitment," *American Journal of Sociology,* 66, July 1960, pp. 32-40.

5. M. Dalton, *Men Who Manage,* (New York: Wiley, 1964), p. 166.

6. *Ibid.,* pp. 203-204.

7. E. Goffman, "On Cooling the Mark Out," in A. Rose (Ed.), *Human Behavior and Social Processes* (Boston: Houghton Mifflin, 1962), pp. 482-505 (pp. 493-95).

8. E. Freidson, *Patient's View of Medical Practice* (New York: Sage Foundation, 1961), p. 176.

9. S. Miller, *Prescription for Leadership* (Chicago: Aldine, 1970), pp. 185-86.

10. H.S. Becker, and B. Geer, *Making the Grade* and *Boys in White,* p. 179.

11. J. Roth, "Treatment of tuberculosis as a bargaining process," in A. Rose, (Ed.), *Human Behavior and Social Processes* (Boston: Houghton Mifflin, 1962), pp. 575-88.

12. G.J. McCall, *Identities and Interactions* (London: Free Press of Glencoe, 1966), pp. 81, 86, 140-42, 149, 156, 170.

13. Carl Backman, "Emerging Role of Bargains," 1968, 1, 3, Summer 7-9.

14. B.P. Indik, and G.M. Smith, "Resolution of Social Conflict through Collective Bargaining: An Alternative to Violence," *George Washington Law Review* 37, 4 (May 1969): p 848-61.

15. J.C. Harsanyi, "Measurement of Social Power, Opportunity and Costs and The Theory of Two Person Bargaining Games," *Behavioral Science* 7, 1 (January 1962): 67-79.

16. J.C. Harsanyi, "The Rationality of Postulates Underlying the Theory of Cooperative Games," *Journal of Conflict Resolution* 5, 2 (June 1961): 179-96.

17. M.C. Joseph, and R.H. Willis, "An Experimental Analog to Two Party Bargaining," *Behavioral Science* 8, 2 (1963): 117-27.

18. S.M. Lipset et al., *Union Democracy* (London: Free Press of Glencoe, 1956), p. 21.

19. A. Strauss et al., *Psychiatric Ideologies and Institutions,* Chapter XIII, "Negotiated Order and the Coordination of Work" (London: Free Press of Glencoe, 1964), pp. 303-315.

20. Homans, "Bringing Men Back In," *American Journal of Sociology,* 1964, 29, pp. 809-818.

21. *Ibid.,* p. 811.

22. M. Deutsch, and R.M. Krauss, "Effect of Threat Upon Interpersonal Bargaining," *Journal of Abnormal and Social Psychology,* 1969, 61, p. 181.

23. M. Deutsch, *op. cit.,* 1960, p. 182.

24. *Ibid.,* p. 181.

25. M. Deutsch, "Trust and Suspicion," *Journal of Conflict Resolution* 2, 4 (December 1958): 278-79.

26. H. Garfinkle, "A Conception of and Experience With 'Trust' as a Condition of Stable Concerted Actions," O.J. Harvey (Ed.), *Motivation and Social Interaction* (New York: Ronald Press, 1963), pp. 187-238.

27. J.L. Loomis, "Communication, the Development of Trust and Cooperative Behavior," *Human Relations,* 1959, 12, pp. 305-315.

28. L. Solomon, "The Influence of Some Types of Power Relationships on the Development of Trust," Ph.D. dissentation, New York University, 1957.

29. Garfinkle, *op. cit.*

30. M. Deutsch, "A Theory of Cooperation and Competition," *Human Relations,* 1949, 2, pp.129-152.

31. E.T. Hall, *The Silent Language* (Greenwich, Connecticut: Fawcett, 1959), p. 101.

32. *Ibid.*, p. 117.

33. *Ibid.*, p. 119.

34. *Ibid.*

35. Garfinkle, *op. cit.*

36. *The World Almanac,* 1965.

37. *Boston Globe,* January 17, 1971, p. 64A.

38. Ben Kocivar, "The New Cars," *Parade Magazine,* October 5, 1970, p. 16.

39. Anne Taylor, "Auto Love Affair on the Rocks," *Boston Globe,* July 2, 1970, p. 18.

40. *Time* June 8, 1970, p. 66.

41. *Parade Magazine,* "Intelligence Report," Lloyd Shearer (Ed.), August 23, 1970, p. 5.

42. Automobiles have undoubtedly altered the style and psyche of the country and this too must be considered. The product that these salesmen are selling is not just any product, but part, at least, a healthy part of the American dream, even if slightly used. (On some sort of unconscious level it might even be reasonable to consider some of the hostility directed toward used car salesmen as a manifestation of the disappointment of having to accept someone else's dream, already enjoyed, savored and cast off as our dream. Fortunately, this kind of hypothesizing is completely unprovable one way or the other but does offer an added, if underlying, dimension to the study.)

43. *Boston Globe,* July 2, 1970, p. 18.

44. *Time* June 8, 1970, p. 66.

45. Peter Fuller Cadillac-Olds radio announcements on Boston radio station WEEI for at least the period January through January 1970-1971. Peter Fuller sells only pre-owned, never-used cars, which is somehow a much classier arrangement

46. A low-ball is a technique used to remove the shopper from the field on the assumption that he is looking for the best deal he can get either in terms of trade-in value for his car or selling price for the car in which he is interested (in reality, two sides of the same coin. All the customer should really be concerned with is the difference between the two, the amount he has to shell out.) The salesman is aware that he is giving an unrealistic figure and that this will induce the customer to return. When he does come back, the salesman's bet is hedged by saying that the price he quoted was good only for that day or that that was for a standard transmission or that that figure didn't include transportation costs or a myriad of other equally feasible sounding alibis. The technique is used primarily on new cars where each unit is virtually identical, but is also occasionally applied to used cars if the customer is shopping for a particular make and model. For more on this subject, see the glossary and the chapter on salesmen, Chapter 6.

47. E.H. Sutherland, *The Professional Thief* (Chicago: University of Chicago Press, 1937).

48. Goffman, *op. cit.*, pp. 482-505.

49. D. Mauer, *The Big Con* (New York: Pocket Books, 1949).

50. As will be emphasized later, it is questionable as to whether any of us ever act as anything other than middlemen in the broadest sense of the term. The important point is not so much whether we are acting as middlemen, but whether we *know* we are acting as middlemen. Some everyday examples of middlemen are presented below. Suffice it to say here that the configuration occurs often enough to be worthy of study in itself. Chapter 5 will deal extensively with this idea.

51. K.H. Wolff (Ed.), *The Sociology of George Simmel* (New York: Free Press, 1950).

52. P.M. Blau, *Exchange and Power in Social Life* (New York: Wiley and Sons, 1967).

Notes to Chapter 2

1. Elliott Krause, to whom I shall be eternally grateful convinced me that any topic looks relatively limited when begun, but expands very quickly of its own volition, so the trick was to pick a manageable topic at the outset and do a comprehensive job on it rather than pick an outrageously broad topic and try to narrow it while justifying the necessary exclusions.

2. P.M. Blau, *Exchange and Power in Social Life* (New York: Wiley and Sons, 1967), p. 3.

3. The advantages and disadvantages of any particular field technique are of central concern to any study. Participant observation is neither new to social science or new to sociology, so rather than iterate in any great detail any more arguments as to its efficacy, suffice it to say that for the reasons described in the text, it was deemed most appropriate (i.e., useful) for this particular study. For a more in depth analysis of this and other sociological techniques, the reader is guided to Denzin's *Sociological Methods* (Aldine, 1970), pp. 363-412, which in particular concern participant observation, advantages and disadvantages by researchers who have used them. Colin Bell, "A note on participant observation," *Sociology* 3, 3 September 1969: 417-18, presents an interesting view from a newcomer's perspective in discussing the four alternate roles of an observer in either an open or closed system so defined because of ease of access with a researcher enacting either an overt or covert role.

For an interdisciplinary approach to the question of researcher's field role, see Gottschalk, Kluckhohn and Angell on *Use of Personal Document,* especially Chapter III, pp. 109-132, on the problems of the anthropologist in the field.

Raymond Gold presents perhaps the most comprehensive analysis (if somewhat idealized) in terms of the observer's choices within the technique of participant observation in "Roles in Sociological Field Observations," *Social Forces,* March 1958, 36, pp. 217-23, in his delineation of roles ranging from complete participant (with the true identity and purpose unknown to the group under study) to the complete observer (entailing no social interaction on the part of the researcher) with the participant as observer (a one visit interview) and the observer as participant as observer (a field relationship with care taken not to "go native") being the intermediate choices. In terms of his schema, I acted as a participant as observer in this study. This analysis on Gold's part closely follows Junker's initial work on the subject relating field work and living in society, especially p. 146 in "Field Work," 1960.

The use of, difficulties with and advantages of the method as seen from a number of different point of view are all conveniently housed in Hammond's anthology of *Sociologists at Work,* with special attention directed to the articles by Dalton, pp. 74-83, Reisman, p. 253 and 260-69, and Geer, pp. 325-41. In addition, the reader is directed to Adams and Preiss, *Human Organization Research,* 1960; Whyte's *Street Corner Society;* Howard Becker, "Problems of Inference, and Proof in Participant Observation," *ASR* 23 (1958): 655-56, among others.

For a more generalized view, note bibliographic entries listed under "Method" following the appendixes and the bibliography following Bruyn's article on "The Methodology of Participant Observation," Chapter 29 in Filestead's *Qualitative Methodology* (Chicago: Markham Publishing Co., 1970). Also Marian Pearsall's "Participant Observation as Role and Method in Behavioral Research," Chapter 31 in the same book. While I do not agree with her analysis (methodology prescribes a role and vice-versa) it is helpful in understanding some of the controversy surrounding participant observation. Chapters 8, 9, 12, 13, 14, 16, 18 (previously mentioned), 20, 22, 23, and 27 are also of interest.

4. H.H. Becker, "Whose side are we on?" *Social Problems* 14, 2 (Winter 1967): 239-47.

An added benefit of this perspective was the insight afforded by the salesmen's vocabulary. While not an adequate basis in itself for assumptions, it can be useful.

5. Ned Polsky makes the point rather graphically in *Hustlers, Beats and Others,* p. 123, that language of a sub-group is strewn with pitfalls if it is taken as sole determinant of the behavior of the group. On the other hand, he rather dramatically misses one of the cogent factors of taboo words and phrases. He cites the point that there are three kinds of possible incestuous relationships and the one least practiced, i.e., more abhorrent, is the only one with an often used term to describe it ("motherfucker" to describe relations between mother and son as opposed to brother and sister or father and daughter). The fact that the taboo word refers to the most taboo form should be predicted. Parenthetically, the spelling of the word as a single rather than double or hyphenated work seems curiously characteristic of obscenities.

6. While access to informants seems to be a generic problem of doing field work as is well documented by Junker, *Field Work,* 1960, pp. 106-111, as denoted by the "rebuff" there seems to be a curious tendency on the part of some groups to be unusually informative. Although seldom discussed, if at all, groups who have a negative social image (I hesitate to call them deviants) seem to be unusually good informants once they establish that you mean them no harm. If a researcher appears sympathetic and friendly, they seem eager to respond. My conclusions are based not only on my own research, but the "quality" of the research of Polsky, *Hustlers, Beats and Others;* Humphrey, *Tearoom Techniques;* Becker, *The Outsiders* (although in this particular case, Becker was more a member of the group than in the other instances cited); Cavan in *Liquor License;* Sutherland in the *Professional Thief;* and Maurer in the *Big Con.* A partial clue to this phenomenon may be found in *Boys in White,* where Becker and Geer remark that the students clearly associated them (the researchers) as nonfaculty since they did and said things that would not be acceptable to the faculty in their presence (p. 29). The combination of having a sympathetic ear for a change and a chance to flaunt authority by performing in front of a researcher seems to give an observer easy access to information from groups who enjoy a less than admirable position in society.

7. Related to the use of participant observation as a technique is the concept of perspective as used by Becker and Geer as the actions and beliefs that go with actions that cannot and should not be described independently (p. 34, *Boys in White;* p. 38, *Making the Grade).* The perspective of a situation is specific to that situation and is only one side of the story. Not infrequently perspectives clash as described by Freidson (p. 176) in *Patient's View of Medical Practice* between individuals involved in interaction which again underlines the need for the researcher to adopt the perspective of only one side in order to be able to adequately delineate it and its effects. For as Shibutani states, a perspective is a pervasive thing: "a perspective is an ordered view of one's world — what is taken for granted about the attributes of various objects, events and human nature . . . it constitutes the matrix through which one perceives his environment." ("Reference Groups as Perspectives," *American Journal of Sociology,* 40, May 1955, p. 564.) Obviously perspective is vital to the researcher who is seeking an in-depth understanding through participant observation.

8. To a certain extent, the problem of being trusted by even one side is always a problem in doing field work (see Gottschalk, Kluckhohn and Angell); entree and rapport are always a problem. The problem is of course compounded when more than one party is present, as is almost always the case, and difficulties increase when parties are adversaries or at least competitive or hostile toward one another. Becker discusses the dilemma in *Whose Side are We On?* and Humphrey, Polsky and others who have done work with groups outside of the law make the point that part of their bargain in anonymity for informants and others observed. While the used car salesmen interviewed and observed were

seldom outside of the law, the situation of the bargain in which outcome was unpredictable made the situation equally touchy in terms of picking a side. There was enough ambiguity present in the salesmen's minds, the customer's mind and the house's mind to require a clear statement of position as to whose side I was on and to stick to that side.

9. B.G. Glazer, and A.L. Strauss, *The Discovery of Grounded Theory* (Chicago: Aldine, 1967).

10. B.L. Wharf, *Language, Thought and Reality* (New York: Wiley, 1956).

11. G.H. Mead, "Cooley's Contribution to American Sociological Thought," *American Journal of Sociology,* 35, March, 1930, pp. 693-706.

12. This particular advantage is often cited by proponents of participant observation — the ability to include long passages of data for the reader's perusal (see Kluckhohn, Becker and Geer, Dalton and others mentioned in note 3).

13. G.H. Mead, *Mind, Self and Society* (Chicago: University of Chicago Press, 1935), pp. 186-92, 244, 329, etc.

14. A. Strauss (Ed.), *The Social Psychology of George H. Mead* (Chicago: The University of Chicago Press, 1956), esp. Chapter 13.

15. Erich Fromm, *The Sane Society* (New York: Holt, Rinehart and Winston, 1964). Fromm makes the point that man is both part and apart from the natural world. He is biologically of the animal kingdom, yet is alone among the animals in being capable of contemplating his own death which sets him uniquely apart.

16. Ironically enough, the only difficulty I ever experienced with this orientation had to do with the fact that I am a young woman and I found myself spending long, uninterrupted stretches of time in the evening with a man or men in small rooms. Occasionally, I was encouraged to become more of a participant and less of an observer. I "solved" this methodological crisis by stern looks (hopefully reinforcing my own role definition), observations earlier in the evening (when most of the car action occurred anyway) and the advent of warmer evenings when conversations could be comfortably carried on outside while waiting for a prospect to appear.

17. Becker, *op. cit.*, p. 241.

18. Glazer, and Strauss, *Ibid.*

19. As mentioned, the research plan was conceived in the field on the basis of data collected. Because salesmen felt that the greatest differences among salesmen fell along the lines of affiliated and unaffiliated dealerships, luxury and "other" priced cars and domestic and foreign dealerships, I included at least one of each of these dealerships in the survey of field work. I did this on the assumption that if the most disparate were similar, then my model would be valid. As the data shows, I found no significant differences between dealerships and because this is the case, data is included without respect to dealership unless the point is relevant to the argument. Unless otherwise stated, comments

included in any section are from different informants on different lots. Field data is the only form of direct quotation that is included without footnote and thus is easily distinguishable from data from "the literature" or other sources which is all footnoted. The majority of the data was collected before analysis was undertaken. The formal research plan is as follows:

Dealerships	6 (four in depth)
Salesmen at dealerships	17
Months in field	4 1/2
Weeks	20
Days per week	3 evenings, 1 Saturday
Hours	2 1/2 to 3 1/2 per session
Sessions	5 per week
Encounters with customers	2 to 3 (approx.) per session
Seminars	2
Salesmen	43
Days	8

Total:

Salesmen	60
In Depth	17
Seminar	43
Sessions	100 (approx.)
Hours	275 plus
Encounters	200 (trade slacked off from the time the original estimate was made)

20. Of particular interest to the researcher who opts for participant observation to one degree or another (see note 3) is the idea of situation or the larger whole of which their study is a part. To a large extent, the first chapter of this study is devoted to just such a concept in an academic sense, the placing of this body of information in an appropriate context. The same procedure must take place in the field in a social sense both for the researcher and for his reader. The question of where does this all fit in must be answered. Carr, in his book *Situational Analysis* (1948), addresses himself to just such a problem and by doing so relates the concepts of participant observation, focus and situation.

He, of course, is an enthusiastic advocate of participant observation on the grounds that "they know what it feels like; they have been there." However he sounds a note of caution by warning that "no body of knowledge can be any more dependable than the method by which it has been obtained." Thus an awareness of the situation is crucial. In its simplest form, a "situation is a focalized pattern of social relationships regarded as a source of actual or potential experience."

Carr based his analysis on the dramaturgical model using for reference a play called *The Dead End.* The following diagram is perhaps more illustrative than simple prose could be.

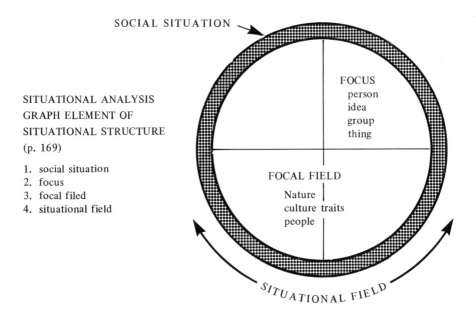

SITUATIONAL ANALYSIS
GRAPH ELEMENT OF
SITUATIONAL STRUCTURE
(p. 169)

1. social situation
2. focus
3. focal filed
4. situational field

SOCIAL SITUATION

FOCUS
person
idea
group
thing

FOCAL FIELD

Nature
culture traits
people

SITUATIONAL FIELD

Goffman defines a social situation as "an environment of mutual monitoring possibilities ... within which an individual will find himself accessible to the naked senses of all others who are 'present' and ... find them accessible to him." (The Neglected Situation, in *Institutions and the Person,* p. 297.)

A social situation exists in a larger context, the situational field composed of what Whyte refers to as an organic whole or what is here defined as composed of nature, culture traits and people. Within any particular social situation, the researcher assumes a focus either an idea, a group, a person, or a thing that exists in the larger context of a focal field. Thus, in my study, the situational field is all human beings who interact with one another for the purpose of arriving at some mutually acceptable solution to their differences. The social situation is that of the bargain, the focus is the used car salesman within the focal field of the used car lot. I am thus going from the generic to the specific in the hopes of being able to enlarge again to the generic.

21. When to leave the field, as I have indicated, is a difficult problem. If a grant is the basis for the study, then time and money often compose the boundary conditions; when neither of these is the case, the researcher's forays being unlimited (at least in theory) this feeling of completeness serves as the guiding principle. Glaser and Strauss are more specific and somewhat analytical in their approach by suggesting that when a model can comfortably include and

enclose all the data that a sufficient analysis has been completed, but the question that is more to the point is when has enough data been collected to justify analysis. Of course, as they suggest, the process of analysis indeed is an ongoing process, but the question as to when to leave the field is still a thorny one. As indicated, I found my own sense of contentment when data began being repetitious, when I had the overwhelming feeling that I had heard it before. Becker and Geer make mention of this idea of "completeness" in their article in *Human Organization* entitled, "Participant Observation and Interviewing: A Comparison,": "Participant observation can thus provide us with a yardstick against which to measure the completeness of data gathered in other ways ..." (p. 28). Although they are referring to a cross-check on other data, the obvious reference to the significance of data being in its completeness cannot be missed. Trow in his commentary on their article, p. 33-35, picks up on the very word completeness. Becker and Geer defended their use of the concept of completeness on pages 39-40, thereby reiterating the importance of a *gestalt* feeling about the data.

The "yardstick" by which to gauge this completeness must rest ultimately with the researcher who can say that while more could be learned about a group or its functioning with more time in the field, the data collected is sufficient to give a rounded, reasonable, accurate, complete picture as far as it goes in describing what it is the researcher set out to describe.

Glaser and Strauss note – on a more humanistic level (*Discovery of Substantive Theory*, p. 7) – that the field worker knows that he knows. Weiss reiterates the point in *Institutions and the Person* in discussing issues in Holistic Research – p. 349. He notes that the issue is double-edged and rests on the ability of the researcher to not only *be* convinced but to convince.

22. Harold Wilensky, "The Professionalization of Almost Everybody," *American Journal of Sociology,* September, 1964, 70, pp. 37-58.

23. The sociology of deviancy has always seemed a bit distasteful and extremely value oriented to me. Deviancy is a term which means on either side of a norm, it denotes only difference. The connotation has become negative and thus, to describe a group as deviant places a value judgment upon it. The other difficulty with the whole concept is that deviancy is context sensitive, i.e., what is deviant to one is not necessarily deviant to another, so the vantage point of the observer must be clearly noted. This is seldom accomplished to my satisfaction, as for instance when Howard Becker describes playing "straight" in *The Outsiders,* 1963, it is clear that he is defining his audience as deviant from the dance musicians of which he fails to mention that he is a member. Since deviancy is in the eye, not to mention mind, of the beholder, I question its utility to serious sociology.

24. D. Maurer, *The Big Con* (New York: Pocket Books, 1949).

25. Blau, *op. cit.*, p. 5.

26. *Ibid.*, p. 8.

27. K.H. Wolff (Ed.), *The Sociology of Georg Simmel* (New York: Free Press, 1950), Chapter 4.

28. Strauss, *op. cit.*, pp. 328-41.

Notes to Chapter 3

1. Webster's New Collegiate Dictionary, second edition, 1960, p. 830.

2. D. Krech, R.S. Crutchfield, and E.L. Ballachey, *Individual in Society* (New York: McGraw-Hill, 1962), p. 67.

3. Stereotypes enjoyed a brief spurt of scientific flurry in the late forties and early fifties, undoubtedly at least partially due to the nationalism aroused by World War II. They enjoyed a brief popularity during the early sixties when civil rights and integration were burning social and sociological issues. L. Wirth, "The Problems of Minority Groups," in R. Linton (Ed.), *The Science of Man in the World Crisis* ([New York: Columbia University Press, 1945]) in his writings on the cities and minority groups along with psychologists S.E. Asch, ("Forming impressions of personality," *J. of Ab. Soc. Psych.*, 41, 1946, pp. 258-90 and *Social Psychology* [New York: Prentice Hall, 1952]), H.H. Kelley ("The warm cold variable in first impressions of persons," *J. Person.*, 18, 1950, pp. 431-9), M. Radke-Yarrow and J.S. Miller ("Children's concepts and attitudes about minority and majority American groups," *Adolescents,* J.M. Seidman (Ed.), [New York: Holt, Rinehart and Winston, 1953], p. 617.) and M. Haire and W.F. Grunes ("Perceptual defenses processes protecting an original perception of another personality," *Hum. Relat.*, 3, 1950, pp. 403-12) are all indicative of the genre along with those who attempted to broaden the scope of the term such as G.W. Allport (*The Nature of Prejudice* [Cambridge, Mass.: Addison Wesley, 1954]), T.W. Adorno, Frenkel-Brunswick, et al., (*The Authoritarian Personality* [New York: Harper, 1950]), L. Festinger ("An analysis of compliant behavior," in M. Sherif and M.O. Wilson (Eds.), *Group Relations at the Crossroads* [New York: Harper, 1953]).

More recently J.S. Bruner and H.V. Permutter ("Compatriot and foreigner: A study of impression formation in five countries," *J. of Abnorm. Soc. Psych.*, 1957, 55, pp. 253-60) and T.F. Pettigrew ("Personality and sociocultural factors in intergroup attitudes," *J. of Confl. Res.*, 1958, 2, pp. 29-42) have attempted cross-cultural studies with special emphasis on blacks in a white culture. The term has fallen into temporary disuse after scientific inquiry determined that stereotyping was "typical" human behavior with a tendency for tenacity.

The more modern trend, especially in the field of the study of social disruption, seems to be a strict avoidance of labelling thereby precluding the study of stereotyping. For example, see T.J. Scheff (*Mental Illness and Social Processes* [New York: Harper, 1967]) D. Matza (*Becoming Deviant* [Englewood Cliffs, New Jersey: Prentice Hall, 1969]), O.E. Klapp (*Collective Search for Identity* [New York: Holt, Rinehart and Winston, 1969]) and B. Kaplan (*The Inner World of Mental Illness* [New York: Harper and Row, 1964]). In fact, a perusal of the most current available issue of *Sociology Abstracts* reveals only seven entries under the heading of "stereotype" including articles by a

Dutchman, a Frenchman, an Indian, an Argentinian, two Poles and a single American writing about the "sexless older years: a sociologically harmful stereotype."

4. A.H. Hastorf, and Hadley Cantril, "They Saw a Game: A Case Study," *The Adolescent*, J.M. Seidman (Ed.) (New York: Holt, Rinehart and Winston, 1953), p. 635.

5. *Ibid.*, p. 645.

6. G.H. Mead, *Mind, Self and Society* (Chicago: University of Chicago Press, 1967), p. 175.

7. *Ibid.*, p. 174.

8. It is of some interest that Mead encounters the same difficulty in trying to explain the initial differentiation of "I" and "me" as Freud does with the "id" and "ego" since in both cases a social awareness is necessary before the social as opposed to the individual part of the human can be formed.

9. Mead, *op. cit.*, p. 176.

10. *Ibid.*, p. 177.

11. E.C. Hughes, "What Other," in A. Rose (Ed.), *Human Behavior and Social Processes* (Boston: Houghton Mifflin, 1962), pp. 119-27.

12. L. Wirth, *On Cities and Social Life* (Chicago: University of Chicago Press, 1964), p. 35.

13. *Ibid.*

14. After a thorough search of "the literature" harvested little substantive information on either bargaining or salesmen in general let alone used car salesmen and their relationship to their customers, I turned to the more popular literature. The journals, newspapers, and other miscellaneous sources perused were chosen on the basis of their accessibility both to me and to the public at large. I skimmed the following for applicable data over an eighteen month period, from July 1969 to January 1971, in addition to my usual reading habits during which I was always on the look-out for usable data:

> *Consumer Reports*
> *New York Times*
> *Wall Street Journal*
> *Boston Globe*
> *Time*
> American Automobile Association Newsletter
> miscellaneous women's magazines

I felt this sample constituted a reasonable cross-section of literature available to the average customer. In addition, I got by with a little help from my friends who would save articles that concerned used cars. It might be noted that all the information thus gathered does not appear in the body of this paper since much of what appeared relevant at one point no longer seemed applicable at the time of write-up and analysis.

15. John Quirk, *The Hard Winners* (New York: Avon, 1965), pp. 450-51.

16. *Ibid.*, p. 454.

17. *Boston Globe,* February 23, 1970, p. 37.

18. *Punch,* 7 January 1970, p. 2.

19. *Consumer Reports,* volume 9, 1970, p. 551.

20. *Boston Globe,* October 5, 1970, p. A-25.

21. *New York Times,* June 21, 1970, p. 41.

22. *Boston Globe,* July 26, 1970, p. A-9.

23. *New York Times,* October 30, 1969, p. 37.

24. *Ibid.*

25. Betty Furness, "The cost of living," *McCall's,* September 1970, p. 124.

26. *Boston Globe,* "Gasoline Alley," by Bill Perry, March 8, 1970, comic section.

27. *Boston Globe,* June 7, 1970, p. 2-B.

28. *Boston Globe,* November 19, 1969, p. 62.

29. Massachusetts Division AAA Newsletter, "Your Guide to Used Car Buying," Fall 1969, p. 11.

30. *New York Times,* "Used-Car Sellers Face Stiff Rules," May 10, 1970, p. 88.

31. *Ibid.*, p. 88.

32. *This Week Magazine, Boston Globe,* October 12, 1969, p. 6-7.

33. *Ibid.*, p. 7.

34. *Boston Globe,* "Drive a hard bargain when buying a new car," by John R. White, June 11, 1970, p. 40.

35. *Boston Globe,* July 27, 1969, p. 18.

36. "Adventures in the iron trade," by Shelby Coffey III, *Washington Post, Potomac,* January 25, 1970, p. 5.

37. *Ibid.*, p. 10.

38. *Ibid.*

39. *Ibid.*, p. 7.

40. *Ibid.*, p. 10.

41. *Ibid.*, p. 8.

Notes to Chapter 4

1. G.H. Mead, *Mind, Self and Society* (Chicago: University of Chicago Press, 1935), pp. 173-204, 273-78, 371-73.

2. G.H. Mead, "Time," Chapter 13, *On Social Psychology* (Chicago: University of Chicago Press, 1964), pp. 328-41.

3. G.H. Mead, *Mind, Self and Society* (Chicago: University of Chicago Press, 1967), p. 89.

4. G.H. Mead, "The Objective Reality of Perspectives," Chapter 14, *On Social Psychology*, pp. 342-54.

5. H.S. Becker et al., *Boys in White* (Chicago: University of Chicago Press, 1961).

6. G.H. Mead, *Mind, Self and Society*, p. 89.

7. This information was gleaned as the result of a questionnaire distributed to each of the twenty-three men in this particular course; in addition, I was shown the results from thousands of responses to the same questionnaire over a period of years. I am indebted to the Ford Marketing Institute for their assistance and cooperation. They allowed me to attend two seminars of two weeks each on automotive selling which they conducted for their salesmen. I was allowed to attend free of charge and was supplied with all class materials (including lunch). The instructor and all participants were extremely cordial and most helpful.

8. Ford Marketing Institute, Advanced Retail Selling, pp. 2-3, 1969.

9. G.H. Mead, *Mind, Self and Society*, p. 5.

10. Arnold M. Rose, *Theory and Method in the Social Sciences* (Minneapolis, Minnesota: University of Minnesota Press, 1954), p. 8.

11. E.H. Sutherland, *The Professional Thief* (Chicago: University of Chicago Press, 1937), p. 176.

12. G.H. Mead, *Mind, Self and Society*, p. 5.

13. Hoffman, *et. al.* ("Tendencies toward group comparability in competitive bargaining," *Human Relations*, 1954, 7, 2, p. 141-59) note that a significant motivation in the bargaining situation in which they were interested (collective bargaining) was the individual's concern about his status in the action relative to the others in the group. He could often be interested to the extent of wanting to equal or surpass their performance. The salesman is well aware of this factor, the effect an audience has on the interaction as well as the competitive nature of the interaction. A "friend" is not a welcome sight.

14. *Ibid.*, p. 12.

15. *Ibid.*, p. 11-12.

16. *Ibid.*, p. 12.

17. Sutherland, *op. cit.*, p. 181.

18. E.C. Hughes, *Men and Their Work*, Glencoe, Illinois: Free Press, 1958, p. 139-44. The section of *caveat emptor* is of sufficient importance to be cited in its entirety:

... In purest form, business goes on among traders. Since the customer is always a trader, he is presumed to be as sophisticated about the object traded in as is the seller. The trading is a game. The principle of *caveat emptor* can apply without injury to anyone. As in all games, however, there are rules designed to allow the game to continue. There is no sense letting anyone in who lacks the resources to make good his deals, or the skill to keep the game going. Hence, stock exchanges have limited memberships. But the state and the public are not especially considered in making the rules of entrance to the game and the rules of play.

Not all business is of this form, for goods are eventually sold to the amateur, a consumer. The consumer may know what he likes, but he is not expected to be as good a judge of what he buys as is the man who sold it to him. He expects some little protection from unscrupulous sellers who would impose upon his ignorance. *Caveat emptor* tends to be limited, but not completely — witness the tongue-in-cheek "pitch" advertising. The consumer often, in moments of annoyance, initiates action to license sellers or to otherwise protect the consumers from them.

The people in a profession make their living by giving an esoteric service . . . The essence of the matter appears, however, to be that the client is not in a position to judge for himself the quality of the service he receives. He comes to the professional because he has met a problem which he cannot handle himself . . . He has some idea of the result he wants; little of the means or even the possibility of attaining it . . . those in the profession do not want the principle of *caveat emptor* to apply.

Notes to Chapter 5

1. E.C. Hughes, *Men and Their Work* (Glencoe, Illinois: Free Press, 1958), p. 139.

2. This concept of commitment is a double-edged sword in this context especially when the value judgment inherent in the concept is realized: "Occupational commitment is one of the chief values of our society. It is a mark of adulthood among us to settle down to a consistent line of activity, a career in a chosen field." (Blanche Geer, "Occupational Commitment and Teaching," *Institutions and the Person* [Chicago: Aldine, 1968], p. 222).

Salesmen consider selling a career while the house considers selling used cars a career so while salesmen feel it is quite consistent to sell other things, the house considers it a mark of a less than "adult" personality. On the other hand, the salesmen themselves realize that a commitment of some kind to a dealership is necessary for as Geer points out: "Once secured, a good clientele makes possible a sense of continuing responsibility, pride and satisfaction not otherwise obtainable, not to mention a continuing source of business." Geer notes that teachers often move around within the field of teaching to administrative positions and the like and thus still demonstrate a commitment to the concept of teaching while not actually teaching. The crucial factor is obviously commitment from whose point of view, as Becker notes ("Notes on the concept of commitment," *AJS*, 66, 1960-61, pp. 32-40), commitment is consistent human behavior and consistency is in the eye of the beholder. He further notes that the concept can be seen as coming into being when "a person by making a side bet, links extraneous interests with a consistent line of activity." This side bet can consist of thoughts about the kind of person I am and the kind of society I live in. Thus the car salesman adopts a view of the universe consistent with his job or vice versa (see Chapter 6) in order to strengthen his commitment to selling and specifically selling used cars.

3. R. Bogdan, "Learning to Sell Door to Door: Techniques and Strategies of Persuasion," April, 1968, Syracuse University, unpublished.

4. A.M. Carr-Saunders, and P.A. Wilson, *The Professions,* Oxford: Clarendon Press, 1933.

5. H.L. Wilensky, "The professionalization of everyone," *AJS,* 5, 70, 32, September, 1964, p. 137-58.

6. R.L. Brooks, *How I Went From Failure to $50,000 a Year,* Los Angeles: Sherbourne Press, 1967, p. 152-72.

7. Bogdan makes the same point in saying that the duper is duped, caught up in the same story he tells his customer whether he's selling vacuum cleaners, encyclopedias, or used cars.

8. Arthur Miller, "Death of a Salesman."

9. Vance Packard, *The Hidden Persuaders,* New York: Pocket Books, Inc., 1957.

10. Ned Polsky, *Hustlers, Beats and Others,* New York: Doubleday, 1969.

11. *Ibid.,* p. 53.

12. Boston Globe, 25 October 1970, p. 76, "At election time, Deus ex machina equals Richard Nixon leaving plane" by Chauncey Howell.

13. Adventures in salesmanship, Sears Roebuck and Company, *The Advertiser's Digest,* July, 1941.

14. E.H. Sutherland, *The Professional Thief,* Chicago: University of Chicago Press, 1937, p. 69.

15. This idea of the customer getting what he deserves because he's either greedy or in over his head or both is discussed by Erving Goffman in "On Cooling the Mark Out," in *Human Behavior and Social Processes,* Arnold Rose, ed., Boston: Houghton Mifflin, 1962, p. 482-505.

16. Sutherland, *op. cit.,* p. 56.

17. This characteristic of distinguishing between members of the profession is not unique to used car salesmen, of course. Because there is competition in nearly any profession, some amount of hostility, competition, back-biting, whatever could be predicted, but many professions as a part of their code of ethics will not give public vent to these feelings, e.g., doctors, lawyers, architects, even most businessmen. (A good example of this practice is the stir Mary Burns caused with her early Rambler ads that named names with regard to other automobile manufacturers and their products; previous to then, it simply wasn't done.) However, when an occupation is unfettered by a professional code of ethics, Simmel's prediction of competition (Simmel, *Conflict and the Web of Group Affiliations* [New York: Free Press, 1964], pp. 57-58) is much more

likely although Simmel warns that "The businessman who succeeds in having his competitor suspects of unsoundness by the public gains nothing if the public's needs are suddenly deflected from his merchandise." (p. 58)

In the case of the used car salesman, the unsavory reputation is already present, so it is more a matter of deflecting it than creating it. Polsky points out the same uneasy fraternity among hustlers (*Hustlers, Beats and Others* [New York: Anchor, 1969], pp. 60-62) as does Becker (*The Outsiders* [New York: Free Press, 1963]) about musicians, especially between commercial musicians and dance musicians (pp. 91-94).

In addition to deflecting unsavory reputations, there are distinctions within any group as to those who are more equal than others; there are higher grade thieves, prostitutes, lawyers, safe crackers, teachers, students, politicians, *ad infinitum.* The point about used car salesmen is that in addition to the usual suspicious fraternity, they have a suspicious public to deal with and their "internal" suspicions can be aired to the customer as a method of differentiating "me" and "them."

18. Georg Simmel, *The Sociology of Georg Simmel* (New York: Free Press, 1950.

19. Max Weber, *Theory of Social and Economic Organization* (New York: Free Press, 1947), pp. 35, 52, 132, 193, 254, 319, etc.

20. Talcott Parsons, and Neil J. Smelser, *Economy and Society* (New York: Free Press, 1956), p. 10.

Notes to Chapter 6

1. G.H. Mead, *Mind, Self and Society* (Chicago: University of Chicago Press, 1967). See also Chapters 2 and 3.

2. Based on the assumption that there are 148 hours in a week in which 8 hours a day or 56 hours a week are spent sleeping and 40 hours a week spent "at work." The percentage is even greater if commuting time is computed.

3. Melville Dalton, *Men Who Manage* (New York: John Wiley and Sons, 1959).

4. Mead, *op. cit.* A brief word is added here as a refresher as to the differentiation of the "I" and "me"; at its simplest, the me is the object, the self seen through the theoretized eyes of society as accepted and acted upon by the ever-present, eternal I supposedly untainted by any "other," a practical impossibility. For a more in depth, less facile discussion, see "Through a Windshield Darkly" (Chapter 3) or Mead.

5. K.H. Wolff (Ed.), *The Sociology of Georg Simmel* (New York: Free Press, 1969), p. 145.

6. *Ibid.*, p. 155.

7. Morris Freilich, "The natural tried in kinship and complex systems," a

revision of "Are kinship studies obsolete?" a paper read at the joint meetings of the Northeastern Anthropological Conference and the American Ethnological Society, Cornell University, Ithaca, New York, March, 1963.

8. H.S. Becker, and B. Geer, *Boys in White* (Chicago: University of Chicago Press, 1961).

9. Dalton, *op. cit.*

10. M.L. Taylor, and R.J. Pellegrin, "Professionalization: Its function and dysfunction for the life insurance occupation," *Social Forces* 38, 2 (December 1959).

11. Gluckman (*Custom and Conflict in Africa* [New York: Barnes and Noble, 1956], pp. 27-53) makes the point in his discussion of government in Africa among the Zulus that the middleman is placed in really an intolerable position; given responsibility without authority. He represents the headman to the people and the people to the headman and thus is blamed by both because he has no control over the actions of the headman and is unable to direct the people. However Gluckman overlooks one point. Not only are intermediaries traditionally in a tenuous position, but they are *intentionally* placed in that position by those in power, i.e., the "establishment," and serve *only* to benefit those in charge. Certainly the intermediary never wins and the people never win because power is invested in only one direction, downward, never upward. A number of examples can be given from my personal experience in such a role. While working for a public agency, I was assigned the responsibility of community liason with a rather militant black group. I was pleased at the prospect of being able to inform the agency as to the feelings of the community, but it turned out that the agency was quite unconcerned with my attempts and instead, unbeknownst to me for a long period of time, fed information (usually misinformation) through me which they wished the community to have knowing that the community would believe me. I was their unwitting pawn. After a respectable interval of time, I figured out the situation and turned "counterspy" and started advising the community of the points of vulnerability of the agency, how best to achieve their demands within the present framework and structure. When the agency, also after a decent interval, figured out that this was what I was doing, I was summarily relieved of my responsibilities in this area.

Used car salesmen are, of course, in the same position. They work for the house and form the valuable function *for the house* of buffering between the customer and house (the house has no nefarious reputation, it is the salesman and the house is where the profit is being made) and while the salesman may think he can take the part of the customer with the salesman, he will be out on his ear if he does it with any consistency. The intermediary is there at the discretion and whim of the group in power, cause man that's who put 'em there in the first place and that's who pays the bills and that's what power is all about.

Another example. So-called grass-root social service agencies were established via the poverty program after a number of long, hot summers in theory in response to the black communities' objection to white paternalism in the ghettos. These agencies were funded by those in power to carry out the functions of those in power, in theory with advocacy to those in power. Of course, the advocacy role has never worked and the intermediaries now inhabit a no man's land where they are neither part of the community nor part of the decision makers, but suspect because they are paid by the establishment and in a very real way act as unwitting spies. There is no advocacy role for them to play.

With respect to the car salesmen, the men do occasionally take the side of the customer against the house and it is part of the game to beat the house, but it should be understood that all intermediary positions are invested, created and controlled from the top, never the bottom and to think otherwise is to be unaware of the nature of power.

12. R. Bogdan, "Learning to Sell Door to Door: Techniques and Strategies of Persuasion," April, 1968, Syracuse University, unpublished.

13. *Ibid.*

14. W.M. Evan, and E.G. Levin, "Professionalism and the Stockbroker: Some Observations on the SEC Special Study," *Bus. Law,* 21, January 1966, pp. 358-59.

15. J.M. Rosenfeld, "Strangeness between helper and client: A possible explanation of non-use of available professional help," *Social Problems* 11, 2 (Fall, 1963).

16. E. Freidson, "Client control and medical practice," *American Journal of Sociology,* January 1960, pp. 374-82.

17. M. Weber, *The Theory of Social and Economic Organization* (New York: Free Press, 1947).

18. This ambiguity at a crucial point in dealings with the public is in no way limited to used car salesmen. The same phenomenon can be observed in the behavior of the urban policeman in his dealings with student riots, the urban ghetto (especially if he himself is black) and other situations in which as enforcer of law and order, he must often choose between the two rather than be able to serve them simultaneously. See M. Banton, "Police Discretion," *New Society,* 48, 1963, p. 2, in which he discusses popular morality vs. the law and the factor that emotional involvement plays in the decisions made. Notice that the car salesmen have the ability to exercise the same discretion with the same results. Banton expands this thesis in *The Policemen in the Community* (New York: Basic Books, 1964), in noting again the place of discretionary action that is highly dependent on role. Dodd in "Police mentality and behavior," *Issues in Criminology* 3, 1 (Summer 1967): 47-67, makes the point that the police are expected to conform to popular morality. Vernon (Fox) notes the same conflicting ethical considerations with role and function being unclear in his article on "The sociological and political aspects of police administration," *Ind. Sociol. R.* 3, 1 (Oct. 1965): 94-100. I. Piliavin and S. Briar note the problem as being particularly acute in "Police encounters with juveniles," *Am. J. of Soc.* 70, 2 (Sept. 1964): 206-214. See also Wm. A. Westley, "The police: a sociological

study of law, custom and morality," pp. 304-313, in *Contributions to Urban Sociology*, W.E. Burgess and D. Bogne (Eds.) (Chicago: University of Chicago Press, 1964). This point was also underlined in a study the author undertook in Houston, Texas, where the role of the rookie cop in the ghetto was extremely undefined; although the new cop might feel that he should be fair and just in his dealing with black offenders, his superiors who had grown up under a different system demanded harsh treatment, and these same superiors were the ones who determined promotions and pay raises.

This kind of role ambiguity could be predicted in any situation in which a middleman is involved, but is particularly acute in the case of the police and shifting societal values and the car salesmen with unclear monetary values. Both, in theory, are expected to be absolute by all concerned and neither are.

19. The house, it will be remembered, is the endearing term used by the salesman to describe the manager and financial backer (usually owner) of the dealership with which he is involved. The owner is usually on the premises at least part time with a sales manager in residence at all times. The sales manager is also a middleman between and owner and the salesman but serves as the functional equivalent to the owner as far as the salesman is concerned. The salesman seldom goes over the head of the manager to the owner (in spite of the example appearing in this chapter) but will seek the man with whom he is most compatible to "sign off" his deals, especially on a close one. Since the study is predominantly from the viewpoint of the salesman, the hierarchy of the house is of little importance since the salesman does not differentiate between the two. Mechanics and the service department in general are considered part of the house since they work on salary and the salesman sees them as siding with the establishment against him especially when it comes to setting priorities in terms of whose cars are serviced first, the salesman's customer's or the house's new ones or unsold used ones.

20. E.C. Hughes, *Men and Their Work* (Glencoe, Illinois: Free Press, 1958), p. 141.

21. G. Simmel, *Conflict and the Web of Group Affiliations* (New York: Free Press, 1964).

22. Simmel died in September 1918.

23. The idea of displacement is taken from psychoanalytic theory as propounded by Freud; see *The Basic Writings of Sigmund Freud,* A.A. Brill, (Ed.) (New York: Modern Library, 1938), pp. 35, 38, 62, 246, 249, 336-39, 361, 656-63, 702-703, 861, 906, and *A General Introduction to Psycho-analysis* (New York: Washington Square Press, 1924), p. 271. While his concept received its notoriety primarily from Freud's analysis of dreams, it is also used to explain associations that occur when a name is forgotten and then remembered incorrectly and when one set of behaviors is substituted for another, the first being presumably either too traumatic or too socially unexceptable to be tolerated by either the actor or his audience.

In a more commonplace context, the results of displaced hostility can be seen in an angry man kicking a chair or throwing something; hard-hats who are suffering a 33% unemployment rate harrassing and beating peace demonstrators or in the example of a man who has been chewed out by his boss coming home and yelling at his wife since it is unexceptable to yell at the boss. One wonders if some of the hostility Becker's dance musicians feel toward a "square audience" is a case of displaced hostility for either a "system" that keeps them from the music they love or themselves for selling out. (*The Outsiders,* p. 91-95 passim [New York: Free Press, 1963].)

24. As noted above, the mechanic is considered part of the house as far as the salesman is concerned since he does not work on commission (although he can occasionally receive a commission on a car) and is not primarily concerned with selling cars. As already stated, the mechanic is seen as being on the side of the house as opposed to the salesman.

25. See note 18 above.

26. W. Edwards, "The Theory of Decision Making," *Psych, Bull.* 51, 4 (1954): 398.

27. Ford Marketing Institute figures assign an average length of less than two years to a salesman's residency with any one house although all manufacturer's and most houses urge a salesman to stay with a dealership in order to build up a following of loyal customers and referrals.

28. Stephen Miller, "The social base of sales behavior," *Social Problems,* v. 12, Summer, 1964, p. 20.

Notes to Chapter 7

1. Stephen J. Miller, "The Social Base of Sales Behavior," *Social Problems,* v. 12, Summer, 1964, p. 22.

2. R. Bogdan, "Learning to Sell Door to Door: Techniques and Strategies of Persuasion," Syracuse University, April, 1968, unpublished.

3. D. Mauer, *The Big Con* (Indianapolis, 1948).

4. E. H. Sutherland, *The Professional Thief* (Chicago: University of Chicago Press, 1937).

5. Miller, *op. cit.*, p. 18.

6. Ned Polsky, *Hustlers, Beats and Others* (New York: Doubleday, 1967).

7. Erving Goffman, "On Cooling the Mark Out: Some Aspects of Adaptation to Failure," *Psychiatry,* 15, November, 1952, pp. 451-63.

8. Erving Goffman, "On Face Work," *Interaction Ritual* (New York: Anchor, 1967), p. 5.

9. Miller, *op cit.*, p. 17.

10. *Ibid.*, p. 19.

11. H. S. Becker, "The Professional Dance Musician and His Audience," *American Journal of Sociology,* 57, September, 1951, pp. 136-44.

12. Eliot Freidson, *Patients' Views of Medical Practice* (New York: Russell Sage Foundation, 1961).

13. Goffman, *op. cit.*, 1967, p. 7.

14. Bogdan, *op. cit.*, p. 24.

15. *Ibid.*, p. 25.

16. *Ibid.*, p. 26.

17. Georg Simmel, *The Sociology of Georg Simmel* (New York: Free Press, 1950), p. 313.

18. *Ibid.*, p. 312.

19. *Ibid.*, p. 316.

20. Bogdan, *op. cit.*, p. 35.

21. *Ibid.*, p. 35.

22. *Ibid.*

23. *Ibid.*, p. 22.

24. *Ibid.*

25. *Ibid.*, pp. 33-34.

26. Ibid., *p. 34.*

27. *Ibid.*, p. 7.

28. *Ibid.*, p. 14.

29. *Ibid.*, p. 15.

30. *Ibid.*, p. 16.

31. Miller, *op. cit.*, p. 20.

32. Bogdan, *op. cit.*, p. 8.

33. *Ibid.*, p. 27.

Notes to Chapter 8

1. T. C. Schelling, *The Strategy of Conflict* (Cambridge, Massachusetts: Harvard University Press, 1960), p. 5.

2. G. C. Homans, "Social Behavior as Exchange," *American Journal of Sociology,* 1958, pp. 597-606.

3. P. M. Blau, "Formal Organization: Dimensions of Analysis," *American Journal of Sociology,* 63, 1957, p. 58.

4. S. J. Miller, "Exchange and Negotiated Learning in Graduate Medical Education," *Sociology Quarterly* (Fall, 1966) pp. 469-79. See also S. J. Miller, *Prescription for Leadership* (Chicago: Aldine, 1970), p. 135.

5. Exchange theory uses the bargain as a conceptual model in which abstractions such as services, obligations and the like are passed between individuals and groups. In this study, bargaining actually occurs on a pragmatic level, i.e., it is not an abstraction but a reality. The emphasis by the former is on exchange theory while in the latter, it is on exchange. (In the case of the former the bargain is the model for social action, while in this study, social action is the bargain.)

6. J. A. Roth, "The Treatment of Tuberculosis as a Bargaining Process," in A. Rose, *Human Behavior and Social Processes* (Boston: Houghton Mifflin, 1962), p. 575.

7. E. Freidson, "Dilemmas in the Doctor-Patient Relationship," in A. Rose, *Human Behavior and Social Processes* (Boston: Houghton Mifflin, 1962), p. 207. See also E. Freidson, *Patients' View of Medical Practice* (Russell Sage Foundation, 1961).

8. "Bargaining Goes to College," *Boston Globe,* Sunday, March 15, 1970, pp. 1 and 18.

9. M. Deutsch, and R. M. Kraus, "Effect of Threat Upon Interpersonal Bargaining," *Journal of Abnormal Social Psychology,* p. 181.

10. Schelling, *op. cit.*, p. 22.

11. *Ibid.*

12. *Ibid.*, p. 5-6.

13. *Ibid.*, p. 22.

14. J. M. Morgan, "Bilateral Monopoly and the Competitive Output," *Quarterly Journal of Economics.* 63: 376, n6 (August 1949).

15. M. Deutsch, "Reflections on Some Studies of Interpersonal Conflict," *American Psychologist* 24, 12 (December, 1969): 1076.

16. Schelling, *op. cit.*, p. 89.

17. Roth, *op. cit.*, p. 583.

18. Deutsch, *op. cit.*, p. 1079.

19. Roth, *op. cit.*, p. 575.

20. W. Edwards, "Theory of Decision Making", *Psychological Bulletin*, 51, 4 (1954): 388.

21. This concept of image management is deftly described by Goffman in such writings as *The Presentation of Self in Everyday Life* and referenced in his other works as well. This conept is discussed in the earlier chapters of this study as well. All this serves as a reminder that image management is something all human beings practice and it has not always had the connotations of unsavoryness that it has acquired since being coupled with R. M. Nixon.

22. Schelling, *op. cit.*, p. 27.

23. *Ibid.*, p. 104f.

24. *Ibid.*, p. 28.

25. Schematically:

A owns the car

B is the mechanic who will originally buy the car

C is the salesman

D is the hypothetical "sucker" who will buy the car after it has been fixed up

A sells to B for $50

B fixes up and sells to C for $175

C sells to D for $200

A makes $50

B makes $175 minus $50

C makes $25

B would only make $125 since he had to buy the car for $50 originally. B decided it was a little risky; he'd have to stand for parts and laqor and he wouldn't get his $175 until AFTER the car was sold (if and when).

26. As is obvious from scrutiny of these notes and the bibliography, Schelling's work has been extremely helpful. Our main difference in considering bargaining is not in the rules, but in how these rules effect the participants. This is probably due to the fact that Schelling is dealing with an assumed military situation with two parties involved in a situation of conflict (war). Thus the more emotional, human, unpredictable quirks of a relatively unrestrained participant such as the used car salesman are contrary to the expectations of Schelling and his participants. Also, Schelling is dealing with either a two or four party situation (a diplomat speaking for his country) rather than a three party situation. In Schelling's situation, participants deal with one another on the basis of necessity, not desire; a diplomat can't shop elsewhere for a treaty or a general for an adversary.

27. Schelling, *op. cit.*, p. 46f.

28. E. Hall, *The Silent Language* (New York: Doubleday Company, 1959), pp. 100, 117.

29. Deutsch, *op. cit.*, p. 181.

30. Fuad Khuri, "The Etiquette of Bargaining in the Middle East," *American Anthropologist* 70, 4 (August 1968): 698-706.

Notes to Appendix I

1. Ned Polsky, *Hustlers, Beats and Others* (Chicago: Aldine, 1967), p. 123.

2. Mario Pei, *The Story of Language* (New York: Mentor Books, 1949), p. 145.

3. Roger Brown, *Words and Things* (New York: Glencoe Free Press, 1958), p. 357.

4. Edwin Sutherland, *The Professional Thief*, (Chicago: University of Chicago Press, 1937) p. 7.

5. Polsky, *op. cit.*, p. 122.

6. Benjamin Whorf, *Language, Thought and Reality* (Cambrdige: Technology Press, 1956).

7. William Goode makes the point that "client choices are a form of social control. They determine the survival of a profession or speciality as well as the career success of particular professionals," "Community within a community: The professions," *ASR*, 22, April 1957, pp. 194-200. Thus shopping around can be seen as a client's method of control over the salesman. The salesman attempts to limit this control as described in the text by taking the buyer off the market in a number of legitimate and "semi-legitimate" ways. By maintaining a trusting relationship with the client after the transaction has been completed, he hopes to make the customer his "own" and remove the shopping element as control.

8. The glossary contained herein is undoubtedly not exhaustive, but I assume that any used car salesman would at least know what any particular expression meant, even if he did not use it himself. All words, expressions, etc., were gleaned from actual conversations with no particular attempts being made to elicit specific jargon other than by occasionally asking for clarification which sometimes resulted in other examples being given. I did not set out to document language patterns of the used car salesmen but began keeping a record of words that I didn't understand or found particularly colorful, strange, ambiguous or contradictory in terms of more common usage. As might be expected, the great number of listings came shortly after I entered the field and tended to taper off as I became more and more familiar with not only the lingo, but the concepts it described and thus less conscious of its "difference" although I consciously attempted to keep sight of vocabulary, as its strangeness diminished, I am sure that my retention did likewise.

As mentioned earlier, the glossary is included as yet another facet of the used car salesman.

Notes to Appendix II

1. *Time* November 2, 1970, p. 14, "Politics and the Name Game."

2. *Time* November 2, 1970, p. 12, review of *The Greening of America* by Charles Reich.

3. Erma Bombeck, *Boston Globe,* p. A-1, Sunday, December 7, 1969, "Playing that new adult game: garage sale."

4. *Psychology Today,* July 1970, p. 71, advertisement.

5. A.H. Copeland, *Bulletin of the American Mathematical Society,* volume 51, 1945, pp. 498-504.

6. J.D. Williams, *The Compleat Strategyst* (New York: McGraw-Hill, 1954).

7. A. Rapoport, *Fights, Games and Debates* (Ann Arbor: The University of Michigan Press, 1960).

8. A. Rapoport, *Two-Person Game Theory* (Ann Arbor: The University of Michigan Press, 1966).

9. R.D. Luce, and H. Raiffa, *Games and Decisions* (New York: Wiley and Sons, 1957).

10. J.F. Nash, "The bargaining problem," *Econometrica* 18 (1950), pp. 155-62.

11. J.F. Nash, "Noncooperative games," *Annals of Mathematics* 54 (1951), pp. 286-95.

12. J.F. Nash, "Two-person cooperative games," *Econometrica* 21 (1953), pp. 128-40.

13. J.C. Harsanyi, "On the rationality postulates underlying the theory of cooperative games," *Journal of Conflict Resolution* 5 (1961), pp. 179-96.

14. J.C. Harsanyi, "Rationality postulates for bargaining solutions in cooperative and noncooperative games," *Management Science* 9 (1962), pp. 141-53.

15. T.C. Schelling, *The Strategy of Conflict* (Cambridge, Mass.: Harvard University Press, 1960).

16. T.C. Schelling, "Bargaining, communication and limited war," *Journal of Conflict Resolution* 1 (1957), pp. 19-38.

17. Eric Berne, *Games People Play* (New York: Grove Press, 1967).

18. H. Garfinkle, *Motivation and Social Interaction* O.J. Harvey (Ed.) (New York: Ronald Press Co., 1963), pp. 187-238.

19. M. Deutsch, "Trust and suspicion," *Journal of Conflict Resolution* 2, 4 (December 1958): 266.

20. M. Deutsch, "Effect of motivational orientation on trust and suspicion," *Human Relations* 13, 2 (May 1960): 123-40.

21. M. Deutsch, "A theory of cooperation and competition," *Human Relations,* 1949, 2, pp. 129-52.

22. Under Deutsch's guidance, L. Solomon, "The influence of some types of power relationships on the development of trust," Ph.D. dissertation, New York University, 1957.

23. E. Goffman, *Encounters* (New York: Bobbs Merrill, 1961).

24. Kenneth Boulding, referenced by Rapoport, *Two-Person Game Theory,* on the cover.

25. Williams, *op. cit.,* p. 5.

26. T.C. Schelling, *Game Theory and Analysis of Ethical Systems,* p. 47.

27. Rapoport, *Two-Person Game Theory*, p. 16.

28. *Ibid.*, p. 17.

29. *Time* November 2, 1970, p. 12.

30. Rapoport, *Two-Person Game Theory*, p. 5.

31. *Dennis the Menace* by Hank Ketcham, *Boston Sunday Globe,* comic section, January 2, 1970.

32. *Time* March 9, 1970, p. 70, in a review of *Poor Devils,* by David Ely.

33. D.A. Schon, *Displacement of Concepts* (London: Tavistock Pub., 1963), p. 191.

34. *Time* November 2, 1970, "Politics and the Name Game," p. 14.

35. *Ibid.*

36. Webster's New Collegiate Dictionary, second edition, 1960, p. 340.

37. Schelling, *The Strategy of Conflict,* p. 83.

38. *Ibid.*, pp. 162-63.

39. Garfinkle, *op. cit.*, p. 190.

40. *Ibid.*, p. 193.

41. *Ibid.*, p. 191. It might be noted that although Garfinkle was not talking about game theory specifically in all cases, his reliance on rules and what other social scientists came to regard as game theory makes his analyses pertinent to the discussion; also the fact that he relied on the concepts of trust and predictability tie him closely to those more directly and outspokenly hitched to game theory.

42. Roger Caillois, "Unity of play: diversity of games," *Diogenes* 19 (1957), p. 99.

43. Goffman, *op. cit.* p. 17.

44. *Time* January 26, 1970, p. 59, a discussion of the findings of Iona and Peter Opie in *Children's Games in Street and Playground,* Oxford University Press.

45. Berne, *op. cit.*, p. 48.

46. *Ibid.*, p. 97.

47. Garfinkle, *op. cit.*, p. 194.

48. *Ibid.*, p. 199.

49. *Ibid.*

50. Deutsch, 1958, *op. cit.*, p. 266.

51. *Ibid.*, p. 267.

52. *Ibid.*, pp. 278-79.

53. *Ibid.*, p. 267.

54. L. Von Neumann, and O. Morgenstern, *Theory of Games and Economic Behavior,* second edition (Princeton: Princeton University Press, 1947).

55. Deutsch, 1960, *op. cit.*, p. 129.

56. Berne, *op. cit.*, p. 172.

Also of interest although not directly quoted are the following:

Braithewaite, R.B., *Theory of Games as a Tool for the Moral Philosopher,* Cambridge: Cambridge University Press, 1955.

Buchler, I. and Hugo Nutini, ed., *Game Theory and the Behavioral Sciences,* Pittsburgh: University of Pittsburgh Press, 1969.

Edwards, W.A. Tversky, *Decision Making,* Baltimore: Penguin Books, 1967.

Schubik, M., ed., *Game Theory and Related Approaches to Social Behavior.,* New York: Wiley and Sons, 1964.

Also additional monographs by Luce, Rapoport, Raiffa, Tinter and others noted in the bibliography.

1. Bargain

Becker, H. "Notes on the Concept of Commitment." *AJS,* 67, 1960.

Davis, F. "Definitions of Time and Recovery in Paralytic Polio Convalescence." *AJS,* 61, May, 1956, pp. 582-87.

Deutsch, M., and R.M. Kraus. "The Effect of Threat Upon Interpersonal Bargaining." *J. Ab. Soc. Psych.,* 61, 1960, pp. 181-89.

Fouraker, L.E. and S. Siegel. *Bargaining Behavior.* New York: McGraw-Hill, 1963.

Freidson, E. "Client Control and Medical Practice." *AJS,* January, 1960, pp. 374-82.

_____. "Dilemmas in Doctor-Patient Relationships." A. Rose, ed. *Human Behavior and Social Process.* Boston: Houghton Mifflin, 1962.

_____. *Patients' Views of Medical Practice.* New York: Russell Sage Foundation, 1961.

Glazer, B.G., and A.L. Strauss. *An Awareness of Dying.* Chicago: Aldine, 1965.

Hall, E.T. *The Silent Language.* Greenwich, Connecticut: Fawcett, 1959.

Hoffman, P.; L. Festinger; and D. Lawrence. "Tendencies Toward Group Comparability in Competitive Bargaining." R.M. Thrall, C.H. Coombs, and R.L. Davis, eds. *Decision Processes.* New York: Wiley, 1954.

Joseph, M.C., and R.H. Willis. "An Analog to Two Party Bargaining." *Beh. Sci.* 8, 2 (1963): 117-27.

Khuri, Fuad I. "The Etiquette of Bargaining in the Middle East." *Am Anthro* 70, 4 (August 1968): 698-706.

Komorita, S.S., and J. Mechling. "Betrayal and Reconciliation in a Two Person Game." *J. of Pers. and Soc. Psych.* 6, 3 (1967): 349-53.

Lipset, S.M., et al. *Union Democracy.* Glencoe: Free Press, 1956, p. 21.

Miller, S.J. "Exchange and Negotiated Learning in Graduate Medical Education." *Sociology Quarterly,* Fall, 1966.

Morgan, J.N. "Bilateral Monopoly and the Competitive Output." *Quarterly J. of Eco.* 63, 376 (August, 1949).

Nash, J.F. "The Bargaining Problem." *Econ.,* 18, 1950, pp. 155-62.

_____. "Noncooperative Games." *Ann. of Math.,* 54, 1951, pp. 286-95.

Neisser, H. "The Strategy of Expecting the Worst." *Soc. Res.,* 1952, 19, pp. 346-63.

Roth, J.A. "The Treatment of Tuberculosis as a Bargaining Process." p. 575 in A. Rose, ed. *Human Behavior and Social Processes.* Boston: Houghton Mifflin, 1962.

Scheff, T. *Being Mentally Ill.* Chicago: Aldine, 1966.

ed. *Mental Illness and Social Processes.* New York: Harper, 1967.

Schelling, T.C. "Bargaining, Communication and Limited War." *J. Con. Res.*, 1, 1957, pp. 19-38.

Siegel, S., and L.E. Fouraker. *Bargaining and Group Decision Making.* New York: Mcgraw-Hill, 1960.

Stone, J.J. "An Experiment in Bargain Games." *Econ.*, 26, 1958, pp. 286-96.

Strauss, A.L. "Negotiated Order." in E. Freidson, ed., *The Hospital in Modern Society.* Glencoe, Illinois: Free Press, 1963.

Walton, R.E., and R.B. McKersie. *A Behavioral Theory of Labor Negotiaitons.* New York: McGraw-Hill, 1965.

Wolff, K.H. *The Sociology of Georg Simmel.* Glencoe, Illinois: Free Press, 1950.

Zeuthen, F. *Problems of Monopoly and Economic Welfare.* London: Routledge, 1930.

2. Conflict

Bauer, R.A. "Communication as a Transaction: A Comment on 'On the Concept of Influence'." **Pub. Opin. Quart.** 27 1 (Spring, 1963): 83-86.

Deutsch, M. "Reflections on Some Studies of Interpersonal Conflict." *Am Psych.* 24, 12 (December, 1969): 1076.

Dollard, J.; L.W. Doob; N.E. Miller; O.H. Mourer; and R.W. Sears. *Frustration and Aggression.* New Haven: Yale University Press, 1936.

Fellner, W. *Competition Among the Few.* New York: McGraw-Hill, 1949.

Foote, N.N., and L.S. Cottrell. *Identity and Interpersonal Competence: A New Direction in Family Research.* Chicago: University of Chicago Press, 1955.

Freidson, E. "Process of Control in a Company of Equals." *Soc. Prob.* 11, 2 (Fall, 1963).

Margolin, J.B. "The Effect of Perceived Cooperation or Competition on the Transfer of Hostility." Ph.D. dissertation, New York University, January, 1954.

Miller, N.E. "The Frustration-Aggression Hypothesis." *Psych. Res.*, 48, 1941, pp. 337-42.

Morgan, J.M. "Bilateral Monopoly and the Competitive Ouput." *Quarterly J. of Eco.* 63, 376, n6 (August, 1949).

Schelling, T. "The Strategy of Conflict." *Conflict. Resol.*, 2, 1958, pp. 203-264.

_____. *The Strategy of Conflict.* Cambridge: Harvard University Press, 1960.

Simmel, G. *Conflict and the Web of Group Affiliations.* New York: Free Press, 1964.

Sjoverg, G. "Strategy and Social Power: Some Preliminary Formulations." *Soc. Sci. Quart.*, 33, March, 1953, pp. 297-308.

3. Economic

Abramsson, Bengt. "Homans on Exchange." *AJS,* September, 1970, p. 273.

Allen, F.R.; H. Hart; D.C. Miller; W.F. Ogburn; and M.F. Nimkoff. *Technology and Social Change.* New York: Appleton Century Crofts, 1957, II. Social Effect of Selected Major Inventions, F.R. Allen, "The Automobile."

Armstrong, W.E. "A Note on the Theory of Consumer's Behavior." *Ox. Eco. Papers,* 2, 1950, pp. 119-22.

Arrow, K.J. *Social Choice and Individual Values.* New York: Wiley, 1951.

Belshaw, C.S. *Traditional Exchange and Modern Markets.* Englewood Cliffs, New Jersey: Prentice-Hall, 1965.

Blau, P.M. *Exchange and Power in Social Life.* New York: Wiley and Sons, 1967.

Chu, Don-Chean. "Morals and the Economic System: Honesty and the Profit Motive." *Ind. Sociol. Bull.* 2, 2 (January, 1965): 68-80.

Coleman, J.S. "Comment on Talcott Parsons' 'On the Concept of Influence'." *Pub. Opin. Quart.* 27, 1 (Spring, 1963): 63-82.

Cox, D.F. "Self-Confidence and Persuasibility in Women." *Pub. Opin. Quart.*, 38, Fall, 1964, pp. 453-66.

Evans, F.B. "Correlates of Automobile Shopping Behavior." *J. of Market.* 26, 4 (Oct., 1962): 74-77.

_____. "True Correlates of Automobile Shopping Behavior." *J. of Market.* 28, 1 (January, 1964): 65-66.

French, C.L. "Correlates of Success in Retail Selling." *AJS,* 66, September, 1960, pp. 128-34.

Freund, J. *The Sociology of Max Weber.* New York: Random House, 1969.

Gibbins, K. "Communication Aspects of Women's Clothes and Their Relationship to Fashionability." *Brit. J. of Soc., Clin. Psych.* 8, 4 (December, 1969): 19.

Hayes, S.P., Jr. "Some Psychological Problems of Economics." *Psych. Bull.*, 47, 1950, pp. 289-330.

Homans, G.C. "Social Behavior as Exchange." *AJS,* 1958, pp. 597-606.

Ito, Rikuma. "Differential Attitudes of New Car Buyers." *J. Advert. Res.* 7, 1 (May, 1969): 38-42.

Kornhauser, A., and P. Lazarsfeld. "The Analysis of Consumer Actions." reprinted in *Language of Social Research*, pp. 392-404.

Marschak, J. "Why Should Statisticians and Businessmen Maximize 'Moral Expectation'?" J. Neyman, ed. *Proceedings of 2nd Berkeley Symposium on Mathematical Statistics and Probability.* Berkeley: University of California Press, 1951, pp. 493-506.

McFarland, R.A., and R.C. Moore. *Values and Ideals of American Youth.* E. Ginzberg, ed. New York: Columbia University Press, 1961, pp. 169-91.

Murphy, J.R. "Questionable Correlates for Automobile Shopping Behavior." *J. of Market.* 27, 4 (October, 1963): 71-72.

Packard, V. *The Hidden Persuaders.* New York: Pocket Book, 1964.

Parsons, T. "On the Concept of Influence." *Pub. Opin. Quart.* 27, 1 (Spring, 1963): 37-62.

——— , and N.J. Smelser. *Economy and Society.* New York: Free Press, 1965.

Samuelson, P.A. "A Note on the Pure Theory of Consumer's Behavior." *Econ.* 138, 5, pp. 61-71 and 353-54.

Simmel, G. *The Sociology of Georg Simmel.* K.H. Wolff, ed. New York: Free Press, 1950, Chapter 4.

Smith, E., and E.A. Suchman. "Do People Know Why They Buy?" *J. of Appl. Psych,* 24, 1950, pp. 673-84.

Sutton, F.X. *The American Business Creed.* Cambridge: Harvard University Press, 1956.

Tanner, J.C. "Comments on Forecasting Car Ownership and Use." *Urban Studies* 3, 2 (June, 1966): 143-46.

Weber, M. *Social and Economic Organization.* New York: Free Press, 1964.

Yoshimo, I.R. "The Stereo-type of the Negro and Hi-priced Car." *Sociol. Soc. Res.* 44, 2 (November-December, 1959): 112-18.

4. Game

Abt, C.C. *Serious Games.* New York: Viking, 1970.

Bernard, J. "Theory of Games as a Modern Sociology of Conflict." *AJS* 59: 418 (March, 1954).

Berne, E. *Games People Play.* New York: Grove Press, 1967.

Braithwaithe, R.B. *Theory of Games as a Tool for the Moral Philosopher.* Cambridge: Cambridge University Press, 1955.

Buchler, I., and H. Nutini, eds. *Game Theory and the Behavioral Sciences.* Pittsburgh: University of Pittsburgh Press, 1969.

Caillois, R. "Unity of Play — Diversity of Games," *Diogenes,* 19, 1957.

Deutsch, K.M. *Nationalsim and Social Communication: Applications of Game Theory to International Politics: Some Opportunities and Limitations.*

Edwards, W. "The Theory of Decision Making." *Psych. Bull.* 51, 4 (1954): 380-417.

_____, and A. Tversky. *Decision Making.* Baltimore: Penquin Books, 1967.

Flood, M.M. "Some Experimental Games." *Man. Science,* 5, 1958, pp. 5-26.

Foster, C., and A. Rapoport. "Parasitism and Symbiosis in an N-person Non-Constant-Sum Continuous Game." *Bull. of Mth. Biophysics,* 18, 1956, pp. 219-31.

Frechet, M. "Emile Borel, Initiator of the Theory of Psychological Games and Its Application." *Econ.,* 21, 1953, pp. 95-96.

Guyer, M., and A. Rapoport. "Information Effects in Two-mixed-motive Games." *Beh. Sci.* 14, 9 (November, 1969): 467-82.

Harsanyi, J.S. "On the Rationality Postulates Underlying the Theory of Cooperative Games." *J. of Confl. Resol.,* 5, 1961, pp. 179-96.

_____. "Rationality Postulates for Bargaining Solutions in Cooperative and Non-cooperative Games." *Man. Science,* 9, 1962, pp. 141-53.

Hastorf, A.H., and Hadley Cantril. "They Saw a Game: A Case Study." *The Adolescent,* J.M. Seidman, ed. New York: Holt, Rinehart & Winston, 1953.

Kuhn, H.W., and A.W. Tucker. "Contributions to the Theory of Games." *Annals of Math. Studies,* 28, Princeton, 1953.

Luce, R.D. "A Definition of Stability for N-person Games." *Annals of Math.,* 59, 1954, pp. 357-66.

_____, and E.W. Adams. "The Determination of Subjective Characteristic Functions in Games with Misrepresented Pay-off Functions." *Econ.,* 24, 1956, pp. 158-71.

_____, and H. Raiffa. *Games and Decisions: Introduction and Critical Survey.* New York: Wiley, 1957, p. 95.

_____, and A.A. Rogow. "A Game-Theoretical Analysis of Congressional Power Distributions for a Stable Two-Party System." *Beh. Sci.,* 1, 1956, pp. 83-96.

McKinsey, J.C.C. *Theory of Games.* New York: McGraw-Hill, 1952, p. 3.

Morgenstern, O. "The Theory of Games." *Sci. Am.,* 180, May, 1949, p. 23.

Nash, J.F. "Two-person Cooperative Games." *Econ.,* 21, 1953, pp. 128-40.

Neisser, H. "The Strategy of Expecting the Worst." *Soc. Res.,* 58, September, 1952, pp. 167-75.

Raiffa, H. "Arbitration Schemes for Generalized Two-person Games." in H.W. Kuhn and A.W. Tucker, eds. *Contributions to the Theory of Games II* (*Annals of Math. Studies,* 28) Princeton, New Jersey, 1953.

Rapoport, A. "Some Game Theoretical Aspects of Parasitism and Symbiosis." *Bull. of Math. Biophysics,* 18, 1956, pp. 15-30.

_____. *Fights, Games, and Debates.* Ann Arbor: University of Michigan Press, 1960, Part II.

_____, and A.M. Chammah. *Prisoner's Dilemma: A Study of Conflict And Cooperation.* Ann Arbor: University of Michigan Press, 1965.

_____. *Two-Person Game Theory.* Ann Arbor: University of Michigan Press, 1966.

Rashevsky, N. *Mathematical Theory of Human Relations.* Bloomington, Indiana: Principia Press, 1948.

Royden, H.C.; P. Suppes; and K. Walsh. "A Model for the Experimental Measurement of the Utility of Gambling." *Beh. Sci.*, 4, 1959, pp. 11-18.

Shubik, M. *Game Theory and Related Approaches to Social Behavior.* New York: Wiley, 1964.

Suppes, P., and R.C. Atkinson. *Markov Learning Models for Multiperson Interactions.* Stanford: Stanford University Press, 1960.

Thomas, H. "Encounter: Game of No Game." Chapter 5 in A. Burton, ed. *Encounter.* San Francisco: Jossy-Bass, 1969.

Tinter, G. "The Theory of Choice Under Subjective Risk and Uncertainty." *Econ.*, 9, 1941, pp. 398-404.

Todhunter, I. *History and the Theory of Probability.* Cambridge: MacMillan, 1865.

Von Neumann, J., and O. Morgenstern. *Theory of Games and Economic Behavior* (second edition). Princeton, New Jersey: Princeton University Press, 1947.

Williams, J. *The Compleat Strategyst.* New York: McGraw-Hill, 1954.

5. Profession

Argyris, C. *Integrating the Individual and the Organization.* New York: Wiley, 1964.

Barber, B. "Is American Business Becoming Professionalized?" Analysis of a Social Ideology, A. Tiryakicin, ed. *Sociological Theory, Values and Socio-cultural Change.* New York: Free Press of Glencoe, 1963.

Baxter, R. "Inquiry into the Misuse of Survey Techniques by Sales Solicitors." *Pub. Opin. Quart.*, 28, Spring, 1964, pp. 124-34.

Becker, H.S. "The Professional Dance Musician and His Audience." *AJS*, 57, September, 1951, pp. 136-44.

Becker, H.S., and J. Carper. "The Development of Identification with an Occupation." *AJS*, 61, January, 1956, pp. 289-98.

_____. "The Elements of Identification with an Occupation." *ASR*, 21, June, 1956, pp. 341-48.

_____, and A. Strauss. "Careers, Personality and Adult Socialization." *AJS*, 62, November, 1956, pp. 253-63.

_____. "Some Problems of Professionalization." *Adult Education*, Winter, 1956, pp. 101-105.

_____. "The Nature of a Profession." N.B. Henry, ed. *Education for the Professions: The Sixty-First Yearbook of the National Society for the Study of Education, Part II*. Chicago: University of Chicago Press, 1962, pp. 27-46.

_____. *The Outsiders*. New York: Free Press, 1966.

_____; B. Geer; D. Riesman; and R.C. Weiss, eds. *Institutions and the Person*. Chicago: Aldine, 1968.

Bogdan, R. "Learning to Sell Door to Door: Techniques and Strategies of Persuasion." April, 1968, Northeastern University, unpublished.

Borow, H. "Development of Occupational Motives and Roles." W. Hoffman and M.L. Hoffman, eds. *Review of Child Development Research, Vol. II*. New York: Russell Sage Foundation, 1966, pp. 373-422.

Brooks, R.L. *How I Went from Failure to $50,000 a Year*. Los Angeles: Sherbourne Press, 1967.

Carlin, J.R. *Lawyers on Their Own*. New Jersey: Rutgers University Press, 1962, pp. 161-64.

Carr-Saunders, A.M., and P.A. Wilson. *The Professions*. Oxford: Clarendon Press, 1933.

Carnegie, D. *How to Win Friends and Influence People*. New York: Simon and Schuster, 1937.

Dalton, M. *Men Who Manage*. New York: Wiley, 1959.

Davis, F. "The Cabdriver and His Fare." *AJS*, 63, 1959, pp. 158-65.

Evan, W.M. "Role Strain and the Norm of Reciprocity in Research Organization." *AJS*, 68, November, 1962, pp. 350-53.

_____, and E.G. Levin. "Professionalism and the Stockbroker: Some Observations on the SEC Special Study." *Bus. Law*, 21, January, 1966, pp. 358-59.

_____. "Status Set and Role Set Conflicts of the Stockbroker: A Problem in the Sociology of Law." *Soc. For.* 45, 1 (September, 1966): 73-83.

Form, W., and S. Nosow. *Man, Work and Society*. New York: Basic Books, 1962, pp. 321-29.

_____, and J.A. Geschwender. "Social Reference Basis of Job Satisfaction: The Case of Manual Workers." *ASR*, 27, pp. 228-37.

French, C.L. "Some Structural Aspects of a Retail Sales Group." *Hum. Org.* 22, 2 (Summer, 1963): 146-51.

Hentig, Hans Von *The Criminal and His Victim*. New Haven: Yale University Press, 1948.

Komarovsky, M. *The Unemployed Man and His Family*. Dryden Press, 1940.

Gold, R.L. "Janitors vs. Tenants: A Status Income Dilemma." *AJS*, 57, March, 1952, pp. 486-93.

Goode, W.J. "Community Within a Community: The Professions." *ASR*, 22, April, 1957, pp. 194-200.

Harper, D., and E. Frederick. "Work Behavior in a Service Industry." *Soc. Forces,* 42, December, 1963, pp. 216-25.

Howton, F.W., and B. Rosenberg. "Salesman: Ideology and Self-imagery in a Prototype Occupation." *Soc. Res.*, 32, Autumn, 1965, pp. 277-98.

Hughes, E.C. *Men and Their Work.* Glencoe, Illinois: Free Press, 1958.

Kriesberg, L. "The Retail Furrier: Concepts of Security and Success." *AJS,* 57, March, 1952, pp. 478-85.

———. "Occupational Controls Among Steel Distributors." *AJS,* 61, November, 1955, pp. 203-212.

Krugman, H.E. "Salesman in Conflict: A Challenge to Marketing." *J. of Marketing* 23, 1 (July, 1958): 59-61.

Kuesel, H. *How to Sell Against Tough Competition.* Engelwood Cliffs, New Jersey: Prentice-Hall, 1957.

Leggett, J.C. "Economic Insecurity and Working Class Consciousness." *ASR,* 29, pp. 226-34.

Maurer, D. *The Big Con.* New York: Pocket Books, 1949.

Merton, R.K.; G. Reader; and P. Kendall, eds. *Student-Physician.* Cambridge: Harvard University Press, 1957.

Miller, S.J. "The Social Base of Sales Behavior." *Soc. Prob.* 12, 1 (Summer, 1964): 15-24.

Miller, S.J. *Prescription for Leadership.* Chicago: Aldine, 1970.

Pederson, C., and M. Wright. *Salesmanship.* Illinois: Homewood, 1966.

Polsky, N. *Hustlers, Beats and Others.* Chicago: Aldine, 1967.

Quirk, J. *The Hard Winners.* New York: Avon, 1965.

Rosenberg, M. *Occupations and Values.* Glencoe, Illinois: Free Press, 1958.

Rosenfeld, J.M. "Strangeness Between Helper and Client." *Soc. Ser. Rev.* 38, 1 (March, 1964): 17-25.

Roth, J.A. *Timetables: Structuring the Passage of Time in Hospital Treatment and Other Careers.* New York: Bobbs-Merrill, 1963.

Roy, D. " 'Banana Time': Job Satisfaction and Informal Interaction." *Hum. Org.*, 18, Winter, 1959-1960, pp. 158-68.

Smigle, E.O. "Interviewing a Legal Elite: The Wall Street Lawyer." *AJS,* 64, 1958, pp. 159-64.

Sutherland, E.H. *The Professional Thief.* Chicago: University of Chicago Press, 1937.

———. *White Collar Crime.* New York: Dryden Press, 1949.

Taylor, M.L., and R.J. Pellegrin. "Professionalization: Its Function and Dysfunction for the Life Insurance Occupation." *Soc. Forces* 38, 2 (December, 1959): 110-14.

Thielbar, G. "Occupational Stereotypes and Prestige." *Soc. Forces* 48, 1 (September, 1969): 64.

Whyte, W.M., Jr. *The Organization Man.* New York: Simon and Schuster, 1956.

Wilensky, H.L. *Intellecturals in Labor Unions: Organizational Pressures on Professional Roles.* Glencoe, Illinois: Free Press, 1956.

Wilensky, H.L. "The Professionalization of Almost Everybody." *AJS,* 70, September, 1964, pp. 37-58.

Wollmer, H.M., ed. *Professionalization.* Englewood Cliffs, New Jersey: Prentice-Hall, 1966.

6. Trust

Blumberg, A.S. "The Practice of Law as Confidence Game: Organizational Cooptation of a Profession." *Law Soc. Rev.* 1, 2 (June, 1967): 15-40.

Brown, J.A. "Gradients of Approach and Avoidance Responses and Their Relation to Level of Motivation." *J. Comp. Physiol. Psych.* 4, 1 (1948): 450-65.

Deutsch, M. "A Theory of Cooperation and Competition." *Hum. Rel.,* 2, 1949, pp. 129-52.

_____. "Conditions Affecting Cooperation." Final Technical Report for the Office of Naval Research, Contract NONR 285, 10, February, 1957.

_____. "Trust and Suspicion." *J. of Conflict Resol.* 2, 4 (December, 1958): 165-79.

_____. "The Effect of Motivational Orientation Upon Trust and Suspicion." *Hum. Relat.* 13, 2 (May, 1960): 123-40.

Freidson, E. "Organization of Medical Practice and Patient Behavior." *Am. J. of Pub. Health,* January, 1961, pp. 43-52.

Garfinkle, H. *Conceptual Systems and Personality Organization.* New York: Wiley, 1960.

_____. *Motivation and Social Interaction.* O.J. Harvey, ed. New York: Ronald Press, 1963, pp. 187-238.

Gouldner, A.W. "Norm of Reciprocity." *ASR,* 25, April, 1960, pp. 161-79.

Griffin, K. "The Contribution of Studies of Source Credibility to a Theory of Trust." *Psych. Bull.* 68, 2 (1967): 104-120.

Hartford, T., and M. Hill. "Variations in Behavioral Strategies and Interpersonal Trust." *J. of Applied Psych.* 23, 1 (2967): 33-35.

Hey, R. N. "May Divergent Values in Counseling be Growth Facilitating?" *Marr. Fam. Living* 22, 3 (August, 1960): 210-13.

Knight, F.H. *Risk, Uncertaity and Project.* Boston: Houghton Mifflin, 1921.

Loomis, J. L. "Communication, The Development of Trust and Cooperative Behavior." *Hum. Relat.,* 1959, 12, pp. 305-315.

Piaget, J. *Play, Dreams and Imitation in Childhood.* New York: Norton, 1962, p. 170, 227.

Rosenfeld, J. M. "Strangeness between Helper and Client: A Possible Explanation of Non-use of Available Professional Help." *Soc. Serv. Rev.* 38, 1 (March, 1964): 17-25.

Solomon, L. "The Influence of Some Types of Power Relationships on the Development of Trust." Ph.D. dissertation, New York University, 1957.

Stotland, E. *The Psychology of Hope.* San Francisco: Jossey-Boss, 1969.

Wirth, L. *On Cities and Social Life.* Chicago: University of Chicago Press, 1964.

7. Method

Adams, R. N., and J.J. Preiss, eds. *Human Organization Research.* Homewood, Illinois: Dorsey Press, 1960.

Becker, H. S. "Interviewing Medical Students." *AJS* 62, September, 1956, pp. 199-201.

_____. "Problems of Influence and Proof in Participant Observation." *ASR,* 23, 1958, pp. 652-60.

_____ and B. Geer. "Participant Observation and Interviewing: A Comparison." *Hum. Org.,* 16, 1957.

_____. "Problems of Publication of Field." A. Viditch, J. Bensman, and M. Stein, eds. *Reflections on Community Studies.* New York: Wiley, 1964, pp. 267-84.

_____. "On Methodology." August, 1969 (in press).

Bell, Colin. "A Note on Participant Observation." *Sociology* 3, 3 (September 1969): 417-18.

Berreman, G. D. *Behind Many Masks.* Society for Applied Anthropology, Monograph IV, 1962.

Bruyn, S. T. *The Human Perspective in Sociology: The Method of Participant Observation.* Englewood Cliffs, New Jersey: Prentice-Hall, 1966.

Black, M. *Models and Metaphors: Studies in Language and Philosophy.* Ithaca, New York: Cornell University Press, 1962, pp. 64-139.

Buckley, W., ed. *Modern Systems Research for the Behavioral Scientists.* Chicago: Aldine, 1968, pp. 304-313.

Cicourel, A. V. *Method and Measurement in Sociology.* Illinois: Free Press, 1964.

Garfinkle, H. *Studies in Ethnomethodology.* Englewood Cliffs, New Jersey: Prentice-Hall, 1967.

Goffman, E. *Encounters: Two Studies in the Sociology of Interaction.* Indianapolis: Bobbs-Merrill, 1961.

Gold, R. L. "Roles in Sociological Field Observations." *Soc. Forces,* 36, 1958, pp. 217-23.

Gottschalk, L.; Kluckhohn, C.; Angell, R. *Use of Personal Documents.* Social Science Research Council, New York, 1945.

Hall, O. "Use of Sampling Procedures and Role Theory in Sociological Research." *Can. J. of Eco. and Poli. Sci.*, 15, February, 1949., pp. 1-13.

Hammond, P. *Sociologists at Work.* Basic Books, 1964.

Hughes, E. C. "What Other." in A. Rose, ed. *Human Behavior and Social Processes.* Boston: Houghton Mifflin, 1962, pp. 119-27.

Lindesmith, A. *Opiate Addiction.* Bloomington, Indiana: Principia Press, 1947.

Mead, M. "More Comprehensive Field Methods." *Am. Anthro.*, 35, 1939, pp. 1-15.

Merton, R. K. et al. "The Focused Interview: A Manual" (second edition). New York: Bureau of Applied Social Research, Columbia University, 1952.

Miller, S. M. "The Participant Observer and 'Over-Rapport'." *ASR,* 18, 1952, pp. 97-99.

Polya, G. *Patterns of Plausible Inference*, Volume II of *Mathematics and Plausible Reasoning.* Princeton: Princeton University Press, 1954.

Schon, D. A. *Displacement of Concepts.* London: Tavistock, 1963.

Strauss, A. L., and L. Schatxman. "Social Class and Modes of Communication." *AJS*, 60, 1955, pp. 329-38.

8. Theory

Becker, H. S., and B. Geer. *Boys in White.* Chicago: University of Chicago Press, 1961.

———. "Whose Side Are We On?" *Soc. Prob.* 14, 3 (Winter, 1967): pp 239-47.

Blumer, H. "The Problem of Concept in Social Psychology." *AJS*, 45, 1940, pp. 707-719.

———. "Society as Symbolic Interaction." A. Rose, ed. *Human Behavior and Social Process.* Boston: Houghton Mifflin, 1962.

Brown, R. *Words and Things.* New York: Glencoe Free Press, 1958.

Cartwright, D. "Survey Research: Psychological Economics." J.G. Miller, ed. *Experiments in Social Process.* New York: McGraw-Hill, 1950, pp. 47-64.

Cavan, Sherri. *Liquor License.* Chicago: Aldine, 1966.

Denzin, N. "Symbolic Interactionism and Ethnomethodology: A Proposed Synthesis." *ASR* 34, 6 (December, 1969): 922.

Denzin, N. *Sociological Methods.* Chicago: Aldine, 1970.

Fromm, Erich. *The Sane Society.* New York: Holt, Rinehart and Winston, 1964.

Glazer, B. G. and A. L. Strauss. *The Discovery of Grounded Theory: Strategies for Qualitative Research.* Chicago: Aldine, 1967.

Goffman, E. "On Face-work." *Psychiatry,* 18, 1955, pp. 213-31.

_____. "On Cooling the Mark Out: Some Aspects of Adaptation to Failure." *Psychiatry* 15, 4 (November, 1952): 451-63.

_____. *Presentation of Self in Everyday Life.* Garden City, New York: Doubleday. Anchor Books, 1959.

_____. *Interaction Ritual.* Chicago: Aldine, 1967.

Goslin, D. A. *Handbook of Socialization Theory and Research.* Chicago: Rand McNally, 1969, Chapter 21.

Goulder, A. W. *The Coming Crisis in Western Sociology.* New York: McGraw-Hill, 1970.

Humphrey, Laud. *Tearoom Trade.* Chicago: Aldine, 1970.

Krech, D.; R.S. Crutchfield; E.L. Ballachey. *Individual in Society.* New York: McGraw-Hill, 1962.

Lewin, K. "Conceptual Representation and the Measurement of Psychological Forces." *Contr. to Psych. Theory*, 1, pp. 41-207.

_____ "Intention, Will and Need." D. Rapaport, ed. *Organization and Pathology of Thought.* New York: Columbia University Press, p. 95-153.

McCall, G. J., and J.L. Simmons. *Identities and Interactions.* New York: Free Press, 1966.

Mead, G. H. "Cooley's Contribution to American Sociological Thought." *AJS*, 5, 35 (March, 1930): 693-706.

_____. *Mind, Self and Society.* Chicago: University of Chicago Press, 1935.

_____. *On Social Psychology* Chicago: University of Chicago Press, 1964.

Merton, R. K. *Social Theory and Social Structure* (rev. ed.). New York: Free Press, 1957, pp. 368-84.

Mills, C. W. *The Vocabulary of Situated Motives.*

Pei, Mario. *The Story of Language.* New York: Mentor Books, 1949.

Pool, I. de S. "Simulating Social Systems." *International Sci. and Tech.*, March, 1964, pp. 62-70.

Rose, A. *Theory and Method in the Social Sciences.* Minneapolis: University of Minnesota Press, 1954.

Rose, A., ed. *Human Behavior and Social Processes.* Boston: Houghton Mifflin, 1962.

Schneider, L. "The Category of Ignorance in Sociological Theory: An Exploratory Statement." *ASR* 27, 4 (August, 1962): 492-508.

Schutz, A. *Collected Papers.* Nijhoff: Stockholm, 1964.

Strauss, A. L. *Mirrors and Masks: The Search for Identity.* Glencoe, Illinois: Free Press, 1959.

Sussman, M. B. "Sociology and Rehabilitation." *ASA* 1965.

Wallace, W. *Social Theory*. Chicago: Aldine, 1969.

Wharf, B. L. *Language, Thought and Reality*. New York: Wiley, 1956.

Whyte, Wm. *Street Corner Society*. Chicago: University of Chicago Press, 1955, Appendix on Method.

Index

Advertiser's Digest, The, 56
American Automobile Association (AAA),
    31, 32, 36
  Newsletter, 152n14
Author's
  concept and organization of study, 1-23
  future study possibilities, 110-112,
    149-150
  rationale, 13, 15-17, 63, 110
  research plan, 148
  technique of participant observation,
    16, 18, 39, 144-145n3, 147n12,
    148n20
Automobiles
  industry vs. U.S. economy, 8
  intrinsic value of, 8-10
  quantity manufactured (1970), 10
  societal value of, 8-10

Bargain, concept of, 2
  expectation of, xiv
  function of, 1
  global implications of, 1, 92, 107, 111,
    164n26
  impression of, xiv
  in labor negotiations, xiv
  lay concept of, 92
  maneuvers (explicit and implicit), 93
  private vs. global implication of, 1, 92
  quasi-military application, 91
  social functions of, 2
  sociological studies and definitions of, 2
Bargaining, Middle East pattern, 5-7
Bargaining situation, defined, 4
Better Business Bureau (BBB), 31
Boston Globe, 31, 152n14
Brokerage schema, 12-13
  goals of, 13
  relationships between buyer and seller,
    21, 65-66, 75, 100-101, 112,
    158n11, 159n18-n19

Caveat emptor principle, 51, 154n18
Chandler, Raymond, 36
Code of ethics, 58, 156n17
Committee on Consumer Interest, 8
Concepts,
  of deviancy, 150
  of responsive interaction, 5
  of term "bargain", 1-2
Confidence Man, The, 56
Conservative Party (England), 28
Consumer Corner, 34
Consumer Interest

Committee on, 8
  licensing of sellers, 154n18
  protection of, 32, 33, 154n18
Consumer Reports, 29, 152n14
Customer,
  function of brute obstinacy, 4
  function of collective bargaining, 45, 46,
    154n13
  list of characteristics, 42
  expectation of salesman's obligations, 45
  linkage of trust and expectation, 81
  view of bargain, xiv
  view of salesman, 26-37

Dealer's mark-up, 9
Dealerships, 58-62
  definition of, 58
  mechanics of, 60passim
Dennis the Menace, 126
Double coding, defined, 107
Duality of roles for buyer and seller, 3-4,
    11-12, 77passim

Emotional implications of "luxury" cars, 9
Exchange theory, 21, 163n5
  classical version, 13
  defined, 21

"Fall guy" symbolism, 64
Ford Marketing Institute, 40, 115, 154n7,
    161n27
Frommian (Erich) universe, 19, 147n15

"Gasoline Alley" comic strip, 30
Gestalt school, 15
Goffman, Erving, 56

Heath, Ted, 28
High Window, The, 36
Humpty Dumpty, 126

I vs. me, 62, 157n4
Interaction between principals, 5-6, 8, 10,
    12, 13, 22, 77-89
  distrust, operative, examples of, 5-6, 77
  emotions, 8, 10, 77-79
  importance of, 12, 22
  resultant control, 13, 79-89

Jonson, Ben, 113

King, Martin Luther, Jr., 25

Language communality, 59-60

183

About the Author

Joy Browne received the BA in Anthropology and Psychology from Rice University and the MA in Psychology and the Ph.D. in Sociology from Northeastern University, Boston.

She has served as a research psychologist with Sperry Rand Corporation, as a systems engineer with Itek Corporation, and as Head of Social Services of the Boston Redevelopment Authority.

Dr. Browne has taught urban sociology at Northeastern and is currently writing a book intended to help expectant mothers handle both obstetrician and child. A third book on labelling theory is also in progress.